AF579307

FABULOUS FRAUDS

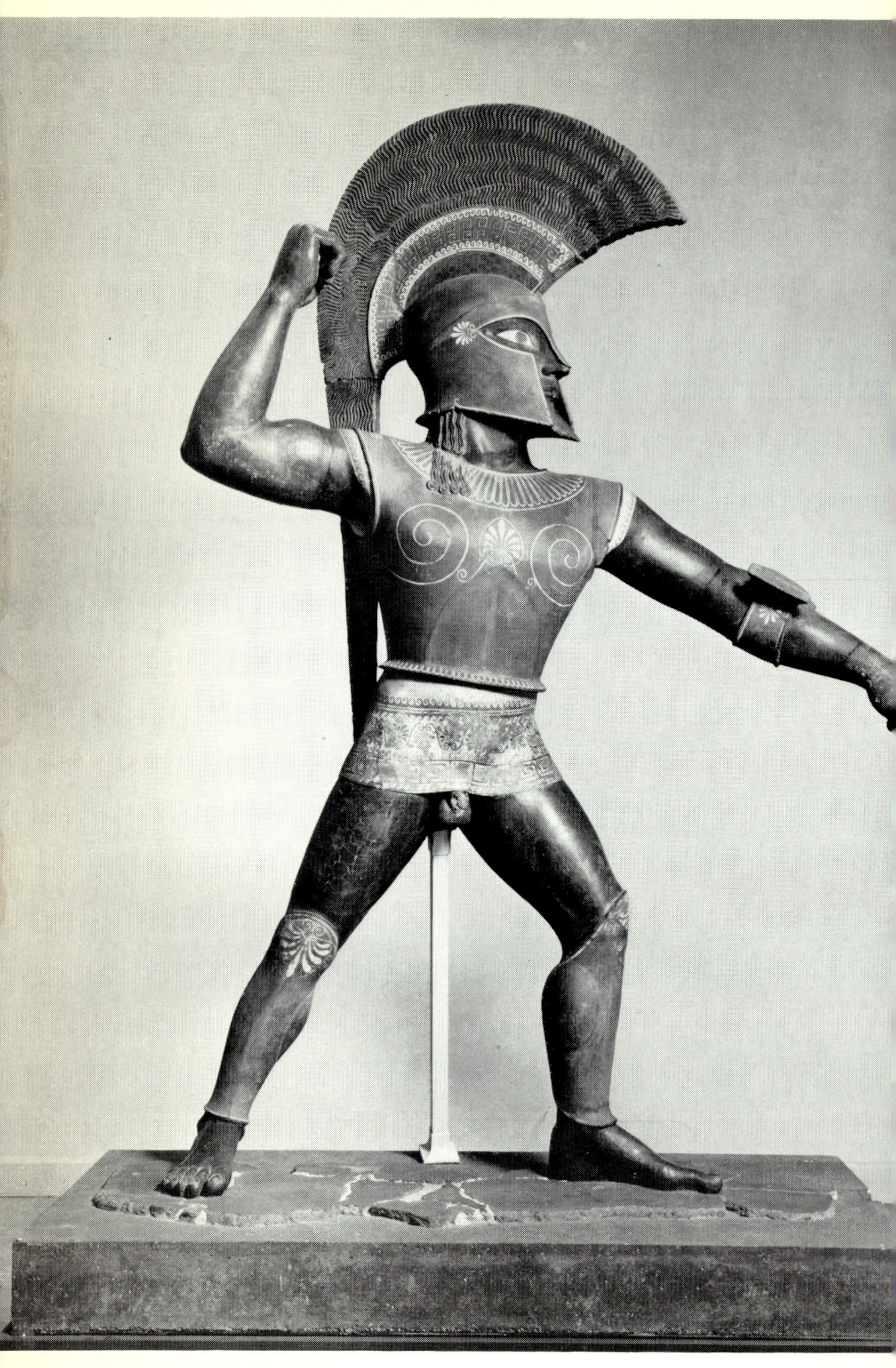

Statue of Mars or Warrior 20th Century A.D. in style of 5th Century B.C. Etruscan work [*By courtesy of The Metropolitan Museum of Art, New York.*]

FABULOUS FRAUDS

A Study of Great Art Forgeries

by Lawrence Jeppson

London Arlington Books

FABULOUS FRAUDS
first published 1971 by
Arlington Books (Publishers) Ltd.
38 Bury Street, St James's
London SW1

Made and printed in Great Britain by
The Garden City Press Limited
London and Letchworth

ISBN 0 85140 138 4

To Frances

In order to detect a forgery, it is best to remember that every object made by man carries within it the evidence of the time and place of its manufacture. It is a challenge to the trained eye of the art historian and to the technical examination of the scientific analyst to penetrate beneath the surface appearance and to discover the truth.

JOSEPH VEACH NOBLE,
The Technique of Painted Attic Pottery

Contents

Preface

Although trained in science and communication, since the late 1950s I have been organizing exhibitions of works by living artists for museums, university salons, and commercial galleries, as well as writing about the artists. Initially I concentrated on contemporary handwoven French tapestries, but gradually my interest expanded to include paintings, original graphics, and sculpture.

I spent three years and thousands of dollars criss-crossing the country to badger the president and general merchandise manager of virtually every major department store in the United States to install a small but *serious* gallery—as a public service if not as a profit-making venture.

In the course of my contacts with artists, gallery owners, educators, critics, and museum directors while organizing more than 200 art exhibits, I have heard innumerable stories of fraud and its cancerous effects on every part of the art world.

LAWRENCE JEPPSON

FABULOUS FRAUDS

CHAPTER I

The Man Who Revisited the Renaissance

One hundred years ago when the young Claude Monet, Paul Cézanne, and Pierre Auguste Renoir were trying to catch the eye of Paris, they met little success, for that eye was transfixed backwards four centuries on the Quattrocento.

So it should come as no surprise that when a Paris collector, Count de Nolivos, loaned to the 1865 Exposition de l'Union Centrale des Beaux Arts an uncatalogued terra-cotta bust into which was cleanly incised the name Hiermus Benivieni (a Florentine poet, philosopher, and friend of Girolamo Savonarola who had been born in 1453 and had lived nearly ninety years) the bust became the show-stopper. Far and wide *Hiermus Benivieni* was hailed as a masterpiece of the Florentine Renaissance.

In Gazette des Beaux Arts Paul Mantz wrote:

> All the subtlety of the Italian character is disclosed in this expressive countenance. It is marked by both good humour and deeply felt experience. The creases at the lips, the precociously furrowed brow, and the intent gaze betoken amazing vitality. Every feature bears the stamp of a striking personality. We have no other portrait of Benivieni. But we could swear that this is a good likeness. The age of the subject and

above all the style of execution suggest that the work should be dated at the earliest in the last years of the fifteenth century or preferably at the beginning of the sixteenth.

Everyone acknowledged the beauty and authenticity of the Benivieni bust, but there was no unanimity about its authorship. Donatello, Andrea del Verrocchio, Desiderio da Settignano, Mino da Fiesole, Antonio Rossellino, and Benedetto da Maiano were cited. Because Lorenzo di Credi had painted a portrait (now lost) of Benivieni, left some drawings in the style of the bust, and was known to have tried his hand at sculpture, Mantz suggested that he was the author, and this became the most widely accepted theory.

De Nolivos decided to sell the bust while critical adulation was at its peak. So in January 1866, the *Benivieni* went on the auction block at the Hôtel Drouot. A fierce bidding contest developed. On one side was the Baron de Triquette, who was serving as agent for the Duc d'Aumale. Pitted against him was the Count de Nieuwekerke, an art lover, sculptor, and, more important, the protégé of Princess Mathilde Bonaparte and director of the Imperial Museum, the Louvre.

In 1820 the state had paid 6,000 francs for the fabulous *Venus de Milo*, which is to sculpture what the *Mona Lisa* is to painting in public awe. But in the bidding for the *Benivieni* this figure was left far behind. Nieuwekerke carried off the prize for 13,250 francs plus another 1,000 francs in auctioneers' charges.

Soon the *Benivieni* was sitting in the Louvre between works by Michelangelo and Benvenuto Cellini.

Three miles north-east of Florence lies the old Tuscan village of Fiesole. On September 17, 1830, a poor peasant family there, named Bastianini, had a son. In spite of the poverty Fiesole was not the worst place in Italy for young Giovanni Bastianini to grow up. He found something intensely interesting inside the cathedral: the monuments to Giovanni Salutati, Bishop of Fiesole, executed by Mino da Fiesole.

He also explored the Monastery of San Domenico—Fra Angelico had been prior there—and the thirteenth-century

Palazzo Pretoria, a small museum filled with antiquities. He marvelled at the beautiful villas of Fiesole, particularly Villa Medici and Villa Palmieri, and the fourteenth-century Castle of Vincigliata.

Young Bastianini had been born with a discerning eye and a pair of hands that could shape what he saw into sculptured masterpieces. But even a discerning eye needs training. So the boy was taken under the paternalistic wing of a Florentine picture dealer, Antonio Freppa. It is not known whether Freppa was already commissioning fakes, but he did sell anything with no questions asked.

Bastianini was seventeen when he began to serve Freppa. The dealer did not, at first, specialize in antiquarian works, but as he became more aware of the boy's abilities he instructed Bastianini to model in the antique manner.

Freppa started Bastianini out with fireplaces and bas-reliefs, not for a long time did he permit the artist to go on to sculpt a series of busts of celebrated women. As Bastianini's work became a more perfect imitation of Renaissance sculpture—Freppa began selling it as antique. The first such sale was a piece representing the Holy Family. It was bought as a Verrocchio.

Note the wording: it was *bought* as a Verrocchio, not *sold* as a Verrocchio. As much as possible, Freppa let his clients draw their own conclusions. He kept the prices low and let buyers exult in the belief that they had discovered treasures that Freppa didn't know he had.

The raiders who made off with the seemingly ignorant Freppa's best pieces were dealers, who turned around and resold them for enormous profits. Their ability to do so must have rankled Freppa on more than one occasion.

A portrait bust that Bastianini sculpted offers an excellent case in point. Using a Florentine medallion as model and inspiration he did a bust of Savonarola. A Florentine dealer named Vincenzo Capponi made off with *Savonarola* for a paltry 640 lire—and sold it for 10,000! The buyers were Banti and Costa. They put the bust on exhibit at the Palazzo Riccardi in Florence in 1864 as a genuine work of the Renaissance.

The counterfeiter of metal sculpture usually takes a plaster cast of the piece that he wishes to duplicate and from it makes new "originals," using various foundry procedures. When a piece of statuary is originally cast in metal, several castings are made, and each is considered an original: the U.S. Bureau of Customs currently recognizes the first six castings as originals. If an unscrupulous person obtains one of them, there is nothing to prevent his making additional copies from it and passing off these second-generation castings as the real thing. Of course he must do more than duplicate the form. If the sculptor has given a certain patina to the originals, the counterfeiter must duplicate this surface treatment.

A counterfeiter who undertakes to duplicate a stone original uses an entirely different technology. He works with a pointing machine, a delicately adjusted device that is suspended over the original at three points. Steel needles, set on adjustable arms, indicate the heights of the surface at those three points. The pointing machine is then moved to the new piece and hung over the corresponding three points. Excess stone is cut away until the three markers fit the new piece perfectly. This procedure is repeated hundreds of times over the surface of the stone, as the dimensions of the original are transferred laboriously to the emerging copy. Problems of ageing and patina remain, of course, once the bulk form has been finished.

The counterfeiter of modern sculpture takes the risk that the prospective buyer may elect to query the artist about the authenticity of a given piece. If the forger duplicates an old piece, he need not worry about the sculptor's unmasking him, but he dare not duplicate a piece known to be unique, such as the *Venus de Milo*.

In using a medallion to model a bust, Bastianini gave himself special problems. Medals are sculptures in miniature, purged of virtually all relief and, practically speaking, offering the subject in two dimensions. The faker cannot copy, cannot rely on either casting apparatus or pointing machine. He must create. He must increase the scale and translate the subject into three dimensions.

Bastianini's *Savonarola* was executed in terra-cotta, which is much easier to work with than stone. It is a ceramic clay which usually contains iron oxide, from which it takes its characteristic reddish colour. Sculpture in terra-cotta is directly fired in kilns. Its surface may then be coloured, glazed, or enamelled in many different ways.

Some of Bastianini's forgeries were in marble. Marble, which is closely related to limestone, varies greatly from quarry to quarry, and with modern laboratory procedures the origin of a marble piece can be traced. Woe to the forger who uses a piece of marble from a quarry unknown to the original artist!

Newly cut marble has a glistening freshness which the forger cannot ignore. This freshness displeased even the early Greeks, and since the golden age of Attica methods of ageing the appearance of marble artificially have been part of the sculptor's heritage. Marble can be immersed in urine or in corrosive ashes; hung in a smokehouse; buried in sour earth (as Michelangelo did with a Cupid that he forged as a young man); washed with a solution of copper, iron, or zinc sulphate; or treated in many other ways. A washing with weak green vitriol (iron sulphate) penetrates so deep that even laboratory observers have been deceived by it. The forger may vary the strengths of his solutions and may incorporate into them colouring agents to impart a variegated surface and make his work appear even more authentic.

The Victoria and Albert Museum in London began acquiring pieces which were really by Bastianini, but they paid more reasonable prices than did Banti and Costa: £80 in 1857 for a marble relief depicting the Madonna with child and cherubs' heads attributed to Antonio Rossellino (1427–1479); £60 in 1861 for a terra-cotta bust attributed to an unknown Renaissance sculptor; and £60 in 1863 for a similar piece.

Bastianini made one statuette, *Giovanna Albizzi*, from pieces of worm-eaten wood glued and bolted and rough-shaped into female form by a joiner; he completed the figure, covered it with gesso paste, and gilded it in the sixteenth-century manner. Eventually a French collector paid a substantial sum for it.

One of Bastianini's most beautiful achievements was *La Chateuse Florentine*, a graceful lady dressed in elegant floorlength robes. She holds a sheet of music in her hands as she sings, seemingly, a Nativity carol. The statuette may have been inspired by the felicitous ladies who visit Saint Anne and Saint Elizabeth in Domenico Ghirlandaio's frescoes in Santa Maria Novella. It was widely admired. Collector Edmond Bonnaffé wrote Freppa in search of something as lovely:

> I should like to inquire, dear Sir, whether you might indicate to me an interesting terra-cotta bust of a young man or a young lady, in short a pleasing subject. I need not stress I am looking for something beautiful by the hand of an artist of the Quattrocento. I should be most grateful if you could give me details of any such bust you may know of, together with its price. A terra-cotta statuette in the style of the figure brought to Paris by M. Castellani [*La Chanteuse Florentine*] about forty centimetres high, would also be most acceptable, providing the subject were interesting and the statuette in a fine state of preservation.

The Castellani who owned the statuette was an intimate friend of Giacomo Rossini, and the composer wrote a letter about *La Chanteuse Florentine* for him:

> It pleases me to declare that this adorable statuette in terra-cotta (which is a part of the collection of my friend Castellani) does not sing my cavatina *Di Tanti Palpiti*, which made Venetians happy in 1813; she hums a melody of the celebrated composer Ludrone, who was born in Padua in 1500; that means (thank God) that she does not sing the seductive music of the future.

Rossini dated the letter April 2, 1866, in Paris. Two days later Castellani sold *La Chanteuse Florentine* as a work of the fifteenth century to the great French collector Édouard André. She went into the Jacquemart-André Museum, as did the letter, and they were displayed together.

Paul Dubois, a sculptor and director of the École des Beaux Arts, had made a long study in Italy of early Renaissance sculpture, and, when he said *La Chanteuse Florentine* was so completely in the spirit of the Quattrocento that no nineteenth-century artist could have done it, everyone believed him. They wanted to.

Now, 100 years later, the connoisseur would not be likely to look at a nineteenth-century Bastianini and believe it to be from Leonardo da Vinci's time. There are many reasons why, and the easiest is that we have now been forewarned. The faker often succeeds with his first good copy, but as his works begin to appear here and there they become susceptible to comparison with one another. When these comparisons start, the creator's idiosyncrasies are discovered, and once they are known, they are likely to be spotted in other of his works which until then have gone unassociated.

In 1922 Paris's original *Benivieni* and London's *Baron von Jenison*, another Bastianini piece done about the same time, were brought together for the first time in a *False or True* exhibition shown in Europe and the United States. Expert and layman alike could see that both works were by the same hand, even though the two busts were of men from different periods and different places.

Today, then, the viewer can easily see that Bastianini's "Renaissance" pieces have only Renaissance veneer. But 100 years ago collectors in Europe actually preferred Bastianini's Renaissance work to genuine objects from the Quattrocento because Bastianini's was closer to what they *thought* Renaissance art had been. It is a peculiar phenomenon that the public frequently responds better to a copy of an Old Master than to the original.

Technically speaking, though, Bastianini was not a copyist. He did not make facsimiles of existing sculptures. He did not, for example, go to Florence and make his own edition of Michelangelo's *David*. He might have used works like the Florentine medallion of Savonarola as sources of portraits for his subjects, but essentially he sculpted original works—in the Renaissance manner. He was, then, a Renaissance sculptor living in the nineteenth century. He sold his works as what they were: modern interpretations.

Unfortunately, Freppa was not quite that scrupulous. He let the buyers attribute the sculptures to whatever Renaissance artists they liked. It was not Bastianini who chiselled the words *Hiermus Benivieni* into the bust that Count de Nolivos bought, and perhaps it was not Freppa either. Pieces of sculpture which left the artist's studio in modest innocence were knighted and even crowned in a not-innocent world. When the truth was finally proved, the artist, who had produced in honesty and innocence, was made to appear a rogue.

Though in all likelihood Bastianini's works would eventually have been recognized as nineteenth century by a majority of scholars, Bastianini himself might have died unrecognized had there not been a falling-out among the unscrupulous.

Everything that had happened to *Benivieni* since de Nolivos acquired it had been sensational: first, the showing in the Salle de l'Industrie, then the heated battle at auction between two well-known rival collectors, the awesome price paid, and finally its enshrinement in the Louvre made the bust a topic of French salon chatter and newspaper attention. And the excitement spread to Italy, home of the statue.

One man who scrutinized every newspaper account about the *Benivieni* was Antonio Freppa. After all, the Count de Nolivos had acquired the bust from Freppa for only 700 francs! When he sold it at the Hôtel Drouot auction for 13,250 francs, his profit was obviously considerable. Yet, according to Paul Eudel in *Trucs et Truqueurs*, 1907, de Nolivos had agreed to give Freppa 1,000 francs more if he should resell the bust at a profit. So Freppa had to decide whether to wait patiently for de Nolivos's payoff or to incur the risk to himself of calling down vengeance on the Count. He waited—for nearly two years.

On December 15, 1867, Freppa finally exploded the whole affair in an article published in *Chronique des Arts* in Paris. In effect, he said: "It's only three years old, your bust. I know the man who made it; I watched him do it. I bought it for 350 francs, and I sold it for 700. The sculptor was Giovanni Bastianini, and the bust is not of Benivieni at all *but of Giuseppi Bonaiuti, a tobacco-factory worker*."

Bonaiuti had since died.

The Louvre brushed off the accusation as the outcry of a crank. No official effort was made to investigate. But the newspapers were not so nonchalant. The episode caused a great debate between the French and Italian press. The French sculptor Eugène Lequesne offered to roll Bastianini's clay for him for the rest of his life if the Italian could prove that he had done the bust. Lequesne published his attacks in the Paris *Patrie*, and Bastianini, who perhaps realized for the first time that he had been used, replied in the *Gazzetta de Firenze*. The debate has been admirably reconstructed by Sepp Schuller in *Forgers, Dealers, Experts*, 1959:

> *Lequesne:* The bust was produced by an antique process, the clay being pressed into a mould and modelled subsequently. Seams are visible on both shoulders and on the back of the neck, where sections of the mould came together. The hair also shows traces of the liquid clay with which the interior of the mould was smeared.
>
> *Bastianini:* The bust was modelled freehand, leaving as much of it hollow as possible. The cast was taken after firing, and that is why the seams and slip show.
>
> *Lequesne:* On one of the curls on the left side of the head the clay was insufficiently bound in, and a small piece dropped off. The place still shows the original fingerprint by which it was replaced.
>
> *Bastianini:* Aren't fingers always used for modelling?
>
> *Lequesne:* The clay differs from that used in Italy today. It has become porous with age.
>
> *Bastianini:* What makes you say that? I'll send you a specimen of the clay ordinarily used here. Neither chemically nor from the artistic point of view does it differ from that used in the Benivieni bust.
>
> *Lequesne:* Patina was applied to the surface by tobacco smoke.
>
> *Bastianini:* Well, as you haven't guessed my method, I'm not giving any secrets away. But I shall be happy to apply the same patina to any terra-cotta you like. I can hardly believe that you use tobacco smoke for the purpose in France. One dealer in antiquities, at least, smiled grimly when he heard of it.

One of Bastianini's friends in Florence, Dr. Foresi, published an account of the scandal entitled *The Tower of Babel*. Paris struck back with a pamphlet by J. Charvet, *The Ass in the Lion's Skin: A Florentine Hoax*.

No contemporary artist could possibly have sculpted so perfect a masterpiece: of this Count de Nieuwekerke was absolutely certain. He was also tiring of the debate. He wanted it ended, but he would not deal directly with the preposterous Italian upstart. So he made an offer anonymously in *Journal du Nord*, a daily newspaper published in Lille. It caused such instant commotion that he was obliged to repeat it with his name attached in the metropolitan press: de Nieuwekerke offered to pay 15,000 francs for a companion piece of equal merit.

Bastianini answered through a letter delivered to Foresi and published in *La Nazione*:

> Deposit your 15,000 francs in safe hands. We will then choose between us a jury, not composed entirely of Frenchmen, and I will for my part guarantee to make a bust, for 3,000 francs, as good as the *Benivieni*. As for the other 12,000 francs, I will be very generous with you, as you are one of the pillars of the Second Empire, by modelling for you busts of the Twelve Caesars at the price of 1,000 francs apiece.
>
> Florence, February 15, 1868

In March Bastianini repeated the offer in *Gazzetta di Firenze*. The Count did not answer.

Three months later Bastianini, only thirty-seven, was dead.

In the weeks following his death on June 29, 1868, the truth slowly came out. Banti and Costa, who had paid 10,000 lire for the bust of Savonarola and had exhibited it in the Palazzo Riccardi in Florence, now found that they could not sell it at any price. So they gave it to the Monastery of San Marco in Florence, where Savonarola had been prior. The monastery had just been converted into a museum, and Bastianini's bust was honourably ensconced in the cell formerly occupied by Savonarola.

After Bastianini's exposure, the Victoria and Albert Museum simply moved his pieces into the room for moderns and continued to purchase his work: in 1869 a plaster cast of the *Benivieni* bust and the fine bust of Baron von Jenison, in 1891 the wax models (for £5 each) of the marble relief purchased by the museum in 1857, and in 1896 another bust of Savonarola. The Victoria and Albert exhibited these works as examples of nineteenth-century neo-Renaissance sculpture.

During his brief life Giovanni Bastianini had created the most beautiful Renaissance sculpture turned out after the Renaissance had ended. An artist of consummate skill and taste, his episode is called by some today "the case of forgery without a forger."

CHAPTER 2

The Man Who Forged in Gold

Israel Rouchomovsky was a goldsmith and engraver of considerable skill.

One day in 1895 a man who said he was from Kerch' visited Rouchomovsky's workroom in Odessa. He was actually Schapschelle Hochmann, a Rumanian dealer in Ukrainian wheat from the city of Ortschakov. He had found a new, more lucrative commodity to sell: history.

Hochmann needed a goldsmith who was not in the trade in antique art objects and who was skilful and naive. Odessa was a long way from London, Vienna, Paris, and Berlin, and an Odessa goldsmith would probably never learn of a transaction in any of those remote cities. From his travels through south-eastern Europe Hochmann knew of the colony of Odessa goldsmiths.

"I want to give something extraordinary to a distinguished Russian archaeologist," Hochmann declared in effect. "Since he is an archaeologist, the object should resemble something of great antiquity. Perhaps a Greek tiara, in gold of course."

"A tiara will take much gold. It will be too expensive. I can do it in silver."

"No, it must be gold. Gold stands the test of time. It does not corrode."

"What should it look like? I have never seen a Greek tiara."

"I will give you some books. And I want this inscription incised in Greek in the design: 'The Senate and People of Olbia to the Great Invincible Saitaphernes.' "

The small colony of Olbia, like Odessa itself, had been established by the Greeks. In the third century B.C. the people of Olbia had erected a strong wall around the town as protection against the Scythian chief Saitaphernes, whom they had tried unsuccessfully to placate with gold.

For eight months Rouchomovsky fashioned a skull-cap tiara in a shape similar to the Persian-style mitre crown that had become the headdress of the popes. He produced it in three pieces, which he then soldered together so skilfully that experts later would declare it had been hammered from a single gold sheet. It stood seven inches high and weighed about a pound.

Visual interest centred on two relief friezes around the circumference. The lower ring depicted scenes of Scythian life. The upper panel, done in a much larger scale, depicted such episodes from the *Iliad* as the quarrel between Agamemnon and Achilles over the slave Briseis. One of the scenes was freely copied from the atlas plate of the *Shield of Scipio*, a fourth century A.D. silver disc in the Bibliothèque Nationale in Paris. The inscription to the Scythian king was on a band separating the frieze panels.

Hochmann paid Rouchomovsky 2,000 roubles for the tiara. The goldsmith then created other works in antique style, among them "Classical Greek" drinking cups, a fabulous solid-gold sculpture of Achilles and Athena, and a necklace in gold relief with pierced ornamentation.

One of his masterpieces was a small gold bottle scarcely three inches high. A central frieze in bas-relief depicted nuptial scenes with small cupids in the style of the Kerch' vases of the fourth century B.C. found in southern Russia. The ornamentation on the bottle consisted of minute granules of gold laid on grain by grain with infinite skill and precision. Rouchomovsky added his own touch by altering the facial types and the postures of the figures, making most of them profiles. From time to time a good friend, another jeweller named Lifschitz, would drop by to watch him work.

One of the first things Hochmann did to the *Tiara of Saitaphernes* was batter it a bit, so that it would not look so perfect, but he was careful not to damage any of the principal bosses.

It was the end of February 1896, and Hochmann lost no time in getting to Vienna with a remarkable collection of ear-rings, finger rings, hornbook clasps, necklaces, and of course his tiara. Probably Hochmann had obtained the less important pieces from other goldsmiths.

Southern Russia was rich in archaeological sites at which outstanding specimens of Greek gold and silver had been found. Hochmann told of new finds in Olbia, near the confluence of the Bug and Dnieper rivers. The tiara was an unprecedented find, a truly important treasure. At the Imperial Museum Hochmann convinced archaeologists Benndorf, Bohrmann, and Schneider, and several collectors, notably Count Wilczek and Baron Nathaniel Rothschild. Otto Benndorf was particularly enthusiastic. He found the tiara a splendid example of pre-Christian goldsmith's art, and he urged the two patrons to buy it for the Austrian Museum of Arts and Crafts. The asking price was substantial: 100,000 gold kronen.

Two directors from the Imperial Museum's Department of Antiquities were dubious. They found it "peculiar and suspicious" that a work of pure gold more than 2,000 years old should exhibit only superficial damage. Hochmann had prepared himself for this objection by claiming that he had had the tiara restored after discovering it, but the curators' warning was sufficient to kill the sale.

Hochmann offered the tiara by letter to Alexander Stuart Murray, director of Greek and Egyptian antiquities at the British Museum, but Murray replied that, "knowing he [Hochmann] was largely occupied with the fabrication of antique objects of art," the affair did not interest him.

Hochmann's thirty-day Vienna visa was about to run out. Frustrated and recognizing that his own reputation among museum people was working against him, he elected to work through two Viennese, Anton Vogel, an art dealer located on

Margarethenstrasse, and a runner named Szymanski. They would have better entrée to the art world.

Hochmann agreed to let the two Viennese have the tiara for 30,000 gold francs, on condition that they share with him the profits from a higher resale price.

In March Vogel and Szymanski went to Paris. Through a high government official they obtained an interview with M. A. Kaempfen, director of Musées Nationaux and the Louvre, and M. E. Herron Villefosse, curator of the Græco-Roman department at the Louvre. Other gentlemen were also called in—and the judgement was unanimous: the Paris experts had no doubt of the tiara's authenticity. Their judgement was corroborated when their research disclosed that the city of Olbia had indeed paid tribute to Saitaphernes.

Since the tiara was priceless, the Louvre had to have it—before there was any Russian move to pre-empt treasure found on Russian soil.

The price had risen to 200,000 francs, and the sellers demanded immediate payment. There was no time to wait for approval (and money) from the Chamber of Deputies. Baron Edmond de Rothschild had warned that he would buy the tiara for himself if the Louvre did not. Two patrons, Édouard Corroyer and Théodore Reinach, loaned the money to the Louvre, and the deal was closed. Vogel signed the receipt and quit Paris immediately. Eventually the spoils were divided (86,000 francs to Hochmann, 74,000 to Vogel, and 40,000 to Szymanski) but they were not distributed right away.

On April 1, 1896, the *Tiara of Saitaphernes* was officially given a place of honour in the Louvre. It is hard to recall another April Fool's joke of such cost!

But even before the Chamber of Deputies could appropriate the funds to reimburse Corroyer and Reinach, clouds were gathering over the tiara. Veselovskii of the University of St. Petersburg declared in the pages of *Novoye Vremia* that the tiara was a modern fabrication typical of the Ortschakov forgers, but the French were not reading Russian journals.

After the acquisition a Munich archaeologist, Adolph Furtwängler, added his condemnation in writing: the colour of the gold was modern, the tiara lacked the reddish-brown coating found on genuine pieces, the style was a mixture of periods and bore no valid relationship to the antique, the figures wore their garments in a modern manner, their faces and gestures suggested modern melodrama, the vessels in the funeral-pyre scene were anachronistic, the human forms were clumsy and ill-proportioned, and Homeric references were certainly suspicious.

In August the Tenth Congress of Archaeology met in Riga, and there the director of the Odessa Museum, Professor von Stern, asserted that the tiara was a clever forgery. He said that the Hochmann brothers had established a workshop that had manufactured not only the Louvre's tiara but also another one then on exhibit in Krakow and many other objects.

Foreign voices were not all against the tiara. The Louvre found on its side Gaugolf von Kieseritzky, keeper of the department of goldsmith's work at the Hermitage Museum in St. Petersburg. He came to Paris to denounce the tiara but after a careful examination became convinced of its authenticity. Finally, the Chamber of Deputies bowed to the judgement of the Louvre and appropriated the reimbursement. Kieseritzky then recanted his declaration of faith, but his defection was hushed up in Paris.

At the beginning of 1897 Hochmann filed suit in Vienna against Vogel and Szymanski, claiming that they had refused to share the profits of the Louvre sale. They replied—apparently without thought of how their answer implicated them—that the tiara and jewels were false. Then they settled out of court.

But Hochmann was also being pursued by a Russian collector, Souroutchane, for selling fake antique-gold jewellery. Souroutchane identified a caster, Morier, and Rouchomovsky as Hochmann's workmen. A thorough search of Rouchomovsky's workshop turned up "exceedingly beautiful designs of antique ornaments and palm leaves similar to those found on the tiara" (*l'Anthropologie*, 1899). Von Stern went to an archaeological congress in Odessa to denounce the goldsmith, but through the press Rouchomovsky stoutly refused the "undeserved honour" of the authorship of the Louvre's tiara.

For seven years the *Tiara of Saitaphernes* continued to sparkle in a Louvre showcase. The controversy merely served to bring people to look at it.

In the early weeks of 1903 Salomon Reinach, patron Théodore Reinach's brother, complained that two runners had offered him a drinking horn and a collar in gold, supposedly from southern Russia but obviously fake. Although still defending the tiara, he declared that these objects appeared to be "of the same workmanship." Some defence can be offered for this position. If the tiara were genuine (or even thought to be) forgers would naturally imitate it in an effort to impart authenticity to their own products.

In March authorities were investigating a Montmartre painter known as Elina (his real name was Mayence) on suspicion of counterfeiting works by Henri Pilles. Elina was not about to admit faking Pilles, but he did declare himself the creator of the *Tiara of Saitaphernes*! He said that he had made it in 1894 for a man named Spitzer for 4,800 francs—and he boasted too of making false mummies. His confession created a sensation.

P. T. Barnum thereupon wired the French government that he would buy the tiara from the Louvre for 250,000 francs—giving the Louvre a 25 per cent profit—on condition that the tiara turn out to be phoney! On March 19 and 21, 30,000 people went to the Louvre to see the tiara.

Lifschitz, Rouchomovsky's old friend from Odessa, had meanwhile established himself in Paris. On March 23 *Le Matin* published a letter from him certifying that his friend Rouchomovsky had made the tiara and that he himself had watched him make it. He insisted that his friend had acted in good faith and had known nothing of the planned false attribution. Lifschitz's assertion was soon seconded by a Russian woman, Madame Nageborg-Malkine, who had spoken to the goldsmith a few weeks earlier. She said that the poor man was very distressed at the misunderstanding that had placed his work in the Louvre.

Le Figaro then directed its Russian correspondent to seek out Rouchomovsky and obtain a statement; the telegraphed reply was set in large type on the front page on March 25:

THE ENGRAVER ISRAEL ROUCHOMOVSKY, 36 OUSPENSKAIA STREET, ODESSA, STATES CATEGORICALLY THAT HE PRODUCED THE TIARA IN 1896

TO THE ORDER OF A PERSON UNKNOWN, RESIDENT IN KERCH'. ROUCHOMOVSKY IS READY TO COME TO PARIS TO PROVE HIS ASSERTION ON RECEIPT OF TRAVELLING EXPENSES AMOUNTING TO 1,200 FRANCS.

(Rouchomovsky had another good reason for wanting to go to Paris at the time. He had submitted a silver sarcophagus to the Paris Salon. It was decorated in relief with symbols signifying the life of man. From the open coffin rose a golden skeleton consisting of 167 separate parts. It had taken nine years to make, and it had won him a gold medal.)

Within three days public pressure became so clamorous that the Minister of Education informed the Senate that an official inquiry would be made; Professor Clermont-Ganneau of the Collège de France and a member of the Institut de France would be in charge. The tiara was removed from public view and locked up.

France divided into two camps, tiara and anti-tiara, and copies sold better than souvenir models of the Eiffel Tower. Men wore tiara cuff links. Newspapers broke into sly verse linking Saitaphernes' fez with everyone from Elina to the Socialist patriot Jean Jaurés.

Because of the furore, Rouchomovsky was to be sneaked into Paris incognito. A room was readied for him under the name Bardès at the Hôtel Centrale.

He was not a conspicuous man either in personality or in appearance. His wavy dark hair was parted in the middle; he had a tiny goatee, a moustache, and flaring nostrils; and he wore oval rimmed glasses. But the secret of his arrival could not be kept, and when the forty-three-year-old goldsmith arrived on April 5 he was besieged by reporters and autograph seekers. He was a hero.

Louvre representatives took every opportunity to demonstrate that Rouchomovsky could not have been responsible for the tiara. After weeks of cross-examination Clermont-Ganneau, who admitted that he had no particular competence in Greek art, could say only that he found the Russian a commonplace person too lacking in intelligence and archaeological knowledge to give reliable testimony.

Rouchomovsky described his sources, the books which had been given to him. He described how he had made the tiara. He described its ornamentation. Clermont-Ganneau remained unconvinced. Perhaps if he had spoken Russian he would not have been so blinded by the craftsman's crude veneer. Angry, first at having been taken in by Hochmann and then at being disbelieved by the academician, Rouchomovsky called for gold plates. And there before the eyes of the unbelievers he fashioned portions of a new tiara—thus quelling Clermont-Ganneau.

The man who only days before had been hailed as a hero was now scorned as a common forger; he returned to Odessa deeply resentful.

Rouchomovsky turned to his craft to show his scorn for Paris. He fashioned a *Saitaphernes of 1895*, seated on a sarcophagus and wearing the tiara, and a counterpart, *Saitaphernes of 1903*, uncrowned and weeping, again seated on his sarcophagus, while children played ball with his tiara.

He was an elegant artist-craftsman, and the world had used him ill. Hochmann probably went on selling new counterfeits. The tiara remains Louvre property, but it is displayed only during rare exhibits of fake art.

CHAPTER 3

Tales of Mona Lisa

The white moustache of the Marquis Eduardo de Valfierno—the name he was currently using—twitched as he picked up his fresh edition of *La Prensa*.

He did not waste a glance on the headlines but riffled the pages rapidly until he reached the obituaries. Valfierno paid no attention to the deaths of women, for he was interested in widows. Soon after a rich man died in Buenos Aires his widow would receive a visit from the mannerly Latin-American Valfierno. A few words of condolence were all that he needed to create rapport. He brought the widow the subtle scolding she needed, for even the best wife thinks of things that she could have done to make her husband's days happier.

When he had the lady properly responsive, he would offer her the solution: "Señora, you could render no greater honour to your husband than to beautify the chapel of your church with a painting in his name. But it should be the work of a special artist. I can offer you a great Murillo—a genuine Murillo, from the hand of Spain's greatest painter. This you cannot deny him."

If the deceased had come originally from another city, Valfierno would suggest that the painting be given to one of the churches there, thus keeping Buenos Aires from becoming overcrowded with Murillos, which would have put an early end to the game. He thus spread works by Bartolomé Esteban Murillo the length of Argentina, from Córdoba to Tierra del Fuego, from Atlantic to Andes.

Valfierno's accomplice, Yves Chaudron, was a Frenchman so thin that his bones showed through his skin. He had originally been a picture restorer, a good one. From this craft it had been an easy step for him to begin painting his own imitations.

According to the Marquis's *Saturday Evening Post* biographer, Karl Decker, the Valfierno-Chaudron factory, "one of the busiest places in Argentina," sold Murillos by the score until Argentina had "more Murillos than it had cows."

Forgery on such a scale is not a modern invention. Even the earliest periods of civilization recorded artistic duplicity of sizeable proportions. Pliny reported an early Egyptian treatise on the fabrication of bogus jewellery. The rare becomes desirable precisely because no one else can have it. To the forger, this situation is irresistible.

As Valfierno and Chaudron were aware, successful art forgery is probably the most highly skilled manufacturing industry in the world. The most fabulous forgeries have usually been the creative work of a single individual or at most of a small ring: a painter, a pusher, an expert or two, perhaps a customs official. Bribery is frequently used to enlarge the circle of co-operation without making outsiders privy to the workings of the ring. Usually the forger produces on speculation, but for Valfierno, Chaudron produced on order.

An oil painting consists of a series of layers. First, there is a support: wood, metal, or canvas mounted on a stretcher. This support is covered with a priming coat to bond subsequent layers of paint to the support. Next comes the paint, which makes the actual picture; it consists of some kind of vehicle—various kinds of oils mixed often with thinners, thickeners, or drying agents—plus pigments. Finally, there is a protective film of varnish or other fixative.

Every artist develops his own techniques for handling different materials. He may paint in a very thin medium so that brush marks disappear and there is no visible sign of his technique. Or he may lay down a thick impasto with brush or knife, an immediate personal identification. The forger must duplicate these techniques, and he is up against the fact that in the past they were often jealously guarded secrets that perished with the artist. In analysing El Greco's *Disrobing of Christ*, for example, one expert has identified more than thirty separate procedures undertaken by the artist before the final image was executed.

Such complexity obliges the forger to take short-cuts, through either ignorance or impatience. He strives for the final effect and runs the risk that careful technological analysis, if undertaken, may unmask him. But, of course, in Argentina at the turn of the century Valfierno and Chaudron had no reason to fear either technological or aesthetic investigation. There were no experts south of the equator to challenge them.

In the factory they turned whirling electric fans on Chaudron's freshly varnished canvases to dry them and to split the shrinking surface into a thousand cracks. They reversed a vacuum cleaner to coat the varnish with 200 years' worth of dust. Finely ground coffee scattered about made passable flyspecks.

If Chaudron had been a less-than-perfect copyist at the beginning, by the end of the Argentine period he had painted so many fakes that he had become exceedingly skilled. When Valfierno finally tired of bilking widows, he left the business to Chaudron and went into finance on a grand scale. He also left Buenos Aires—suddenly and with a quarter-million dollars in gold—and set up operations in Mexico City. Unable to run the old business alone, Chaudron soon joined him.

There was already a famous Murillo in Mexico City. The Marquis didn't think it was a very good one—if indeed it was a Murillo at all—but the guidebooks extolled it, and everyone in the city was convinced of its authenticity.

Valfierno lived in a large hotel frequented by foreigners, mostly North Americans. He was pleasantly surprised to discover the relatively large number of people—"collectors"—who would buy anything that they were persuaded to admire, even though they could never under any circumstances resell it, exhibit it publicly, or even show it to a few close friends and would have to keep it forever hidden.

The gift of the confidence man lies in being able to spot people susceptible to corruption. When they had one, Valfierno and Chaudron would sneak a fresh copy of the painting into the building where the Murillo was hanging and slip it inside the frame behind the original. Both pictures faced the same direction; an unsuspecting person would think that he was seeing the back of the original when he was really looking at the back of the duplicate. Inside a heavy frame in a poorly lighted location the double thickness was never noticed.

At a quiet hour when few people were about, Valfierno would take the buyer to see the picture. "There's your picture," he would whisper. "Like the guidebook says, Murillo never painted a better one. The price we have asked is really not enough, but we'll stick to our end of the bargain. We're fools, you see. We run a lot of risk."

"You'll deliver it—out of Mexico?"

"That's included in the price."

"I don't see how you're going to get it."

"That's our worry."

"It's a deal then."

"Do you have a pen?"

"Yes."

Valfierno would pull the painting away from the wall. He always made a point of keeping his eyes aimed not at the Murillo but outward towards the room. "Take your pen," he would say to the customer, "and sign your name on the back. I can't see what you're doing. Make any mark you wish—just so you can be certain when you get the painting that we have delivered *your* Murillo." Upon Valfierno's insistence each customer would make his mark on the back of what he thought was the Murillo; some signatures were flourishing and as unfakeable as a bank officer's name on a cashier's check, others ingenious ciphers hidden in a corner. An especially suspicious customer might even snip off a few centimetres of thread to match with the canvas when the Murillo turned up at home. Every customer received the precise canvas that he had signed.

During a good week Valfierno might close several such sales. The Marquis had a large supply of undated Spanish and English clippings declaring that on the previous day some black scoundrels—*Yanquis* no doubt—had ripped the famous Murillo from its frame and that it had disappeared. Valfierno mailed them to his customers, claiming that they had been clipped from Mexico City papers. If there was any chance that the purchaser might return to Mexico City, Valfierno would hint that the Mexicans were probably going to hang a copy in the original's place while the investigation continued.

Business was so good that Chaudron hired native talent to help him paint the Murillos. He himself had become very bored with re-executing the same canvas. But the Mexicans were too talkative to fit well into a confidence ring, and word leaked out. When grafters and crooks tried to muscle in, Valfierno and Chaudron moved to Paris.

Every year thousands of works by Jean Baptiste Camille Corot, Jean François Millet, Titian, and Murillo were sold in Paris, and the forgery field was overcrowded. Valfierno's pride demanded something more prestigious and more daring. Using his profits from Argentina and Mexico, he set about underwriting the supreme coup in art forgery, for which he recruited from the vast number of confidence men he knew three of the very best: a monocled Englishman of impressive nonchalance, a Frenchman who had all the right connections, and an American who knew a sizeable percentage of those listed in the Social Register.

The ring set up headquarters in a villa near the Place de l'Étoile; their target area included a score of luxury hotels in that expensive quarter of Paris. They entertained lavishly—with apéritifs, fine French cuisine and wines, champagne, Napoléon brandy in huge snifters, rich Havana cigars. As hosts the four were carefully careless talkers, given to intimations, nonchalant innuendo, blatant boasting. They could do anything for their friends; a friend had only to ask. Did he need a string pulled in the French bureaucracy? Did he want to meet the star of the Folies Bergère?

Their delivery of these little services quickly certified the conspirators' skill and reliability, and, once confidence had been established, Valfierno's crew sold various treasures from the Louvre. Nothing was ever actually stolen, though the purchasers believed otherwise. A buyer who showed interest in a particular painting and was willing to pay the price soon found it delivered to his doorstep, usually outside France. The coveted object would arrive with a sheaf of documents on Louvre stationery and a harvest of official Louvre seals and ribbons. The documents always included at least one marked "confidential" which reported that the particular masterpiece had disappeared and that a replica of the stolen object had been hung temporarily to keep the scandal from the public and to facilitate capture of the guilty parties.

For three years the ring continued to sell fine things from the Louvre. Then one evening, when the foursome and an American collector they were entertaining were far along the champagne trail, one of the ring suggested that they might steal the *Mona Lisa* for their guest.

"Why not?" asked the American.

Valfierno and the others had expected a rebuff from the collector. They were stunned by his instant response to this outrageous proposal.

"Why not?" the American asked. "It has never been done, but that is no reason it could not be done, and, knowing Paris as you do, you should be able to manage it."

In June 1910, a month after the expensive bargain was struck, the American had his *Mona Lisa*. He was told, as usual, that a copy had been substituted in the Louvre. The purchaser was satisfied at first. But either because he wanted to boast of his possession or because he wanted to smoke out some corroboration of the authenticity of his painting, he dropped a few hints here and there. Soon *Le Cri de Paris*, an obscure weekly, picked up the rumour. Then an anonymous writer in the same weekly declared that the *Mona Lisa* hanging in the Salon Carré at the Louvre was a copy that he had seen in the hands of dealer Louis Heuzy in St. Étienne—a copy identifiable by two small green spots that the writer had spilled on the painting while he was restoring it for Heuzy in 1902. (Thirteen months later—after

August 21, 1911—the paper recanted: it had published the story only to arouse public indignation over lax security in the Louvre!) Soon experts were flocking to the Louvre to inspect the painting and to declare that it *was* the authentic picture purchased from Leonardo da Vinci by King François I.

These assertions caused no little trouble for the ring until Valfierno used his connections with several amenable Paris journalists, who renewed the claim that a copy had been substituted and parried the experts with friendly Gallic sarcasm. The American believed the rumour, but this experience taught the ring a harsh lesson: they had to change their methods if they wished to sell fakes of anything as well-known as a da Vinci.

In 1911, as now, the *Mona Lisa* was considered by many to be the greatest painting in the world. So bewitching has the subject's smile appeared to some that the Louvre—in 1911—was receiving impassioned fan mail addressed to her. The painting is of Lisa di Anton Maria di Noldo Gherardini, third wife of a Florentine merchant, Francesco Bartolommeo di Zanobi del Giocondo, to whom she was espoused at thirteen. In most countries the picture is known as *La Gioconda*.

Da Vinci began painting her in 1503 and continued the work into 1506. How can a portrait take so long? It was no simple portrait; it became, rather, an expression of deep psychological affinities between the painter at fifty and his twenty-four-year-old model. X-ray photographs reveal three completely different conceptions under the final painting, the surface of which consists of perhaps hundreds of infinitely thin glazes.

Leonardo kept the painting, and it was one of three of his own works he possessed when he moved into the little castle of Cloux near Amboise as the guest of King François I of France. François purchased the portrait. The price usually mentioned is 12,000 francs—about $9,200—but at least one source claims that the amount actually paid to Leonardo was 4,000 scudi, estimated at nearly twelve tons of pure silver, worth about £140,000—more than $500,000 today! Whatever the arrangement between Leonardo and François, the value in 1911 may well have been the $5 million cited by the newspapers. It would be far more than that today.

The Duke of Buckingham tried to purchase *Mona Lisa* from François in 1623, and the French King would have sold it but was dissuaded by his court. Buckingham plotted to steal it but abandoned the idea. At the time it was hanging in Fontainebleau. During the French Revolution it was moved to the Louvre.

In spite of the painting's fame, the Valfierno ring had several substantial ambiguities working for them in their efforts to sell the *Mona Lisa*. First, there had long been a question about the authenticity—or at least the *uniqueness*—of the Louvre painting.

Leonardo's first biographer, Giogio Vasari, who had been a young boy when the painter moved to France, said that the *Mona Lisa* which he had seen had been unfinished, a term that does not describe the Louvre *Mona Lisa*. Might Leonardo have painted at least *two* versions: the first commissioned by Francesco del Giocondo, which was still incomplete when copied in a sketch by Raphael in Leonardo's Florentine studio in 1504; and the second, requested later by Giulio de' Medici after Mona Lisa had become his mistress, which Leonardo kept for some reason and later turned over to Cardinal Luigi d'Aragona and his secretary, Antonio de Beatis, representative of François, in the castle of Cloux?

Leonardo's own words add to the ambiguity. He said that he had painted her *facta di naturali*, "according to nature." But that could mean either that he painted her from life or that he painted her in the nude. And nude *Mona Lisas* do exist in the world. In fact the world abounds in *Mona Lisas*, many purporting to be by Leonardo. All that Valfierno had done in selling a Chaudron copy was to add to the supply.

For example, the following collections are known to contain copies:

Quimper Musée Municipal des Beaux Arts—a copy given to the city by the Count of Silguy in 1869 but catalogued as a copy from Leonardo's time.

Tours Musée des Beaux Arts—two copies, both from the sixteenth century.

Mulhouse Musée des Beaux Arts—a copy "probably by a pupil of Leonardo."

Musée Ingres, Montauban—a complete fake that came from Ingres's estate and may have been done by Paul Balze, a student of Ingres; scientific examination revealed that it had been executed on paper and showed false cracking because of the glue.

Musée de l'Ain, Bourg—a copy claimed to be from the period and even better than that in the Prado.

Prado, Madrid—probably the best copy of all (if the one in the Louvre is real), considered to be the work of Andrea Soli, a pupil of da Vinci, though Bernard Berenson said that it might have been done in the sixteenth century by a Spaniard; when the Louvre's *Mona Lisa* was stolen, this version was widely heralded as Leonardo's preparatory study; José de Armas still argues that it is the real one.

Chamber of Deputies, Rome—a copy from the collection of Cardinal Silvio Gonzaga and probably by Bernardino Luini.

Nasjonalgalleriet, Oslo—a seventeenth-century copy signed Bernardino Luini but probably painted by Philippe de Champaigne!

Walters Art Gallery, Baltimore—a sixteenth-century copy.

Panacothek Museum, Munich—a seventeenth-century copy.

William D. Vernon collection, New York—a well-documented version that is stubbornly declared by the family to be the *original* and valued at $2.5 million; it came from the personal collection of Marie Antoinette and in 1793 was given by the Queen to a young American, William Henry Vernon, who had been introduced at court by Benjamin Franklin. It now belongs to the Otis Art Institute of Los Angeles County.

Hekking collection, Nice—a copy known variously as the "Gioconda of Nice" or the "Gioconda of Cannes" and intermittently declared the real thing by Riviera papers; its provenance is unknown.

Lord Brownlow collection, Grantham, England—a copy that is withheld from public view and photography; Guy Isnard wonders whether or not it is one of the *seven* copies which once belonged to the Reynolds collection!

Lord Spencer collection, Northampton, England—a nude version, *La Belle Gabrielle*, probably painted by a student of Leonardo in the sixteenth century.

Paolo Weiss collection, Rome—another nude version claimed by Federico Hermanin to be an authentic Leonardo but by others to be from the sixteenth or seventeenth century.

Carrara Academy, Bergamo—a seventeenth-century nude framed by tapestry flowers.

The Hermitage Museum, Leningrad—a kind of striptease Lisa which has been attributed to Leonardo and to Cesare de Sesto.

In 1952 in connection with the 500th anniversary exhibition of Leonardo's birth, Michael Florisonne and Sylvie Béguin mentioned sixty-one known copies of *La Gioconda*, and this list may not have included the late Marcel Duchamp's dadaist version with moustache. But even so it had to be limited to copies of some skill, age, and recognition, for a few years ago a copyist in the Louvre completed his *one thousandth* portrait of this patient woman.

After its coup the extravagantly self-confident ring could no longer be content with selling lesser objects. But if it was to sell another counterfeit of *La Gioconda*, the buyer would have to be absolutely convinced that he had purchased the painting which had hung in the Louvre. Meanwhile, Chaudron was put to work painting a new *Mona Lisa*.

The Louvre *Mona Lisa* was not painted on canvas but on a wooden panel made of three slabs of heavy, close-grained Italian walnut 1.5 inches thick. The panel measures 30.32 inches by 20.86 inches and weighs eighteen pounds. In 1911 it was braced and secured against warping by a massive cradle that weighed another 110 pounds. The Renaissance frame added twenty-five pounds. A heavy glass shadow box had been attached to protect the picture from vandalism, and it added forty pounds more, bringing the total weight to almost 200 pounds.

The frame, cradle, and shadow box were unimportant to Chaudron, but the structure of the panel and the quality and verisimilitude of the painting were crucial. In European museums, from the Louvre to the Prado, copyists are allowed to set up easels in the galleries and to copy or interpret any paintings they like, but they are not allowed to make any copy of the same size as the original. Chaudron set himself up in the Salon Carré, and there day by day he painted a masterly, though reduced, *Mona Lisa*, which would serve as his guide for the full-size copy he would do in the privacy of his studio. To obtain aged Italian walnut for the panel, an antique bed, itself a priceless antique from Leonardo's period, was sacrificed.

When Chaudron's full-scale copy was complete, he turned it over to the ring, and before long the painting was in the United States, where it went through customs easily as a copy. Since the original was hanging in the Louvre, the copy aroused neither interest nor attention. By then Chaudron had started on another *Mona Lisa*. In the meantime, Valfierno and his three friends were hard at work selling *Mona Lisas*—for future delivery in the United States.

By the time Chaudron had finished six *Mona Lisas*, the ring decided that it dare not delay much longer in delivering the promised merchandise. Chaudron could go on making copies, and the ring might be able to sell them, but they risked loss of their first clients and also loose talk from disgruntled customers. As one of the most respected art historians of all time, Max Friedländer, once observed, "Forgeries must be served hot as they come from the oven." It was time to act, and Valfierno's next move was to recruit Vincenzo Perugia.

Perugia had been born in Jumenza, Italy. Although he loved Italy, he nevertheless had moved to France, where he soon ran foul of the law. On June 23, 1908, he was sentenced to a short prison term in Macon for attempted robbery; on February 9, 1909, he was arrested for illegal possession of weapons. As a result the French police had twice put his fingerprints on file.

Perugia's prison term was only about thirty days; in July 1908 he went to work for a firm of house painters and glaziers in Paris. In October 1910 Louvre officials decided to put their greatest masterpieces under glass. This move was strongly debated by the French art community. Glass cut down the visibility of the art and was therefore undesirable; but even less desirable on a painting, the Louvre maintained, were finger marks, an acid bath, or a knife slash.

Perugia's employers were given the contract to put the *Mona Lisa* under glass, and he was one of four men assigned to the task. He was in and out of the Louvre constantly, and learned the building, the workmen, the rules, the procedures. The job was complex and had to be done four times before the museum was satisfied. It was completed in January 1911. Then Perugia quit to work for another firm. Though no longer assigned to the Louvre, he returned from time to time to visit his friends.

Perugia had worked for the Marquis Valfierno before and was recruited into the ring, which was at last ready to steal the real *Mona Lisa*. Perugia knew nothing of Chaudron's fakes and assumed that the *Mona Lisa* itself was to be sold. The day of the actual theft was Monday, August 21, 1911.

At that time the Louvre was closed to the public on Mondays, which is cleaning day. A workman's white blouse was a carte blanche to come and go without challenge. Although curators, photographers with special assignments, and art historians with passes could wander freely through the usually darkened galleries, the security force was reduced from 120 to 12. These twelve included none of the roving plainclothes detectives on the force.

About 4.00 p.m. Sunday, August 20, Perugia and two accomplices drifted into the Louvre among the thousands of other visitors who crowd the museum on the Sabbath to the point that copyists are not permitted to clutter the galleries on Sundays.

On days when the copyists do work, their easels, camp-stools, and canvases are gathered up by the staff and taken after the museum closes to a little room between the Galerie d'Appollon and the Salle Duchâtel. The door to this room was concealed, but Perugia knew where it was, and the three men were hidden there when the museum closed on Sunday afternoon. It was not a place into which a watchman would poke his head, and they spent an unmolested though uncomfortable night.

When the Louvre workmen began flocking in at 6.30 the next morning Perugia and his friends put on smuggled-in white blouses. They slipped out and pretended to be busy with assigned tasks. Unfortunately the head workman, Picquet, had started a group on some repairs in the Grande Galerie, adjacent to the Salon Carré. He was in and out constantly, and Perugia dared do nothing until Picquet went off to another part of the building.

At 7.20 a.m. precisely—as he later told investigators—Picquet entered the Salon Carré with two of his men and said to them, pointing to the Leonardo, "That is the most valuable picture in the Louvre." When Picquet came back, just before 8.35 a.m., he noticed that she had taken a little vacation!

She had, in fact, been taken off the wall within five minutes after he had passed through at 7.20. Because of his work making the shadow box, Perugia knew how she was fastened to the wall, and he also knew how heavy she would be. The weight gave the thieves some trouble, but they soon had the painting unhooked.

Three men carrying a painting on a working day—in 1911—would hardly arouse the interest of other workmen in the Louvre, except perhaps that of Picquet, who was not around. Photographers regularly asked that various paintings be brought to museum studios next to the Salle Duchâtel, where they could be photographed under better lighting.

A vacant spot on the wall is not in itself suspicious, and even Picquet did not raise an eyebrow when he noted the *Mona Lisa*'s absence. In fact, he quipped to his workmen, "I guess the authorities have removed it because they thought we would steal it!"

The three thieves lugged the painting into the Grande Galerie and turned right into the Salon de Sept Mètres and out through a corner door to a cramped stairway used only by the staff. There they removed the wooden panel and abandoned the rest. There too Perugia left for the police a beautiful left thumbprint on the glass that had shielded the *Mona Lisa*.

Then disaster struck. From a wax impression Valfierno had made a key for the door at the bottom of the stairway, but Perugia had never tried it in the lock. The key did not work. Furious, Perugia yanked a screwdriver from his pocket and set about stripping off the lock itself. He had removed the bronze knob and was twisting out the second screw when his accomplice outside the door to the Salle de Sept Mètres stuck his head through and whistled. Someone was coming. Perugia stepped back. He dropped the doorknob into his pocket, hid the *Mona Lisa* under his blouse, and waited.

The intruder was Sauvet, the official plumber. Perugia lost no time in complaining that some dolt had swiped the doorknob and that he could not open the door. Obligingly Sauvet thrust in his key and unlocked the door, then twisted the knob bar with a pair of pliers. "Better leave the door open so it won't bother anyone else," Sauvet suggested.

He went on his way, and Perugia's accomplices ran down the stairs. The three went out into the Cour du Sphinx. They quickly crossed the Salle d'Afrique to the Cour Visconti, and there they found a door wide-open to the street. The guard had gone off for a bucket of water to wash the vestibule.

Perugia wrapped his white blouse around *Mona Lisa* and took off down the street, not even pausing when he flung the door-knob into the old moat-like dry ditch beside the Louvre. An automobile was waiting, and within fifteen minutes Perugia and *Mona Lisa* were at the ring's new headquarters on the Left Bank. No one else from the ring had been near the Louvre, and all had ironclad alibis.

The theft was not noticed until Tuesday! Exactly twenty-four hours to the minute after Picquet had last seen the *Mona Lisa* in place, Brigadier Poupardin of the Louvre guards passed through the Salon Carré and observed that the painting was not there. At 9.00 a.m. a painter named Louis Beroud arrived. He was painting a picture of the gallery itself and complained of the absence of the Leonardo.

"It is being photographed," Poupardin explained. When he passed by again before noon, Beroud asked him to have the photographer bring it back so that he could continue with his project. Poupardin returned within minutes. "The picture is not there," he reported. "They know nothing about it."

He promptly called Georges Bénédite, curator of Egyptian antiquities, who was acting head of the museum during the vacation of archaeologist Théophile Homolle, curator of the Louvre and director of the national museums. Homolle would be fired. Bénédite called Louis Lepine, prefect of the Paris police. Lepine closed the museum and flooded it with detectives. Lepine went personally to report the theft to the Minister of Interior before going to the Louvre to take command of the investigation. The consensus was that the thieves would keep the original and return an imitation to the Louvre, but other theories also abounded, and the press soon added numerous others. A tiny announcement of the theft appeared in the 5.00 p.m. edition of

Le Temps, and a general press conference was convened at the museum at 5.30.

The next morning—Wednesday—the world was rocked by the news of the theft, the most insolent deed in the whole history of art! By then the ring was ready to embark for the United States. During the next few weeks ocean liners would be subject to thorough search. *Le Champagne*, which sailed Tuesday for South America, was virtually torn apart, and so were *Kaiser Wilhelm II* and *Oceanic* when they reached New York. But the ring's copies were long since in the United States, and the ring's members soon joined them. The men quickly made their appointed rounds and sold all six Chaudron copies at $300,000 apiece, with no questions asked; each buyer was certain that he possessed the authentic Louvre *Mona Lisa*, and none would ever dare solicit an expert appraisal.

According to one account, that was supposedly related to Decker by Valfierno, Perugia, seeking more profit for himself, subsequently stole the painting back from the ring. Valfierno did not go after it again, as the effort would have increased the risk of being caught; besides, Perugia had no contacts for selling it. Indeed, when he did try to sell it he demonstrated the weaknesses of the amateur. In November 1913 he wrote to the Florentine dealer Alfredo Geri offering to sell the *Mona Lisa* so that it could be restored to the Italian people, to whom, he insisted, it rightfully belonged.

Inclined at first to treat the letter as that of a crank, Geri eventually thought better of it and answered. Within a few weeks Geri; Giovanni Poggi, director of the famous Uffizi Gallery in Florence; and the Italian police had both Perugia and *La Gioconda* in custody. By the end of December the painting was reinstalled in the Salon Carré to a welcome worthy of a conquering Napoléon returning home.

Perugia was an embarrassment to French police. During the original investigation they had interrogated everyone who had had access to the Louvre when the paintings were being glassed. They had interviewed—and dismissed—the Italian. They had two complete sets of fingerprints on file from his arrests in 1908 and 1909, and Alphonse Bertillon—the man who founded the science of fingerprint identification—had found a perfect thumbprint on the piece of glass that had covered the *Mona Lisa.* But the print happened to be from the left thumb, and if *any* search was made through all the 750,000 sets of criminal prints on file the police checked only for right thumbs!

Perugia went to prison briefly and maintained he had worked alone.

In spite of the return of the painting, rumours about the *Mona Lisa* were hardly over. Such stories will never cease. Based upon revelations borrowed from the London *Sunday Express*, *L'Oeuvre* reported on November 20, 1926, that an accomplice of Perugia, Jack Dean (one of Valfierno's ring?), had made six copies and had sold five. The *Mona Lisa* that Perugia had stolen—hence the version returned to the Louvre—had been the sixth copy! Dean had kept the *original*, which at one time he had tried to sell as a copy in Paris for 200 francs. Another version of the same tale claims that Dean sold it to a merchant in Algiers.

In 1949 another *Mona Lisa* was found in the majestic disorder of an antique shop on the Côte d'Azur, and a local journalist used two columns to plead that Leonardo might have painted two. And why not? In 1950 an American, a Dr. Yodston, claimed that infra-red investigation had proved that his *Mona Lisa* was older than that in the Louvre and therefore the original—a thesis promptly denied by Florentine experts Roberto Longhi and Roberto Papini. If there is another real *Mona Lisa* by Leonardo, it most likely is either that in the Vernon collection or that in the Prado, probably the former.

CHAPTER 4

The Aristocrat of Three-Dimensional Forgery

Gently, Alceo Dossena tapped the granite griffin into place. At last he had shaved enough from the left shoulder so that the sculpture slipped into place as perfectly as a key into its own lock. It was just what he wanted, the craftsman's perfection. Dossena was usually a fast worker, but he had wasted too many days studying the blunted remains of the original griffin and then fashioning, from his imagination, a latter-day replacement. Stylistically the new gargoyle could hold its own with its centuries-older, more weathered companions on the cathedral spire.

The craftsman sat back on the scaffolding and through half-closed eyes looked wearily at the griffin smirking snugly in its niche. His piece was perfect. But it was too perfect—too shiny, too sharp, too new. It looked like a modern replacement. It needed to have its nose flattened a little and its sheen darkened. Only then could he mortar it in place.

Ageing a gargoyle was no problem. Alceo knew the secrets, and he had intended to do it all along. He could do it the easy way with a little carbon black. This gargoyle might be his last job. He couldn't tell, and he was worried. He could not work rapidly for when the work was done he might be done too. The war had dried up funds for church restoration, funds that had previously enabled him to ply his trade in so many parts of Italy.

He had been born in Cremona on October 8, 1878 to a family of general artisans, who were by turns—and by their wits—sculptors, architects, and painters. He had learned all their skills. By the age of six he could make an extraordinarily fine drawing of a classical head. He had served two formal apprenticeships, the first as a cartoonist for a silk weaver beginning at age twelve, the second as a marble mason. From the first experience he had learned principles of design and from the second the discipline and skill of physical execution. Immensely capable with his hands, he had even made violins, according to Schüller, "said to have been as good as the highly prized old instruments." His first jobs had required him to repair old marble balustrades, columns, and statues in Cremona, Ferrara, Parma, Milan, and Bologna, work which demanded an imperceptible marriage of old and new.

Restoration had frequently meant creation of new works to replace pieces beyond repair; he had created tombstones, fountains, mantels, statuettes, and decorative plaques of his own design. To absorb the style and meaning of the Renaissance, he had gone into the churches for first-hand study of sculptures, a study that had purified his taste.

When Italy jumped into World War I the year after it began, painters were made to hurl grenades, and sculptors to drag howitzers up impassable canyons.

Perhaps because he loved Madonnas and disliked gargoyles, Alceo Dossena was destined to be numbered among the luckier ones. For a time after restoration funds expired he was broke, but the conscription machinery soon took him off the streets, and he found himself in the imperial army. The younger, stronger men had been taken first, but the war was not going well, and less able, older conscripts were eventually called up. Dossena was one of them.

Although the pay was lamentable, Dossena at least had plenty of pasta, a dry place to sleep, and warm though ill-fitting and scratchy clothes. Spared the rigours of the front lines, he was assigned to garrison duty at Poggio-Mirteto, where he had enough free time to create artistic objects from wood and stone. He traded them as best he could for money or privileges.

Nevertheless, as Christmas of 1916 approached, Dossena, then thirty-eight, was so broke that he could not buy gifts for his family. He did have one unsold piece, a stone Madonna and child in bas-relief and perfected with the same meticulous care that he had lavished on his griffin. There was no point in trying to dispose of it in the barracks; they were filled with men as broke as he.

At the last moment he obtained a pass, and Christmas Eve found him in the artists' quarter in Rome. But his quest for a buyer was fruitless. When he entered the Frascati wineshop in Via Mario de Fiori for a Chianti, he was tired and despondent. He had been carrying the newspaper-wrapped Madonna under his slate-green cloak, and with a melancholy gesture he laid the unwieldy package down before him. Desperately, he hoped the curious wineshop owner would buy it.

"I'm not interested," Frascati replied cruelly. "Look about you, soldier. My walls are covered with religious bric-a-brac. How can I use another Madonna? But it is Christmas Eve, isn't it? Maybe I can help."

Frascati trotted across the street and fetched Alfredo Fasoli, a goldsmith. The wineshop owner hoped to get a finder's fee from Fasoli if the soldier's piece was worth anything.

Fasoli hedged. He scowled and shook his head in the manner of centuries of hagglers. "No, this doesn't look interesting. Where did you get it?"

"I'm selling it for a friend in the fort," Dossena lied. "He can't get out over Christmas."

Fasoli figured that either Dossena or the friend, if he existed, had stolen the sculpture from some church. It was an admirable piece of workmanship, a lovely antique. They argued on, and finally Dossena accepted 100 lire.

Back in his shop Fasoli looked at the new Madonna more closely. It was a beautiful steal! But, as he turned it over again and again, he realized that it was not an antique. There was nothing that he could put his finger on specifically as wrong, but it was a fake! He was certain that Dossena had sculpted it! He was sure that he would have no trouble selling it as an antique. But he did not know who the soldier was or where to find him.

But a few days later he bumped into Dossena accidentally.

"I can use more pieces like the one I took off your hands the other day. You are very clever. Of course I saw right away that it was a modern piece." Fasoli drew closer to Dossena. "You can make more, can't you?"

Dossena was unsure of the goldsmith's game and did not reply.

"You're very clever. I'll take everything you can do. There's just one thing. . . ."

"Yes?"

"Can you put a few more whiskers on your work? The older it looks, the easier it is to sell.

"I can, if that's what you wish."

That was what Fasoli wished. Every piece of stone that Dossena brought in, Fasoli would turn to gold. He began with that first Madonna and child, displaying it in the most prominent spot in his shop, where it was quickly spied by a collector. "It's an absolutely authentic piece," Fasoli bubbled. "It's of signal rarity, a perfect antique." The collector offered a princely sum to convince Fasoli that he should part with the sculpture.

Dossena abandoned all personal work and during his off hours in the army began to make things for Fasoli. His first commissioned sculpture was a medieval figure. He received 200 lire for it and worried that the dealer would lose money. Fasoli did not tell Dossena that he had sold the piece immediately for 3,000 lire—2,000 of it in gold.

Dossena's talent was too much for Fasoli to handle alone. He turned to a fellow Roman, Romano Palesi. Palesi did a big business in phoney antique furniture—he was called "the wormwood king"—and was exactly the kind of man Fasoli could trust.

After the war the new partners invited Dossena to move to Rome, where they could keep their eyes on him; they offered him a steady income of about $200 a month. So in 1919 Alceo

Dossena took a studio on Via del Vantazzo, not too far from Fasoli's shop and the Piazza di Spagna. Despite their promises, Fasoli and Palesi did not always pay promptly. They wanted Dossena as cheaply as they could get him and thought that by complaining of not yet being able to sell his things they could discourage him from seeking other arrangements. They commissioned him to do a variety of sculpture.

Neither Fasoli nor Palesi could have anticipated the breadth of Dossena's ability. Most forgers are prisoners of a limited period or style. They are forced into tight boxes by limited abilities and psychological quirks. The forger who can make a passable fake Picasso most likely will botch a Dufy, and what he would do trying to imitate an Ingres or a Delacroix is too horrible to imagine. Dossena's unscrupulous dealers must have realized this. They gave him new assignments hopeful that the results would be satisfactory, but they had no right to expect Dossena to do as well as he did.

One by one they added new artists to the craftsman's repertoire—Niccola and Giovanni Pisano, Simone Martini, Lorenzo Vecchietta, Donatello, Mino da Fiesole, Bernardo Rossellino, Desiderio da Settignano, Gianlorenzo Bernini. In amazement, they asked him to do Gothic sculpture in wood. They commissioned ancient Greek statuary. Dossena moved back and forth among media—stone, wood, bronze, terra-cotta. He moved back and forth in time too, his work spanning a millennium and a half. And he achieved a success unmatched in the annals of artistic imitation by any other known individual. One day the brilliant Max Friedländer would call Dossena the "aristocrat of forgery."

Dossena's achievement on behalf of Simone Martini (1284–1344) is especially interesting. Martini was a painter, but never, as far as was known, a sculptor. Dossena studied his painting *The Annunciation* and then proceeded to translate the two-dimensional portrait into a three-dimensional seated *Madonna* in wood. Unsuspecting experts acclaimed the bust as a major discovery, and art historians immediately modified their Martini lectures.

The wooden *Madonna* was supposedly 600 years old, a treasure. It was acquired for the Frick Collection in New York (as were Dossena versions of Donatello and Vecchietta). Another "Martini," a marble, was sold to the Frick—according to Harold Parsons, a buyer for American museums who subsequently compiled a dossier on Dossena—for an incredible $225,000! It is now owned by the University of Pittsburgh.

Dossena created new pieces for Pietro da Rho, a fifteenth-century painter and sculptor who had lived in Cremona, pieces that, according to Illemo Carnelli, director of the Museo Civico of Cremona, enhanced the fame of Pietro. The Celle Palace in Cremona received "Renaissance" bas-reliefs by Dossena.

Pedigrees did have to be concocted, to overcome the uncertainties of more cautious buyers. By the time that a Dossena Madonna reached its ultimate owner, it was blanketed in documents, opinions, and testimonials. Many of these opinions were honestly given by experts who had been tripped up by the manoeuvres of manipulators farther back in the line.

Describing marble reliefs that he supposed to be by Vecchietta, the renowned W. R. Valentiner, director of the Detroit Institute of Arts, declared:

> The noble, slightly melancholic types are completely filled with the tender lyric atmosphere of Sienese art and spread out their luxurious robes with such richness and beauty that we are reminded of Greek relief of the fifth century B.C. . . . Vecchietta was influenced by classic art . . . when he was in Rome in 1464. Soon after this it was in Rome that these reliefs were probably made. They show a great advance over the marble figures by this artist in the Loggia dei Nobili in Siena of the year 1458–60. (*Art in America*, February 1924)

It is significant that Valentiner found in the Dossena imitations *superiorities* to the genuine article. As we have seen, this often is the case with good forgeries.

As the magnificently aged works tumbled out of Dossena's studio—scores of pieces selling for from a few thousand dollars to $225,000—Wormwood King Palesi embroidered his tale more with each telling: Somewhere on Mt. Amiata there was an abbey that had been buried in an earthquake towards the end of the seventeenth century. A priest, Don Mario, had discovered the location, but because of certain peccadillos he had been banished to a small convent near Siena. From Don Mario Palesi had obtained a map—a floor plan really—showing where the precious buried sculptures had been exhumed. But, in order to keep Italian authorities in ignorance of the discovery, Palesi had agreed to sell only abroad and in greatest secrecy. He couldn't take anyone to the site: "We can't risk making the priests and politicians suspicious."

There was always a plausible explanation. Greek sculpture was passed off as secretly excavated provincial pieces from parts of Magna Graecia where archaeologists might logically expect to find such things. Wooden Renaissance sculpture had supposedly been found in old monasteries.

Dossena was careful in selecting his materials. For Renaissance sculpture he used marble from Carrara; for Greek sculpture, he used Pentelic marble that he found in ancient ruins, since a great deal of it had been brought to Italy in the heyday of the Roman Empire. But in carving his Greek works he was handicapped by having to depend upon photographs and ancient Roman copies, rather than on the originals.

One high relief, *The Holy Family*, well certified as from the fifteenth century, went off to dealer Durlacher in London for 3 million lire. A *Mutilated Athena* sixty-three inches high was placed with New York and Paris dealer Jakob Hirsch. It was one of Dossena's finest pieces, a life-size Athena ready for battle, with helmet, breastplate, and circular shield.

Hirsch's reaction to *Athena* was passionate. His willingness to pay soared, and he finally won her for 30 million lire. Then the enraptured dealer took the figure in his arms and kissed her marble mouth.

Of *Athena* Augusto Jandolo, Dossena's friend, later said:

> It is a work of art perfect in every respect, equal to the *Apollo of Veii*, the *Charioteer of Delphi*, and the Aegina sculptures. It is enough to dumbfound any connoisseur. The false patina is the finest ever seen, yellowish in colour, with traces here and there of a chalky deposit so hard as to be impervious to the sharpest steel.

To impart his patinas, Dossena sank a cement-lined tank into his studio floor and filled it with an acid formula whose composition he never revealed. He used a winch to dip the 600-pound

Athena into the bath and raise her forty times; each submersion cut the dazzling white of the marble and left an ever-deeper golden tone. The original Greek sculptors themselves had abhorred the bright reflection of freshly modelled stone. That they intentionally toned down colours and surface glares is well documented. They called their process for handling marble "ganosis."

Any restorer of stone sculpture must be a student of artificial ageing; otherwise new work, as we have seen, will stand out like a naked white gargoyle against a blackened cathedral. The usual finishing procedure was to saturate a statue in silicate-base substances. Today silicon or methacrylate bases are more likely to be used. But these treatments impart a surface discolouration only superficially simulating that of the ages, whereas Dossena's procedures produced a discolouration and hardness in depth that was not removable in water and therefore completely fooled the experts.

Technicians have surmised that Dossena used fire to induce crackle in his marble, and no doubt some signs of ageing—those involving disfigurement rather than patina—were achieved with sandblasting.

Gothic wood sculpture was often painted, and Dossena had to simulate these polychromed surfaces. He found old pieces of relatively worthless statuary and picture frames and soaked their paint off. The flecks were then painstakingly reapplied to Dossena's new sculpture, which had, of course, been executed in the old wood. These splotches of polychrome were supplemented with gold leaf, in some places three layers deep. He carefully tooled the gold to give it the appearance of great age.

Giovanni Pisano (*c.* 1249–1314) gave to Fasoli and Palesi an opportunity for success similar to that they had achieved with Martini. There was no known wood statuary by Pisano. But in the Cathedral of Pisa was an ancient pulpit known as *Apera del Duomo* carved by Pisano. It had been completed in 1311 and taken to pieces about 200 years later. Fragments survived in the cathedral and in a Berlin museum. In the pulpit Pisano (presumably) had incised the legend, "glorious works in stone and gilded wood." The antique art world thus had every right to hope for discovery of wooden sculpture by Pisano, which would be almost priceless.

To create a wooden *Madonna and Child* in the style of Pisano, Dossena took a seventeenth-century wooden sculpture of the same subject and cleverly transformed it, taking the old carving back 400 years in time. He fused bits of wood to the statue and then reshaped the whole and polychromed it. The fusing required nails to hold blocks together, but they were all internal and could not be seen. The *Madonna and Child* was sold in 1924 to the Cleveland Museum of Art by a reputable dealer for $18,000.

In his book *Fakes*, 1967 edition, Otto Kurz says.

> Dossena's performance as Giovanni Pisano is remarkable. It is one of the rare cases in which a forger actually succeeded in catching the fundamental facts of an artist's personal style, together with an almost correct expression. If Dossena had limited his activities to this sculptor he would probably never have been found out.

As dealers grasped the notion that somewhere in Italy an important collection was being liquidated, it was natural for them to try to identify some link in the chain. Perhaps they could identify no one more important than a collateral dealer or a runner. Even if they had traced the chain as far back as Fasoli, they would have had no way of knowing how much farther back it might stretch. But if the eager outsider approached one of the "in" dealers with something more specific—"I've got a client who wants a Gothic Madonna"—he stood a better chance. These specific requests played into Fasoli's hands: all he had to do was to stall the buyers until Dossena could execute the pieces.

It should not be supposed, however, that Fasoli and Palesi sat around waiting for someone inadvertently to commission a piece. Nor did Dossena. They were all creative. They concocted things like the Martini sculptures that dealers in the market would not have dared to dream of. As they became more successful, their aspirations became ever bolder. Dossena went so far as to construct a huge Italian arch in the cinquecento style, which was to have been discovered built into the wall of an ancient provincial building. He projected the completion of an entire archaic

Greek temple pediment, with figures portraying the mythological gigantomachia, the battle between gods and giants. Given the time and enough manpower, he might have created an "original" Roman Colosseum.

From Florence came an order for an early Renaissance tomb carved in the style of Mino da Fiesole. The dealer said that there was evidence that the Savelli family had once had such a tomb, and an inscription referring to the family should therefore be incised in the stone. After the tomb had been delivered, the dealer planted it in a dilapidated church on the old Savelli estates, where it was discovered by a Florentine scholar of suitable repute. Doubly miraculous was the discovery of a receipt signed by Mino da Fiesole acknowledging payment for the tomb by a Savelli.

The Florentine expert appears to have been Elia Volpi, then about seventy years old. His role in the scheme is not clear. He was already known in the United States for alleged false attributions. Volpi had begun his professional life as a restorer for a man named Bandini, for whom he had worked thirteen years before becoming a dealer himself.

Palesi offered the tomb discovered by Volpi to Miss Ellen Frick, heiress and curator of the famous Frick Collection in New York. She already owned several Dossena pieces, though of course she did not know it. She was on the verge of buying the tomb, but her agents were unable to locate the ruined church or the supposed intermediaries, and so she backed off. The *Tomb of the Savelli* then passed through the hands of a Venetian dealer named Balboni and was finally sold for 6 million lire. Dossena received only 25,000.

The tomb, also called simply *Sarcophagus*, eventually came to the United States. It passed from Fasoli and Palesi in Rome through Volpi and Balboni to the Boston Museum of Fine Arts, which acquired it in 1924 for $100,000. Detractors later claimed that stylistically the tomb was a composite modelled from the Tornabuoni tomb by Mino da Fiesole in the Church of Santa Maria Sopra Minerva in Rome and recumbent figures from the tomb of The Blessed Villana by Bernardo Rossellino in the Church of Santa Maria Novella in Florence.

Volpi—who had sold the Martini *Madonna* to Miss Frick—hoped to sell the Boston Museum two life-size Renaissance angels, which would have made splendid guardian protectors for the *Sarcophagus*. The way was being paved with enormous publicity in the American art press. The spring supplement of *Art News* reproduced the angels in a full page.

Within six or seven years Dossena's work penetrated the Western world's greatest museums and collections. Later *The New York Times* estimated the American loss at $1 million. European sales swelled this total to $2,175,000.

By 1927 chinks had begun to appear in the Fasoli-Palesi superstructure. In the United States suspicion was growing about many works that had been offered but not purchased. No one yet suspected that behind so much fine work lay a single artist. Works rejected in the United States at least once included an entire small temple, complete with Madonna, infant, and saint and attributed to Donatello; four archaic Greek marbles ostensibly of 600 B.C.; a three-foot *Athena;* a gilded wooden statue supposedly by Giovanni Pisano; a gilded wooden statue supposedly by Vecchietta; three Tuscan-marble angels three feet high; a larger than life-size *Madonna and Child* in polychromed wood; a *St. Catherine* and a *St. Agnes*, each six feet tall, in marble; a holy-oil bracket attributed to Martini; six marble reliefs of saints and angels; and two Tuscan bas-reliefs of the *Annunciation*.

Some time after the Cleveland Museum of Art had bought the *Madonna and Child* in the style of Giovanni Pisano, the museum began to study the piece more carefully. Examination by X-ray revealed the twentieth-century nails inside. Believing that the dealer himself had been duped, the museum arranged to return the sculpture to him in exchange for another $18,000 object of undisputed quality. There was thus no loss to the museum. Ironically in the very same month (May 1927) that the Cleveland Museum removed from exhibit this spurious *Madonna and Child* by Dossena, it purchased Jakob Hirsch's marble *Athena* for $120,000! *Athena*, of course, was also by Dossena!

At the time of the purchase Cleveland curators were fully aware that *Athena* did not conform in all respects to known Greek types, but they believed it to be part of a whole group of similar statuary produced by a provincial school in a Greek colony. This theory was fully supported by leading American and European archaeologists, who vouched for the authenticity of the *Athena*.

This was the last and biggest known sale of a Dossena piece in this country, for he was just then striking the match under the cardboard houses of Fasoli and Palesi.

Early in 1927 Dossena's wife, Teresina, had become mortally ill. By then he had frittered away all his money. He liked wine and girls, and he had protracted periods of much play and little work. Bills for doctors and medicines accumulated. In May Teresina died, and Dossena could not pay her burial bill. He appealed to Fasoli for financial aid, but Fasoli's reply was incredibly stupid.

To peddle phoney art successfully for so long demands brilliant insight into human frailties. If Fasoli had not read human nature perfectly over the previous decade, he at least had done so with exceptional good luck. But, whether he was complacent, stubborn, suffering from indigestion, or simply tired of Dossena's nagging, Fasoli refused the craftsman any kind of loan or advance. "Bring me a new statue, and I'll buy it from you. We've already paid you for things you haven't yet delivered," Fasoli, by then a wealthy man, replied.

When Fasoli refused the money for Teresina's funeral, Dossena went to a lawyer, and he took with him photographs of work that he had done. The lawyer called upon Fasoli and threatened to make the entire affair public so that Dossena could have the recognition that he deserved. Dossena was ready to stand on his own as a genius.

Apparently, Fasoli decided that Dossena was bluffing and that no one would believe him in any event. But already there were Americans searching for him, though they had no notion at first that so much fake art could have been the work of a single man.

Shortly before Signora Dossena died, a prominent dealer had offered the Metropolitan Museum of Art two life-size figures. One was a *Striding Athena*, the other a youth carrying off a woman in the manner of a famous piece from Eretia in Greece. Both were supposed to have come from an early pediment. In fact, it was intimated that the figures had come from the same site as had a superb goddess then ensconced in Berlin. The price demanded was high.

The pieces were shipped from Europe on approval. After studying them for several days, the Met curators disappointedly concluded that they were examining modern forgeries, not ancient Greek works. Too bad. The pieces had been sponsored by prominent European archaeologists, and there had been every hope. But, in accordance with the policy of the Met, the curators could not mention their reasons for declining the purchase unless they were specifically asked to do so by the sellers. They were not asked.

At the time of this refusal, in 1927, John Marshall, a consultant to the museum and one of the world's foremost archaeologists—he was largely responsible for the museum's fine Classical collection—was in Europe. There, a year before, he had been offered a Greek group that had, so it was claimed, just been unearthed and was in fragments. Marshall had thought the lot suspicious and had turned it down. The Met people in New York now wondered whether or not the statuary that they had examined in their workrooms was the same as the fragmented group previously offered to Marshall? He mailed photographs of what he had seen to New York. The groups were identical.

This incident was particularly interesting to Marshall because the pieces had been offered to him by the same Italian dealer from whom he had purchased a marble statuette for a small sum in 1926: a Greek maiden of the type known as "kore," a broken figure about three feet high draped in a himation and in the rigid archaic pose; both arms were missing, and the figure itself was broken about the knees and reset so that the fracture was obvious. The Met had dated this Dossena piece at about 500 B.C., but Marshall had become mildly suspicious after the sale, and the piece had never been put on display. About that time also, Hirsch attempted to sell his *Athena* to the Metropolitan. But *Athena* did not strike the Met curators as quite right, and they declined. Hirsch then completed the sale to the Cleveland Museum.

The Met's suspicions were focused entirely on the Greek copies. Marshall asked the aid of a friend, Captain Piero Tozzi, a painter and subsequently a dealer in Florence and New York.

Tozzi had been a member of the Italian legation in Washington, D.C., and an investigator of art frauds. He agreed with Marshall that Hirsch's *Athena* looked like a modern work, but he could not identify its origin.

Marshall devoted his entire time to the investigation. He was certain that the abduction group, the Met's little kore, *Athena* and another Greek piece that had appeared in Rome were all from the same hand. Cleveland shipped its *Athena* to Europe so that it could be compared on the spot with the other pieces. Cleveland had made the purchase on the recommendation of Harold Parsons, who operated in Europe as a consultant for the Cleveland Museum, the William Rockhill Nelson Gallery in Kansas City, and later the Joslyn Museum in Omaha, much as Marshall did for the Met. Parsons, too, began to follow the track back to Dossena.

It was at this point that Dossena came on stage for his own cause. His pressure on Fasoli and Palesi began subtly. He appeared nowhere for interviews, did not reveal himself or his name, but he let the word circulate, so that the Italian press began to tell of a native son who could turn out antique art of such genius that it passed easily for the real thing.

The story first broke in September 1927: the newspapers reported that a certain Venetian dealer [Balboni] had invested heavily in frauds and should come to Rome to verify that an unknown sculptor was their originator. Pictures of allegedly phoney work began to appear. Hirsch, who had a reputation to protect, rushed to Venice and closeted himself with his friend Balboni. But by that time Tozzi had found Dossena.

One night in Rome, according to a story filed later by the New York correspondent for *Corriere della Sera*, the son of the director of a Roman art academy and a former student of Dossena, spotted a truck loaded with statues parked in front of Dossena's house. He had heard of sales made abroad by Palesi, and he recognized the licence number of the truck as from the district where Palesi lived. He immediately told an antiquarian whom he knew, who in turn alerted an American dealer, a competitor of Palesi. Evidently, this dealer was Hirsch.

Initially Hirsch had dismissed the rumours and allegations as malicious stories spread by competitors: the art dealers' world was a dirty one. Besides, newspaper accounts had dealt mainly with Dossena's quattrocento and cinquecento copies. But now he had to face the possibility that Dossena had ventured into pre-Christian Greek!

From Venice Hirsch and Balboni stormed Rome, traced Dossena to a cheap hotel, and confronted him, a privilege that Marshall never obtained. Hirsch had a fistful of clippings, which he thrust under Dossena's nose. Dossena glanced through them and quietly acknowledged that he had produced all the things cited. An unbelieving Hirsch produced a photograph of his beloved *Athena*. Dossena looked at it silently and made no response. But when Hirsch demanded that he admit he had had no part in this perfect work, Dossena said that he had carved it.

Hirsch exploded. Dossena was a fraud, a publicity seeker, a talentless stonecutter laying claim to masterpieces to attract attention to himself so that he could escape his squalid existence. He was a parasite. The two men hurled invective at each other until they burst out into the public street.

Dossena led Hirsch and Balboni to his nearby studio. He pawed through a heap of discards in a corner—and produced the amputated left hand of *Athena*! No statue of such antiquity could have passed through the centuries intact. So on Fasoli's advice Dossena had broken off her hand—but he had kept it!

Hirsch and other dealers who had been taken in by Dossena statuary rose as one body—in savage rebuttal. Dossena, they cried, was a restorer, no more. Certainly Dossena's studio was filled with working drawings and photographs of important pieces of art. But he could not have done them himself in so many materials, as so many artists, from so many periods. He had cleaned them, repaired them—nothing more. He was a restorer for Fasoli. Every piece attributed to or claimed by Dossena basically was an original. The fake was the old man himself—Alceo Dossena.

Early in 1928 Marshall made a trip to Munich to try to persuade an assembly of experts of Dossena's authorship of the Greek objects. In the midst of his efforts, in March, he died suddenly in Rome. Alceo Dossena himself continued the battle. In late 1928 *The New York Times* carried this story:

> In the basement of the Metropolitan Museum of Art stands a little statue, smiling. Perhaps it smiles because it slipped into America's greatest museum, past all the barriers raised to keep apocryphal works out. It was bought for the museum several years ago as a genuine piece of archaic Greek sculpture. Now it is known to be just another example of the work . . . of Alceo Dossena of Rome.
>
> Until recently it had been accepted that the Metropolitan Museum had not purchased any works by Dossena, whom telegrams from Italy ten days ago reported as admitting he had carved wood and marble sculpture sold to the Frick Collection here and the Boston and Cleveland Museums as genuine Renaissance and archaic Greek work. On the day that the first news of the situation came from Italy the Metropolitan Museum gave out the statement:
>
> "The museum knows nothing more about the matter than report and rumour, and has nothing of its own to give out."
>
> Accumulating evidence, however, indicated that a piece of the sculpture had entered the Met, although it had never been exhibited nor its acquisition announced. When this evidence was presented to the museum yesterday the facts were corroborated.

Dossena filed a deposition describing his activities, threw his studio open to the press, gave demonstrations, turned many of the photographs of his forgeries over to Parsons, and filed suit against agent Alfredo Fasoli and dealer Romano Palesi, charging them with fraud. Dossena claimed that he had not been properly recompensed for his efforts. He declared that he has always thought that his employers were selling his works as imitations, that he had never participated in their misrepresentations, and that they owed him the equivalent of $66,000 in back wages. When questioned by reporters Dossena admitted having received about $30,000, which wasn't much for his ten years' work. He said that he had another $100,000 worth of work under contract.

Fasoli tried political reprisals: he charged that Dossena was an anti-Fascist agitator, in other words, a Communist. Dossena countered by engaging one of the biggest guns imaginable, the secretary of the Fascist Party, Farinacci, to defend him. The

Fascist press gave him new publicity. (On April 28, 1945, Farinacci was executed by Italian partisans alongside Benito Mussolini, Clara Petacci, and fifteen others.)

The American Art Dealers Association, enraged, declared that it had "voted to do everything in its power, through propaganda, authenticating service, and other legitimate channels to put a curb on the faker and dealer in forgeries."

More laconically, an editorial in *Art News* stated:

> There is no great museum, no matter how carefully guarded, which has not had its share of spurious works: There are few if any which do not still include them in their catalogues. The faker is always with us, and his agents cover the earth. . . . No matter how great his scholarship no man can say with absolute certainty that an undocumented piece of sculpture of fine quality is or is not by a given man.

Sorting out what Dossena had forged and had not forged became an exercise in Solomonizing. Things were attributed to him that he had never dreamed of doing, and in all likelihood a few Dossena pieces are still attributed to Old Masters here and there. Leo Planiscez, curator of the Museum of Fine Arts in Vienna, made an early count of forty-five known frauds. The staff of the Kaiser Friedrich Museum in Berlin was obliged to state publicly—and accurately—that "The Attic goddess acquired from the Altes Museum in 1925 for 1 million marks is an original work, definitely not an imitation by Dossena or any other type of fake."

Edsel Ford had spent $120,000 for a marble bust supposedly by Mino da Fiesole. It had been purchased as a gift for the Detroit Institute of Arts on the strength of testimony by three experts: the former director of the Museo Nazionale in Florence; Wilhelm von Bode, head of the Kaiser Friedrich Museum in Berlin and considered the world's greatest connoisseur of Italian sculpture; and W. R. Valentiner, head of the Detroit Institute itself and an authority of world standing. Valentiner later decided that the piece was a forgery and arranged an exchange with the dealer. The piece was attributed to Dossena, but some people thought it older than that.

The greatest controversy, however, involved the Boston

Museum of Fine Arts' *Sarcophagus*, the one acquired for $100,000 from Balboni in 1924. For three years it was exhibited in the Stone Room of the Evans Wing. In 1928 it was transferred and reassembled in the fifteenth-century Italian gallery of the new building in readiness for the formal opening of this structure.

The tomb was not carved from a single piece of marble, but consisted, like a box or chest, of marble slabs fitted together. Both end panels bear the Savelli family coat of arms. An inscription (which Kurz calls "a howler") begins "Obiit enim praefata Maria Catharina de Sabello Anno Christi MCCCCXXX" ("But the aforesaid Maria Catharina de Sabello died in the year of the Lord 1430"). "Praefata" does not make much sense, as if someone who did not know Latin had copied the words and had thought it some kind of title. In its masculine form, it refers to a military rank; in the feminine it is as meaningless as "captainess" in English. In his suit against Fasoli, Dossena claimed that the inscription had been added after the tomb had left his studio.

On December 17, 1929, Boston Museum officials received a confidential letter from their Vienna representative, who had been sent to Rome to investigate the entire Dossena affair. The museum's trustees were summoned to an emergency meeting the next day. They authorized Director Edward Jackson Holmes and the museum's attorneys to initiate legal action against Volpi and Balboni.

Dossena had claimed authorship of the tomb at least two months earlier, but, of course, the museum could not act until it had reliable proof. Even after the report some museum officials remained unconvinced of Dossena's claim. They took Hirsch's view—at least as far as the tomb was concerned—that Dossena had at best merely restored it and that the work was genuine.

Because the staff could not give a definitive verdict, the museum neither returned the tomb nor exhibited it. The *Sarcophagus* was buried in the cellar. One writer speculated that the museum might be having difficulty obtaining its money because the dealer involved had a brother who was a high official in the Fascist government.

The controversy continued for years. When George Harold Edgell became director of the museum in 1935, he asked the committee on the museum for permission to bring the tomb out of limbo and to place it on exhibition again. He thought it a beautiful object and argued that it was the purpose of a museum of fine arts to exhibit beautiful objects. The committee was willing but not until the staff would declare the tomb to be either antique or a modern forgery. The public was entitled to a firm opinion from the museum. By then more reliable scientific analysis could be undertaken on the premises because of an upgrading of laboratory equipment.

The investigation was undertaken by William J. Young, then a restorer on the technical staff and today head of the research laboratory. Binocular-microscopic examination of the carved faces on the tomb revealed two surfaces, one higher than the other. The lower surface appeared new and unfinished, whereas the shallower surface appeared finished and aged. Evidently parts of the tomb had been rechiselled. It seemed unlikely to the investigators that a forger would carve and age a surface and then carve away part of what he had aged. It seemed more likely that a restorer had sharpened a design grown dull with age.

The next procedure called for examination of the outer crystalloid structure of the marble for physical and chemical changes caused by centuries of exposure to weathering and atmospheric gases. Young used a procedure that had proved reliable in more than 200 examinations of other objects. Small specimens were taken from fourteen separate points on the tomb and ground down with a metal lap and carborundum powder to a thickness of .03 of a millimetre. These pieces were so thin as to be translucent—in places transparent—thus revealing the crystalline structure of the specimen. Specimens, magnified 250 times, were studied under ordinary light and polarized light. The procedure revealed that long exposure had aged certain parts of the tomb, notably the tomb proper, both console brackets, the left-hand panel bearing one of the Savelli coats of arms, a small block next to the right-hand panel, and the fascia of a cornice. The inscription, the right-hand panel bearing another coat of arms, and both pilaster capitals proved to be modern.

Through crystalline analysis it was determined that most of the tomb had been fashioned from Carrara marble. The left-hand panel with the Savelli arms, however, was of Greek marble from quarries near Olympia in the Peloponnesus. Young concluded:

> I do not hesitate to state that the tomb is ancient, and it is my opinion that the left-hand panel bearing the Savelli coat of arms, although ancient, was not part of the original tomb. This panel was incorporated later, the modern right-hand panel added, and the false inscription cut to simulate a Savelli obituary record. Surrounding sections of the tomb were then rechiselled in an attempt to equalize the surface, after which the tomb was impregnated with wax to impart a uniform tone.

When the tomb was replaced on exhibition in 1937, Edgell wrote:

> The director would like to emphasize . . . that the tomb is put on exhibition because it is a beautiful object. The public is entitled to the opinion of the Museum as to its condition and authenticity, which the Museum hereby announces. If, on the other hand, scholars are still unconvinced, they are of course entirely welcome to their opinions. The authorities of the Museum would not feel injured to find themselves in disagreement with any honest scholar. Nobody . . . would deny the beauty of the tomb and therefore the propriety of its exhibition.

But this propriety was disputed by the subsequent director, Perry T. Rathbone, who thought that the tomb fell below the museum's standard. Soon after he was appointed in 1954 he banished the Savelli tomb to the storage catacombs.

For a brief period Dossena was a fad. A film made in Dossena's workshop by Dr. Hans Curles, Director of the Institute for Cultural Research in Berlin, would be shown, and it was hoped that Dossena would himself appear. Dr. Curles described the experience of making the film, *The Creative Hand:*

> We watched Dossena modelling for a long time before we filmed him He was working on a life-size clay group of three mourning women for a war memorial at Cremona. His technique was scrupulously academic. The figures were first modelled accurately from life, a pair of large wooden dividers being frequently used to measure length of limb, head, and distances on the model and to transfer [the measurements] to the clay figure. Later Dossena draped a robe over the model and did the same in clay to his nude figures. . . . As if for relaxation from this arduous work,

he then spent days modelling fourteen reliefs of the stations of the cross, which he had been commissioned to execute for the Vatican.

And here we witnessed the most amazing example of a sculptor at work. Unhurriedly, but in the space of a few minutes and without any plastic or two-dimensional sketch, figures in high and medium relief came into being. Everything happened so quickly and unexpectedly that we could scarcely move the camera into position in time. The ancients must have exercised a similar facility when they improvised stucco decorations for the ceilings and walls of castles and churches. With equal unconcern Dossena modelled daring and imaginative architecture, city gates, and walls whose large plane structures projected from the background in bold perspective.

We were naturally very keen to see Dossena at work on an archaic statue. When he inquired what he should make, I asked him for a Greek goddess. He offered us the choice of a standing or seated figure, and, while we were deciding on the former, had already selected a few pieces of wood and was building the armature. Half an hour later we were looking at an Attic goddess, some two feet tall, modelled in clay, with the captivating beauty that springs from the only slightly relieved rigidity that we admire in the best genuine pieces. It is noteworthy that this work ensued directly—and without more of a pause than it took to utter our wishes—after the Passion relief just described. The goddess, too, was first modelled in the nude and then draped in her robe. The head took shape with equal fluency, and quite suddenly a smile dawned on the face of a woman to whom the Greeks had prayed 2,500 years before. We filmed Dossena working with mallet and chisel on the reclining figure of an early Greek warrior, the complete master of his technique and entirely unconcerned about the final result. We also filmed him drawing a head of Christ crowned with thorns, which he conjured up in light and shade with charcoal on a dark, stumped ground.

We watched Dossena for many days. He worked with a complete lack of affectation and mystery, from time to time singing an air from an opera or smiling at us in friendly fashion. In fact, the abnormality of his work became so natural that it only later occurred to us that we had witnessed the reincarnation of a Renaissance master and an Attic sculptor.

On March 9, 1933, a public auction of Dossena's works was sponsored by Manhattan's National Art Galleries in the grand ballroom of the Hotel Plaza in New York. The collection comprised thirty-nine pieces, including the "Martini" *Madonna*. Each successful bidder received an official document from the

Italian government testifying that the work was a genuine fake.

Alfred M. Frankfurter, whose editorship of *Art News* made it the most authoritative American publication in its field, wrote in the preface to the catalogue:

> I find this sculpture of Dossena of absorbing interest not only for its beauty as a work of art, but also for the first imitative work which I have seen in which I have not been disturbed by an obvious intent to copy and deceive. . . . It is really this quality of sincerity in Dossena, the almost incredible ability of the man to have worked without affectation and without malevolence in the spirit of the dead past and its masters, which seems to me to make his work as valuable, to the collector and museum, for artistic achievement as for scientific documentation.

But the prices realized at the sale were low.

Dossena's glory had come and gone.

Yet perhaps he had a last triumph. In the winter of 1936–1937, Dossena created a *Diana the Huntress.* It was sold and disappeared on the Roman art market but not before being broken, temporarily reassembled, and photographed by Dossena. It left Italy with an export permit from the Italian government as a "modern forgery in the style of ancient Etruscan sculpture of Veii," with a declared value of $125. According to Parsons and an impressive list of European experts, this was the same *Diana* acquired by the City Art Museum of St. Louis in 1952 for $56,000. In spite of attacks the museum continued to exhibit it as genuine Etruscan work. It has since been removed from public view.

Alceo Dossena had died penniless in a pauper's hospital in 1937. Funeral expenses had been borne by his parish. According to Schüller, his death seemed so unimportant that now no one even seems to know where he is buried.

CHAPTER 5

The Battle of the Van Gogh Experts

In 1924 Otto Wacker, who at twenty-six had already failed in three careers—as a picture dealer, nightclub dancer, and taxi-cab owner—sold his first Van Gogh in a private transaction and thereby realized the capital to open a new gallery. He found his spot on a noble old Berlin street, the Viktoriastrasse. On the same street, at number 35, a fine house sheltered one of the most respected showrooms in Berlin, the Paul Cassirer Gallery. Before long Cassirer found itself working with the newcomer—for, however mediocre the bulk of the paintings offered by Wacker, his gallery achieved immediate standing because of the large number of Van Goghs it had to offer.

When questioned about where he had obtained the Van Goghs, Wacker alluded to a nobleman's estate. He protested that, as he had been sworn to discretion, he could not offer firm evidence of provenance, but he claimed another, surer way to test the authenticity of his wares.

A Dutch expert, J. Baart de la Faille, was then compiling a catalogue of the complete works of Vincent Van Gogh. Any attempt to catalogue every known work by Van Gogh is full or pitfalls and booby traps. Probably no art historian beginning a catalogue raisonné on any artist ever imagines that by himself he can locate every painting which should be included. He must call upon other people to help him. Through advertisements, news stories, letters to the editor, and correspondence with museums, collectors, and dealers he publicizes his project and invites owners of the artist's works to make contact with him.

Otto Wacker had answered de la Faille's appeal, and, when the monumental *L'Oeuvre de Vincent Van Gogh: Catalogue Raisonné* appeared in the autumn of 1928, it beautified thirty paintings which had come from Wacker. These paintings were thus authenticated.

By then some of Wacker's Van Goghs had already been purchased by Germany's best dealers—Perls, Goldschmidt, and Matthiesen in Berlin, Thannhäuser in Munich, Kommeter in Hamburg—and by Hodebert in Paris. Through them and through Wacker himself the paintings had passed into the hands of notable collectors on both sides of the Atlantic.

By paying small appraisal fees—40 to 80 marks—Wacker obtained supplementary certificates of authenticity not only from de la Faille but also from other experts on Van Gogh: Julius Meier-Graefe, Hans Rosenhagen, Leo Blumenreich, and H. P. Bremmer. Each painting was considered genuine. There were no reservations.

De la Faille's certificate for a *Self-Portrait at Easel* sold to Chester Dale of New York read:

> The undersigned declares that he has examined the painting reproduced on the other side measuring 58 centimetres in height and 46.5 centimetres in width painted on canvas. He considers it as an authentic and characteristic work of Vincent Van Gogh, painted in 1888 during his sojourn in Arles. It will be described and reproduced in his catalogue raisonné of the work of the master. Berlin, July 20, 1927. [Signed] J. B. de la Faille.

Three other certificates were issued for this painting, by Rosenhagen, Bremmer, and Meier-Graefe. The statement by Meier-Graefe, dated March 27, 1928 went further: "one of the most important works by Van Gogh."

Bremmer was a professor of applied æsthetics at The Hague. As a consultant, he had helped Frau Kröller to organize her exemplary collection of 143 Van Goghs, which today are the heart of the collection in the Rijksmuseum Kröller-Müller in Otterloo. He purchased *Sea View from Sainte-Marie* from Wacker for the Kröller collection. Meier-Graefe was art reviewer for the authoritative *Frankfurter Zeitung* and a Van Gogh authority of great prestige. Rosenhagen and Blumenreich were art historians.

Otto Wacker did not hang all of his Van Goghs on his gallery walls at once but exhibited only a few of them. When he sold one, he would hang a replacement. Many of the paintings were of the same subjects, and he did not put more than one of each up at any time.

The Cassirer Gallery had been founded before the turn of the century by Paul Cassirer and had exhibited Auguste Renoir and Paul Cézanne. Since Cassirer's death the gallery had been operated by Walter Feilchenfeld and Grete Ring.

In their first collaboration Wacker was to stage an exhibition of Van Gogh drawings while the Cassirer Gallery ran a parallel show of Van Gogh oils. Both exhibitions were to be held under the patronage (official, non-financial sponsorship) of de la Faille. Wacker sold a drawing from his show to Berlin's National Museum. He also sent four of his oils to Grete Ring on consignment. The Cassirer show was drawing from many sources—mostly on loan—and only a few of the nearly 100 paintings were available for sale.

Grete Ring looked at the four Wacker Van Gogh oils and did not like them. Her reaction was instantaneous: they were fakes. She called in Feilchenfeld to examine them, but to avoid prejudicing him she did not express an opinion. He too pronounced them phoney.

The four "Van Goghs" were sent back to Wacker with word that they were fakes. But he rejected the judgement and went on showing them in his own gallery. After all, he had certificates of authenticity from de la Faille, Meier-Graefe, Bremmer, and others.

The exhibitions were held in January 1927. De la Faille's book was not to appear until autumn of 1928. He would have had plenty of time to change his book had protests been made directly to him or had he done more investigating on his own. But Grete Ring and Feilchenfeld were in Berlin, and de la Faille was buried in his manuscripts and photographs in Holland.

Because of Wacker's solid certificates of authenticity—and the laws of slander and defamation—the Cassirer management had to be circumspect about doubting Wacker out loud. Perhaps, though, it was they who notified the police, for soon two investigators—Inspector Uelzen and Commissioner Thomas from the Alexanderplatz headquarters—began to probe surreptitiously.

Through Meier-Graefe, who was having second thoughts, word finally leaked across the Dutch border to de la Faille that something might be amiss. Meier-Graefe proposed that they undertake a discreet and thorough examination of the Wacker Van Goghs and publish their findings together. De la Faille agreed.

Soon afterward the art world was stunned by a laconic third-person press announcement issued by de la Faille: he had rescinded his imprimatur without informing Meier-Graefe:

> The editor of the *Oeuvre* catalogue of Van Gogh, Dr. Baart de la Faille, finds himself compelled to append a supplement to his work designating thirty works, described in the catalogue as genuine, to be dubious forgeries. Dr. de la Faille has arrived at this conclusion only after exhaustive study and acknowledges his error with deep regret.

But the supplement was not yet ready and the expert had not announced *which* Van Goghs were dubious forgeries. More than one Van Gogh owner panicked. After all, the sensational revelations of Dossena had just occurred. No piece of art seemed safe from being branded as a fake.

Otto Wacker knew which paintings de la Faille was preparing to condemn and tried in vain to obtain a court injunction forbidding him from publishing his list. Persistent investigators for the *Amsterdam Telegraaf* finally extracted from de la Faille the names of the thirty discredited paintings:

Catalogue Raisonné Number	*Subject*	*Owner*	*Origin*
383	*Self-Portrait*	M. Silberberg, Breslau	Wacker
387	*Still Life with Roll of Bread*	M. Thannhäuser, Munich	—
418	*Seascape near Sainte-Marie*	Wacker Gallery	—
421	*Sainte-Marie*	M. J. Gildemeister (acquired from Perls), Hamburg	—
521	*Self-Portrait*	M. Thannhäuser, Munich	—
523	*Self-Portrait at Easel*	Chester Dale, New York	—
539	*The Zouave*	Otto Kramer, Holzdorf	—
577	*Garden*	Wacker Gallery, Berlin	—
614	*Cypresses*	Wacker Gallery, Berlin	—
616	*Cypresses*	B. E. Wolff (acquired from Perls), Hamburg	—
639	*Alpine Path*	M. Thannhäuser, Munich	—
685	*Peasant* (after Millet)	Wacker Gallery, Berlin	—
691	*The Sower*	Matthiesen, Berlin	—
705	*The Sower*	Hugo Perls Gallery, Berlin	—
713	*Olive Tree*	Gildemeister (acquired from Kommeter), Hamburg	—
729	*Sunlit Landscape*	Matthiesen, Berlin	—
741	*Cypresses*	Hugo Perls Gallery, Berlin	—
812	*Fields*	Hodebert Gallery, Paris	—
813	*Fields*	Hugo Perls Gallery, Berlin	—
823	*Cornfield*	Otto Kramer (acquired from Perls), Holzdorf	—
824	*Trees in Landscape*	Hugo Perls Gallery, Berlin	—
418a	*Small Boats, Sainte-Marie*	Private Swiss Collection	Presum-
527a	*Self-Portrait*	—	ably
539a	*Portrait of Zouave*	—	Wacker
625	*Rising Moon*	—	but no
681	*Vase of Flowers*	—	docu-
710a	*Olive Trees*	—	mentary
715a	*Olive Trees*	—	evidence
736	*Haystack*	—	—
741a	*Two Cypresses*	—	—

Wacker issued a statement promising to sue de la Faille for branding the Wacker Gallery Von Goghs fakes. He let it be known that he would sue anyone else who dared to spread the allegation. Then he disappeared—only to surface in Holland in the best thriller tradition. He said that he had come there to show two of his paintings to Dutch experts and thereby find new supportive evidence for his Van Goghs. But his flight was as much in self-defence as in defence of his paintings.

He telephoned to Dr. Heltzer of the Berlin police to say that he would return to the German capital presently. He said he feared that if he remained in Germany, he would be sued by Russian agents, and that, because he had originally smuggled the pictures from Switzerland into Germany, he was alarmed by nightmares of German tax and customs authorities descending upon him.

Probably Otto Wacker had never smuggled either himself or a single picture across the Swiss-German frontier. But when he went off to Holland he had managed to take *nine* pictures across the German-Dutch border unnoticed.

German authorities howled. Wacker's coup had deprived them of nine vital pieces of evidence that they intended to use against him. And, despite an order from the German police, he did not go back himself. From abroad he protested that he was in no way an art expert and therefore had to rely on the judgements of men who were. He pointed out that, even after the question of the Van Goghs had been raised in public, Meier-Graefe and Bremmer had remained convinced of the genuineness of his paintings.

Wacker had merely to repeat all his corroborative evidence and to insist that de la Faille had been erroneous in his second judgement: all the certificates that Wacker had accumulated still proved the authenticity of his Van Goghs.

The drama quickly became a battle of the experts.

Meanwhile Meier-Graefe was incensed. De la Faille had broken their agreement. Meier-Graefe charged that by rushing unscientifically based conclusions into print de la Faille had acted irresponsibly and had caused unnecessary commotion in the art market.

Stenhoff, director of the Rijksmuseum H. W. Mesdag in The Hague and also an expert of international standing, called de la Faille's action "a little unusual" and said that he should have submitted the case to a committee of experts instead of to the court of public opinion and newspaper sensationalism.

De la Faille threw a sop to opposing experts, patting himself on the back at the same time: "The paintings are so excellently made as to make the imitation very, very hard to determine." He claimed that on March 2, 1928, he had taken a Van Gogh self-portrait to the National Museum in Berlin to compare it with one already there and had decided that without a doubt the one he had carried was spurious. This conclusion had gradually persuaded him that the other Wacker pieces were also fakes.

De la Faille, then, by his own account had been convinced of a Van Gogh forgery in March, six months *before* his catalogue raisonné came out. Certainly it had not been too late to make changes, even if they meant delaying publication. If de la Faille had been convinced of fraud after his studies in the Berlin Museum, then he had no excuse for not doing so.

When de la Faille's list of condemned paintings was published in the *Amsterdam Telegraaf*, dealers Matthiesen, Thannhäuser, and Goldschmidt moved to protect themselves. Before the scandal had broken, Zatzenstein, proprietor of the Matthiesen Gallery, had let Wacker have a genuine Van Gogh, *Garden of the Olive Trees*, from the Mauthner collection, to sell on commission. He was amazed when a second version of this painting was subsequently offered for sale by Wacker.

When Wacker did not respond satisfactorily to the three dealers' inquiries, Matthiesen brought formal action against him through the Association of German Art Dealers and Antiquaries. Wacker's Berlin lawyer, Ivan Goldschmidt—presumably no relation to the picture dealer—told his client's story in the *Frankfurter Zeitung*: the paintings had come from a Russian living in Switzerland. Because of probable reprisals in Russia if the origin of the works became known, Wacker could not under any circumstances break his word and reveal the original owner's identity.

When Wacker returned from Holland on October 3, he

brought masses of new supporting data—but he left behind in The Hague his most valuable evidence, the nine Van Goghs. It was Saturday, and he was met by Inspector Uelzen, who read him the charges filed by Matthiesen Gallery. "This is a squabble between experts. It does not really concern me," Wacker protested to Inspector Uelzen. "I represented the paintings as they were represented to me."

"Where did you get the paintings?"

"From a nobleman whose name I am pledged not to reveal."

"A Russian?"

"The family in question was related to the Czar. The mention of names would mean their death. You can understand why I just cannot say more."

But Wacker *had* revealed more: until then the Czar had never been mentioned. Wacker claimed that part of the baggage his Russian friend had salvaged from Russia was the family's art collection, some of it sneaked out of Russia during the Revolution. The collection was filled with Old Masters now hidden from thieves and Soviet agents in storage vaults in Switzerland. The Van Goghs had been smuggled out.

When the interrogation ended a long statement was drafted. It established neither that Wacker had known the paintings were bogus nor that they were bogus at all. Wacker signed the innocuous document and went home.

The police beat him to his gallery on Monday morning. The two officers awaiting him when he arrived wanted another look around, this time in the proprietor's presence. They found two paintings signed Van Gogh but had no excuse for seizing them.

They examined the gallery's books, which introduced another frustration. The books were kept by a salesman named Renkiewitsch, a friend of Wacker's who doubled as secretary-treasurer of the gallery, making do with what little data Wacker provided him. There were no proper records, only ledgers with a few summary notes and the rare entry of a miscellaneous sale. There were notations on scraps of paper and miscellaneous bills. No record of purchases or sales could be reconstructed with any accuracy. There were no bank statements, transportation vouchers, customs certificates, or indications that money had ever been paid to previous owners for works sold. Evidently the original Russian owner was perfectly willing to have Wacker keep his money!

The three complaining dealers then demanded further inquiries and gave Wacker until December 14 to reveal the whereabouts of his Russian confidant. They demanded that Wacker present them with full documentary evidence authenticating the paintings by the end of December.

Matthiesen's formal complaint had thrown wide the door for the Berlin police. Nonetheless the criminal investigation department could do nothing until the paintings had been proved to be false. Ludwig Justi, director of the National Museum, was appointed to pass upon the genuineness of the Wacker Van Goghs. Justi called upon the aid of his own staff, particularly a curator named Ludwig Thormaehlen.

In December 1928 de la Faille himself issued the authorized supplement to his catalogue raisonné, specifically deleting all the Wacker Van Goghs. Most of the German art dealers who had sold paintings bought from Wacker accepted their return by their clients. But Hugo Perls insisted that the pieces he had purchased were genuine and refused to make refunds.

The Berlin police seized every suspect painting that they legally could and turned them over to Justi and the National Museum for safekeeping.

As the experts quarrelled, de la Faille sought to prove to the world—and no doubt to himself—that he was the supreme expert on Van Gogh. As quickly as he could compile it, he rushed into print with another volume cataloguing not only Wacker's thirty pieces but a total of 178 Van Goghs which he declared were bogus. He called false works that he himself had listed as genuine in his catalogue raisonné and some that he had authenticated in another book, *The French Period of Van Gogh.* This new book was eventually of enormous use to Justi and the German courts. No sooner was it in print than Élie Faure, the French art historian and writer, challenged de la Faille's reliability in the pages of *L'Art Vivant.* He described a personal encounter with the Dutch scholar.

During World War I Faure had purchased a Van Gogh

drawing from a reputable Paris dealer. It had been "constantly admired" by the painters, curators, and art historians who came to Faure's house. In 1925 de la Faille had asked permission to see the Van Gogh drawing. Faure had been delighted to oblige. De la Faille had examined the drawing carefully and had even taken away a photographer's proof. Then for two years Faure had heard nothing from de la Faille. Then he had received a letter from Florent Fels asking to see the drawing: "M. de la Faille tells me you possess a drawing by the painter."

The next year a well-known dealer named Dru had written that he was preparing a show of Van Gogh drawings and that de la Faille had given him a list of collectors including Faure's name. Faure had willingly agreed to lend his drawing. Dru had then asked Faure for the title of the drawing, as it was destined to appear in the catalogue. When the show had opened in June, Faure's Van Gogh had not been in the catalogue; it had not even been hung.

Surprised and hurt, Faure had written to Dru asking for an explanation, and a few days later he had received this reply:

> I asked you for the drawing under the auspices of Mr. de la Faille. Then when I sent him the list of drawings which were to be added to those which he was getting for my exposition, Mr. de la Faille said to me that he could not put yours in the catalogue because it was not by Van Gogh.

"My surprise became stupor," Faure observed. "How could de la Faille, who had expressed no doubt to me and who had successively and recently recommended the drawing to Fels and Dru as a Van Gogh, suddenly, *without looking at the work again*, change his mind?"

Faure wrote immediately to de la Faille to ask how he could have so lightly denounced to a dealer—and thus to the public—a work that no one, not even he, had ever before disputed. How could anyone discredit a work "so lackadaisically," perhaps definitively, without trying to see it again, without even informing its owner—a work that on three occasions he himself had called authentic? Faure demanded proof.

De la Faille's reply acknowledged his previous actions but offered no satisfactory reason for turning thumbs down on the drawing. He had looked at his photographs, he said, and had suddenly decided that the drawing was a forgery. He said that, even though three years had passed since he had seen the drawing itself, he could remember it well enough not to need another look.

Faure retorted in print, "Mr. de la Faille justifies his new opinion because he retains a sufficiently fresh memory!" Yet in spite of this claim, the Dutch expert had admitted that he had taken a last look at all the photographs. It was then, for the first time, that he had realized that the drawing was a fake.

The photograph de la Faille had taken from Faure was poor. In fact, Faure declared, the photographer himself, after seeing the proofs, including the one that de la Faille took, had insisted that the drawing be reshot.

Faure derided de la Faille as very careless. This carelessness, Faure exploded, had never been more apparent than when Faille had declared the thirty Wacker paintings to be authentic—and then precipitately declared them phoney. "Should not a wholesale error of this enormity disqualify an expert?"

Faure took pains to quote the searing criticism of a prominent but unidentified French painter: "Mr. de la Faille has an habitual illness of authentication by photograph!" It was by the same method, Faure went on, that de la Faille had declared authentic a Van Gogh work owned by a famous Paris collector, without ever having seen the painting, though it was easily accessible. And he had used a photograph to brand as a fake a painting sold by Théodore Duret to an American, a painting that Duret had received directly from either Van Gogh or his brother, Theo. When the latter's wife had heard of the incident, she had simply declared de la Faille "to be a fool." Faure speculated that by attacking a Duret painting which had gone to America, de la Faille could once again assert his authority without great risk of serious challenge. The painting, a square still life of two herring, a slice of melon, and a pitcher, was in the *Faux Van Gogh* catalogue as plate 78, but it could be admired as plate 91 in the catalogue of the first exhibition in Manhattan's new Museum of Modern Art (in November 1929), an exhibition which Faure accused de la Faille of having helped to organize.

Faure told of de la Faille's reliance on photos, which convey no sense of material, colour, tonal relation, harmony, or values; he accused the Dutchman of "a myopia little proper to the exercise of the profession of an expert—even occasionally!"

Of course de la Faille struck back. In *L'Art Vivant* he complained that Faure's letters to him had been threatening and remarked that he was not surprised that Faure had tried to muddy de la Faille's efforts:

> Mr. Faure is mad because I'm the horsefly that dared to bite him. . . . When I saw the drawing in Faure's, I did not discuss the authenticity. Only later, after finding other drawings by the same hand, all presenting the same peculiarities and characteristics, which differed totally from the drawings of Vincent van Gogh, did I become certain that here was a series of fakes. The photograph I have of Mr. Faure's drawing is excellent, [so good] that there is no need to see the original again. . . . Do not forget the question concerns a drawing, not a painting. . . . As long as I considered it genuine, I so designated it to Fels and Dru. As soon as I had a contrary conviction . . . I could not fail to oppose it. . . . Faure completely ignores my studies, researches, my comparative material, etc. . . . Does he know how much time is required to form a conviction? . . . How can he say I suddenly changed my mind?

The German police plodded on, methodically building a case against Wacker. Dr. Justi was furious because he had not been able to obtain all the Wacker Van Goghs. Besides those that had been spirited to Holland, some of the paintings sold in Germany were unavailable to him because their owners still refused to surrender them for inspection and the police could find no legal means to seize them. The case had to be built largely around a dozen paintings. Inspector Uelzen went sleuthing to Leiden. He returned empty-handed. Commissioner Thomas went to The Hague . . . and found nothing but more blind alleys.

On January 29, 1929. Justi published a full-page exposé in *Vossiche Zeitung*. His contention all along had been that scientific examination is far superior to æsthetic judgement and would answer the Wacker question once and for all. He was ready at last to declare to the Berlin police that *every* Wacker Van Gogh—thirty-three of them, three more than had originally been included in the de la Faille catalogue—was a forgery, even though the report from the chemist who was analysing the paint had not yet been given to him. Nor had he yet received for examination two paintings from the United States, one from the Buffalo Fine Arts Society and one from Chester Dale.

According to Dr. Justi:

> In the spurious works the brush strokes are timid, as if the imitator had feared that he might shoot beyond the length of the original that he had copied. In the genuine work the strokes are bold and executed with the self-assurance of one who knew exactly what he wanted to do. Another interesting point is that all the Wacker Van Goghs are what, in professional language, are called "reprises," that is, returns to earlier motives. Now, although it is true that Van Gogh sometimes used earlier subjects for second works, it is very curious that among the entire thirty-three disputed paintings there is not one new idea or subject.

Wacker vanished again. The day after Dr. Justi's article appeared, Wacker was found unconscious from unknown causes in the corridor of a Leiden house belonging to Bremmer's sister! He was rushed to a hospital, where his condition was pronounced critical. There was no hope for a speedy recovery. In co-operation with their German colleagues, the Dutch police seized Wacker's baggage and intercepted his mail.

Düsseldorf police searched the studio of his brother Leonard. They discovered a copy of one of the pictures offered for sale by Wacker in Berlin—the paint was still tacky!—and a study for one of the purported Van Gogh forgeries. Both objects were confiscated. They did not prove the origins of the disputed works, but they offered a strong suggestion that Wacker's collaborator was not a Russian émigré but his own brother.

Otto Wacker, however, persistently reaffirmed the existence of his Russian. His detractors asked for proof. Wacker replied that he was certain the Russian would not consent to meet anyone from the police, but he made a counter-offer: he would take Meier-Graefe to Switzerland to meet the Russian. Wacker himself trusted Meier-Graefe—enough so that he had shown the

6—FF * *

art critic one of the Russian's letters, after covering the address and signature to protect the Russian's identity. Meier-Graefe later commented, "The handwriting certainly looked Russian, and the contents were encouraging."

To make certain that the Russian would consent to such a meeting, Otto Wacker sent a secret inquiry to Switzerland. He discovered that his Russian friend had gone to Egypt. The only way to get a message to him was to write to an equally mysterious second party in care of a Paris club. Unfortunately, this letter was never collected.

The experts were divided into two camps on more or less national lines, the Germans declaring the paintings fakes and the Dutch, except for de la Faille, declaring them genuine. But even de la Faille's views had taken another wild turn. His book on the 178 phoney Van Goghs had not yet been published when he began to declare privately that five of Wacker's Van Goghs smuggled into Holland were *authentic*! But he did not alter the text.

German detractors accused Bremmer of having persuaded Madame Kröller to buy *Sea View from Sainte-Marie* as a desperate act to preserve his reputation. A Dutch restorer summoned by Wacker claimed that all the pictures were authentic because the paint was at least thirty to thirty-five years old, which would date them to a period when no one had been forging Van Goghs because they were then worthless.

For eighteen months after his voluntary return to Berlin Otto Wacker dropped from the newspaper pages. During this period of calm Dr. Justi demonstrated the value of a real Van Gogh by paying $50,000 for *Daubigny's Garden*. Wacker had sold his Van Goghs for only $12,000 each.

The police seemed to have insufficient evidence to move against Wacker. Not until nearly three years after the Matthiesen Gallery's original complaint did the public prosecutor's office in Berlin announce an indictment "for persistent fraud and breach of contract." The indictment named both Otto and his brother Leonard. Otto Wacker was accused of selling, between 1925 and 1928, thirty paintings as Van Goghs, "of which it could be established that none had been painted by Van Gogh."

The indictment was handed down on September 4, 1931. The trial of Otto and Leonard Wacker began in the Central Lay Assessor's Court on April 6, 1932. Among those on hand to testify were de la Faille, Justi, Bremmer, Meier-Graefe, Feilchenfeld, Grete Ring, and Zatzenstein.

Also on hand was a collector from Utrecht named W. Scherjon, who had pursued the question of authenticity by scrutinizing all the available Van Gogh letters. Scherjon claimed that de la Faille was wrong. A letter to Theo van Gogh was offered as evidence of the authenticity of certain questioned paintings. Scherjon also invoked æsthetic considerations in defence of Wacker's Van Goghs.

The directors of the New York branch of Wildenstein & Co. Inc., of the Hodebert Gallery in Paris, and of the Thannhäuser Salon in Munich; painters Leo von Koenig and Eugen Spiro; technical experts Kurt Wehlte, Thormaehlen, and Helmuth Ruhemann (then chemist for the state museums of Berlin); art historian Brittner; and, most important, Van Gogh's own nephew, Vincent Wilhelm van Gogh, were all present.

Otto Wacker's own testimony was largely autobiographical. He was by then thirty-three. He reiterated the story of the unidentified Russian. He explained that there had been frequent traffic in paintings between Berlin and Düsseldorf because his brother did restoration work for him. This explained why a painting found there by the police was sticky.

Then Vincent Wilhelm van Gogh testified that the only significant group of Van Gogh works in Russia that he knew about was the collection of about twenty pieces in the Moruschov Gallery. Furthermore, the detailed notes kept by his uncle contained no reference to a Russian collection. In rebuttal Ivan Goldschmidt, still representing Otto, asked if it were not true that piles of the artist's work had lain about the attic as if it were waste paper and had later been hawked from junk carts. The witness replied that this was true only of work from his uncle's Brabant period.

An official from the Soviet government testified that no such collection had ever existed in Russia.

De la Faille did what he could to explain his own shifts. He indicated that he was prepared to issue a supplement to his supplement to his catalogue: five paintings first declared true and then declared false would be re-declared true!

After affirming his own good faith and describing his efforts to go to Switzerland with Wacker, Meier-Graefe stunned the court by announcing that some of Wacker's Van Goghs were of such high quality that, if proved false, no expert in the future would ever be able to distinguish between true and fake Van Goghs with any certainty.

Bremmer, Spiro, and von Koenig all testified as experts. Whereas Justi had said that all the paintings were fakes, these witnesses said that some of the paintings were genuine, some fake, and some indeterminate. They did not agree on which were which. Meier-Graefe had previously testified as an ordinary witness. Now he requested to be heard as an expert. Again he stunned the court, this time by saying: "Anyone who buys pictures and pays enormous prices for them on the strength of expert opinions alone deserves to meet with disaster!"

Ruhemann introduced comparative X-ray photographs of an undisputed Van Gogh oil, *Reaper in a Cornfield*, and of Wacker's Van Gogh of the same subject to show Wacker as a fraud, but Ruhemann's interpretation of the X-ray data was vehemently disputed by Meier-Graefe and Spiro, with the help of defence attorney Goldschmidt. Ruhemann then produced enlargements of the X-ray photos, to show that genuine Van Goghs remain recognizable when X-rayed, whereas fake Van Goghs do not. Van Gogh's paintings are built up according to coherent plan: the final modelling was usually applied on the top of a thick impasto. This structure remains visible even under X-ray examination. Van Gogh applied pigment straight from the tube, but the Wacker forgeries employed layers of stucco, painted over.

Lawyer Goldschmidt demanded to know whether or not the chemists who had tested the pigments had reached the same conclusions as had Ruhemann from his X-ray examinations.

Ruhemann said absolutely yes—and A. M. de Wild, a Dutch expert whose great fame was to come at the trial of Han Van Meegeren a decade later (see Chapter 8), said absolutely no.

By the end of the trial there had been so much acrimonious disagreement among the experts that Presiding Judge Neumann wondered aloud whether the court might not be better served by asking the first policeman off the street to decide which pictures were genuine and which fake.

After two weeks of testimony Otto Wacker was found guilty and sentenced to twelve months' imprisonment "for persistent fraud, partially coincident with grave and persistent falsification of documents." The court declared that the brothers had operated a shuttle service of phoney pictures between Berlin and Düsseldorf.

Both Otto Wacker and the public prosecutor thought the judgement incorrect, for opposite reasons, and appealed. A new hearing began in Berlin's Supreme Court on December 6, 1932; it lasted seven weeks. Wacker's art operation appeared to have been even more extensive than had previously been supposed, and so the court stiffened the penalties: he was sentenced to nineteen months' imprisonment, a fine of 30,000 marks, and forfeiture of civil rights for three years. Nonpayment of the fine would add 300 days to the imprisonment.

Disputes over the paintings did not cease with the trial. In 1939 de la Faille amended his opinion again, deciding that six, not five, of the paintings were genuine.

The origin of the Wacker fakes has never been clearly established. Otto Wacker maintained his story about the Russian. No one had ever seen Otto paint a picture, and there was no evidence that he was a forger. The evidence that Leonard Wacker, who earned his living as a taxidermist, was the forger was largely circumstantial. In fact writers on the case have entirely forgotten Leonard. Only in one source have I found mention that he was indicted with his brother, and no one mentions his presence at the trial. The court records have not been accessible. The war destroyed much. Hugo Perls, alive and active at eighty-three, does not recall Leonard, the man who seems most likely to have been the forger.

Of the disputed paintings most frequently described as genuine, *Self-Portrait*, which had been acquired by Chester Dale now hangs in the National Gallery in Washington, D.C.; another hangs in the Louvre. But both are shrouded in mystery. Where would Otto Wacker have obtained genuine Van Goghs? Did he actually get them from some Russian?

The proliferation of Van Gogh fakes by one painter or another did not stop with Wacker's conviction. As one example, in 1948 several hundred drawings and eighty oil paintings were brought to the director of the Boymans-Van Beuningen museum in Amsterdam for verification. All were forgeries.

For many years Vincent Wilhelm van Gogh tried to track down and unmask paintings falsely attributed to his uncle. But he had to abandon his efforts and capitulate to the forgers. He said, "I had indisputable proofs of their activities in my hands, but I found myself faced with impregnable defences erected by rich and powerful persons in whose interest it was that certain secrets should not be revealed."

CHAPTER 6

The Millet Family Affair

In the summer of 1964 I was poking about the hidden, sooty, and airless corners of Paris, seeking out and selecting a small group of French artists. In the course of my search two good gallery friends made an appointment for me to see a particular painter in his studio. They gave me a piece of paper with his name and address.

I arched an eyebrow. "Millet?"

"Yes, Millet," was the discreet answer.

"Which Millet?" I asked coldly.

"The same family as Jean François Millet." My shudder must have been visible, for my informant added quickly: "But you're not supposed to know that. He's very sensitive and doesn't want to be linked with the family. You must never mention it to him."

Young Millet's studio was the top floor of an old barn. The painter was tall, thin, hungry looking. Two painter friends were with him. All three unfolded their work: a desperate, biting mixture of George Grosz, Robert Rauschenberg, and Neapolitan graffiti translated into images. Certainly there was no Jean François Millet in any of it. As my own associations with the work of the elder Millet was so strongly prejudiced, I blandly interpreted young Millet's drift from his ancestor's work as a manifestation of the same distaste.

But actually the young artist had a double reason for family dissociation: although Jean François Millet's fame might embarrass the descendant who wanted to win his own reputation, the infamy of one J. C. Millet would be more than sufficient to taint the whole family name in family-conscious France. For Jean François Millet's grandson started one of the most notorious of fake-art cabals.

In 1824 Claude Aligny and Philippe le Dieu wandered out from Fontainebleau, supposedly to visit a friend in a porcelain factory. Actually, they were looking for woodland material to sketch, and they became lost in the forest. A friendly shepherd led them to the hamlet of Barbizon, where he permitted them to sleep in the straw with his sheep, the best accommodation that he could offer. In the morning the artists were so impressed by the beauty around that they stayed to paint. Such were the humble beginnings of the Barbizon school, which by 1830 included Jean Baptiste Camille Corot, Théodore Rousseau, Narcisse Diaz de la Peña, Jules Dupré, and a little later Jean François Millet, Charles François Daubigny, Constant Troyon and Charles Jacque.

Corot became the most successful of all the Barbizon painters, and his success made him one of the two or three most counterfeited artists of all times. Millet's work, on the other hand, generally defied the skill of the forger, for it had a certain personality—touch, colour, arrangement, and technique—that was baffling to many would-be imitators.

Millet was born in the village of Gruchy in 1814. He learned to draw with burnt sticks on a white wall. Although his parents were Norman peasants, they were interested in their son's potential. The father took some of Jean François's early sketches to nearby Cherbourg to show to Monchel, a painter who had been taught by Jacques David. Monchel was excited and took the boy as a pupil. In spite of his bucolic origins Millet became the most urbane and well-informed artist, except for Eugène Delacroix, in mid-century France.

Millet had long periods without income, and, even though he was quite famous by 1850, his financial troubles did not cease until 1865, when he turned from canvases glorifying the moral superiority of hard labour—which the middle class condemned as revolutionary—to landscapes. He then produced more than 100 pastels, "which combined his greatest gift, drawing, with a palette of high-toned colour." His range was far wider than most people suppose.

While the French were still ignoring him Millet found an appreciative audience in the United States, where the Puritan ideal of work was a fundamental part of the national mystique, as was a feeling for open spaces and deep forests as typified by the area of Barbizon. William Hunt Morris, a talented idealist, lived briefly in Barbizon and became a disciple of Millet. He introduced Barbizon to American collectors who mattered: Quincy Adams Shaw, William H. Vanderbilt, J. P. Morgan, the Potter Palmers, John G. Johnson.

Only one figure is needed to show how the public attitude towards Millet changed. In 1859 he sold his *Angelus* for $400. In 1889, only fourteen years after his death, it was sold to the collector Chauchard, director of the Louvre Department Store, for $150,000!

By then fake Millets had already become a problem. All by himself one Notlay signed more Millets than Millet had ever painted. The Louvre, seeking to establish a collection of Millets, purchased and displayed Notlay's *Paysanne Allaitant*. One of Millet's sons denounced it, for the painting, a peasant piece, was dated 1841: *Le Vanneur* had been Millet's first peasant work, and it had not been painted until 1849! Forger Notlay had committed a stupid anachronism.

In 1891 the owner of the Château of Tourlaville near Cherbourg was in the shop of the local frame maker when a man entered with a painting under his arm. "Give a look, Masson," he said to the framer, "at this picture I found in the home of a relative at Gréville, Millet's birth ground. Is it worth anything?"

"That's a pure Millet. That's worth gold."

The newcomer thanked him and left, followed quickly by the

château owner, who bought the painting after considerable dickering and took it to Paris for appraisal. It was a fake. He had been set up. With a sworn complaint the police of Cherbourg searched Masson's place and found fifty bogus Millets.

Charles Chaplin, the painter, rests in obscurity, forgotten—but he painted in the manner of Millet. In 1885 an unscrupulous dealer cleaned Chaplin's name off an oil and added that of Millet, an act which must have been perpetrated all too often. In 1934 this particular painting, showing a herd of swine descending a sharp slope of the Cévennes, was sold in Amsterdam for 100,000 francs.

Jean François Millet had a son, Charles Louis Millet, who became an architect. Charles Louis in turn had a son, John Charles, a designer and painter. As a young boy John Charles learned to forge his grandfather's signature; his parents thought it a cute trick.

To help keep them untangled, let us call these three principals Painter Millet, Architect Millet, and Grandson Millet.

The exact story of the Millet plot is difficult to piece together, for the prime participants never told the same stories. But in 1921 Grandson Millet was walking along a Paris street when he saw his grandfather's *Oedipus and the Sphinx* in a shop window. He examined it and stormed into the shop. He cornered the proprietor, Paul Cazot, a house painter from Avignon, and protested that the painting was not genuine. Cazot insisted that it was. The argument was heated, but despite anger and recriminations, some mysterious spark touched both men.

Grandson Millet came back for a second visit. The two men spoke with less hesitation and discovered that they could be enormously useful to each other. Cazot discarded caution and led Millet into the back room, where he showed a number of fake pictures which he boasted that he had painted himself. Although Grandson was himself a Millet, he could not paint as well as Cazot. But Grandson had a gift for signatures.

Their joint procedure was simple enough. Cazot would take the *métro* to the Porte de Clignancourt and walk into the flea market, where he would buy old and worthless paintings of the

Barbizon period. On these canvases he would paint new "Millets."

Usually he would then deliver the paintings to Grandson Millet, who would sign and date them—and also provide authenticating documents. Many of these certificates bore the forged signature of Architect Millet.

As long as a painter is living he is considered the expert on his own work, but under French law when he dies this right passes to his heirs. Sons, nephews, spouse, mother—though they may be ignorant of what the deceased painted and unable to judge the authenticity of works attributed to him—suddenly are regarded legally as competent and qualified experts, and their opinions carry greater weight in the courts than do those of government-accredited experts. More than one mistress—considered a relative under French law—has found her path thus opened to sudden fortune.

Grandson Millet's certificates warmed the hearts of the most circumspect collectors. Consider these inscriptions attached to the back of three Cazot pictures:

> Millet, architect 23 rue Caumartin, Paris 9e. The drawing shown on the other side, *Étude d'Homme*, is an original by my father that was part of a group of drawings that were left me at the death of my father, J. F. Millet. This is to serve as a guarantee of authenticity.—Louis Millet, 8 August, 1887.

> Barbizon, 24-4-1930. This drawing, *Berger Appuyé sur son Bâton*, is a fine drawing whose authenticity is not doubted. It is indisputably by my father-in-law, J. F. Millet.—M. Ch. Millet [Madame Charles Millet]

> [A double certificate] Original drawing by my father J. F. Millet—F. Millet fils. By the present I guarantee the signature of my brother and the originality of the drawing *Femme Portant son Enfant*, on canvas, marked in red, at the lower left, with the cachet of approval of the atelier of my father.—Ch. Millet.

Frequently such certificates were written on letterhead stationery belonging to Architect Millet and purloined by Grandson Millet. Besides forging papers Grandson could perform another task better than Cazot: he could peddle the factory output.

With so many Millet forgeries by Notlay, Masson, Chaplin, and others still in circulation, gallery proprietors, museum directors, and collectors had to be careful not to be duped. But when pieces came to them from the Millet family itself, the authority seemed unimpeachable.

Usually Grandson Millet sold the paintings to legitimate galleries and had little contact with the ultimate purchasers. On an average a good Millet would bring him about $4,000, which he split with Cazot. He did not confine his merchandising to Paris, however, but soon crossed the English Channel and built a substantial business with London dealers. He was astounded by the ease with which he seduced the English. But on one occasion, as described later in the London papers, he made the mistake of trying to fool a dealer who was one of the principal experts on French painting in Britain.

"These two paintings are works of my grandfather," Millet explained.

"My dear sir," the dealer replied, "there must be some mistake. These are certainly not Millet's work."

Millet replied heatedly, "If you take that view, of course, it's impossible to do business."

"I take that view."

In other galleries, though, Millet had better luck, and money filled his hands—and slipped through his fingers. He frequently spent Cazot's share before he could deliver it. To protect his interest, even at the expense of his productivity, Cazot took to accompanying his partner across the Channel and collecting his share immediately upon completion of each transaction.

Occasionally, Grandson did have an opportunity to retail a work directly to a collector. In one instance the prospective buyer was an Englishman who spoke no French, Spanish, or Italian. Millet was acquainted with a Spanish-Italian guitarist, Rudolph Pérez y Montalbo, who did not know a word of English. So one morning when the prospect was coming for another look at the picture, Millet arranged for Pérez y Montalbo to dress in his best clothes and come to visit. Millet introduced the guitarist as a famous picture expert who was in the city for a few days and then asked the musician what he thought of the painting in question. Since the Englishman could not understand the answer, Millet obligingly translated: it was a fine picture, absolutely authentic, and available at an exceptionally reasonable price. When questioned by police in 1930 Pérez y Montalbo said that he knew nothing about art and was no expert; Millet generously concurred.

Grandson Millet's most successful outlet in London was the Thompson Galleries, which bought not only Millets but also the certificated works of other artists by the score. Millet collected $40,000 from Thompson and claimed that Cazot had received $20,000 of it, but Cazot cried not so: he had received only $3,200. Thompson did much better. The gallery reportedly sold a single Millet for $60,000 (some reports said $70,000).

Grandson also sold a considerable number of fakes to Barbizon House in London. On the back of each was a false inscription of origin: "Collection La Doucette, The Hague."

On one occasion after Millet had spent his money too quickly, he went to a bank for a loan. He offered a painting by his grandfather as security and claimed that it had great value. Bank officials granted the application—and were greatly surprised when the painting was not redeemed. The bank offered the painting for sale, but when an expert summoned by the bank declared the picture was a copy negotiations were dropped.

After Millet was arrested, the police followed the trail of this picture, which, mysteriously, the bank could not produce. Inquiry revealed that it had been sold secretly to an American, but the bank refused to identify him, and the police could not determine whether representatives of the bank or a third party had been responsible for what appeared to have been a dishonest sale.

Perhaps Millet and Cazot's most noteworthy transaction was the one that put the pseudo Millet *Les Botteleurs* into the National Gallery of Scotland, Edinburgh; the most spectacular was the sale of twenty Millet canvases to the Musée de Barbizon, which specialized in Millet.

Painter Millet did three versions of *Le Vanneur*. The best version of it, I would like to think, was the one sold to an American and later destroyed in a fire in the United States. The other versions, including the one that is so often poorly reproduced, went into the Louvre. Using the Louvre pictures as models, Cazot painted a new *Vanneur*, which his wife delivered to Grandson Millet one night in July 1929. She asked him to impose the painter's signature, cachet, and date. Cazot had painted the picture on new canvas, which would have been a giveaway. He had therefore glued it, through a process called *marouflage*, to a piece of old canvas, so that anyone looking at the back of the painting would be able to detect only the old canvas.

Young Millet proceeded to manufacture a complete and authentic history for the new *Vanneur* and provided documentation from a first exhibition in the Paris Salon in 1848, through a mysterious disappearance, until its miraculous discovery in an attic in the village of Maisons Laffitte in 1922. The painting had been purchased, so the history declared, by politician Alexandre-Auguste Ledru-Rollin, who had died in the locality of Houilles, not far from Maisons Laffitte. The fake history included critical press reviews supposedly written at the time of the Salon by Censier and Théophile Gautier. Written and printed by Millet, the clippings may have been aged by being toasted over a candle or steeped in tea.

This forgery should have been the crowning achievement of the careers of Cazot and Millet. Christened *Vanneur au Bonnet Rouge*, it was sold on April 15, 1930, by a Paris dealer named Bourzat to a collector named Michaux for 150,000 francs. But for Millet and Cazot it was a very costly picture: it turned out to be the mistake that finished them.

Grandson Millet had unthinkingly signed it at the top, which Painter Millet had never been known to do. This oddity eventually raised suspicions and led to investigation.

There is another explanation, infinitely more French, of what first led the police to Millet and Cazot. Supposedly the latter's estranged wife stole one of her husband's imitations, forged Millet's signature herself, and tried to sell it. When apprehended, she had only to give her name and address to lead inquisitive police to the workshop door.

At any event, the Millet-Cazot structure had already begun to crumble. The Musée Barbizon had become suspicious and had stopped buying from Millet eighteen months earlier; Millet had misappropriated Thompson Galleries property and had passed bad cheques; and a disgruntled Cazot had been acting more and more on his own.

The Millet signature stamp was found in Cazot's possession. He declared to police that he was merely holding it as security on a 200-franc loan that he had generously extended to Millet. When brought before the police Millet and Cazot each tried to dissociate himself from the other and to minimize the quantity of bogus art on the market. In a declaration to newspaper reporters on May 5, 1930, Millet attempted to throw all the blame on Cazot. He said, in effect: "Cazot sold me two copies of paintings by my grandfather, which he swore were originals. Later he confessed to me he had copied them, but by then I had resold them and spent the money. I was forced to continue in the traffic. I have never given any false certificates, and for the past two years I've had nothing whatever to do with this man."

Cazot declared that prosecution would be absurd as it would kill the picture trade in France. Furthermore, Millet was the real culprit, he declared, because it was he who had forged his grandfather's signature and had sold the pictures as authentic.

Technically Cazot was correct. In most countries art forgery in itself does not constitute a defined crime, as does counterfeiting money, documents, and goods. This problem was examined in considerable detail at an international symposium held by the Institute of Criminology in Leiden, in 1962. Participants observed that, historically, forgery had first become recognized as a crime in late Roman law, but definition had remained ambiguous. For art forgery to be punishable by law, said the symposium, it has to "constitute a danger to the community and a threat to the *publica fides*." It seldom does.

The exposure of Millet and Cazot gave police a major headache. To track down all the fakes passed by the pair was an impossible task. The *Chicago Tribune* said that Millet had confessed to having marketed 3,600 forged canvases! Other accounts said 4,000. Numerous pieces were still in dealers' hands, but most had been sold and often could not be traced.

Five years passed before the Millet-Cazot case came to trial, and two more were absorbed in appeals and counter appeals. Millet and Cazot were both cocky throughout their trial and treated the whole history of the previous ten years as a big joke. In the end Millet bore the brunt of the punishment.

In the meantime, in 1930 Millet was arraigned for passing bad cheques. In France counterfeiting money carried a mandatory life sentence, but issuing bad cheques carried a maximum imprisonment of one year and a fine of only 50 francs.

In passing sentence—for Millet was found guilty—the judge scolded: "I wish I could give you more than a year. I consider passing bad cheques the same as counterfeiting money. In America bad-cheques passers get twenty years in jail."

Millet shrugged his shoulders and smirked. "I shall know better than to give bad cheques if I ever go there."

CHAPTER 7

Stamps, Money, and Fra Filippo Lippi

Flag (a lovely contraction of Francis Lagrange) was the only child of an itinerant engraver and picture restorer, self-proclaimed "one of the best in Europe," whose services were constantly in demand by museums and private collectors throughout the Continent. It was the father's job to make old paintings look as good as new, to research and discover the techniques of the original artist, to submerge himself in them, and actually to "become" the original painter. It was hard work, but good restorers were in demand. Flag grew up with his father in the various workshops, toiling on the same paintings, and learning every trick the older man knew.

A successful restorer of old paintings must be equal parts historian, practical chemist, detective, and painter. He must also be creative, but not in the sense of introducing new order or beauty. His creativity must lie in developing new means of duplicating aged effects. At that time the chemistry and physics of painting were shaky arts, not exact sciences. Every Old Master had developed materials, formulas, and complicated techniques of his own.

Usually the restorer is interested only in final effects. A knowledge of the original artist's techniques and materials guides him, for he knows that ignorance or modern short-cuts may do irreparable harm. His job is either to prevent further deterioration of the painting or to make it look (somewhat) like new.

In 1913 the elder Lagrange banished his wife and Flag to Hamburg to isolate the young seducer from the daughters and wives of clients. But when war clouds gathered he commanded them to return to France. Flag, by then turned twenty-one, had fallen in love with nineteen-year-old Maria Bauer, the daughter of a wealthy German family, whom he had met at a gallery opening. As he later recounted in *Flag on Devil's Island*, her parents were strongly opposed to him. German friends kept warning Flag to leave, and he finally took their advice and crossed the frontier moments before it was closed by declarations of war.

Flag lost no time in enlisting in the French army: the best way to win back his girl was to finish the war by defeating the Boche. Because he spoke German he was assigned to intelligence as an interpreter.

When the war ended, few foreigners were permitted into Germany. So Flag persuaded the French War Ministry that it needed a spy in Hamburg. He had no intention of spying seriously, but his duties were light. He was to report three times a year and be available for special assignments, for all of which he would receive a modest annual retainer.

Flag found his Fräulein happily unencumbered, but Bauer family antipathy to him had not lessened because of German defeat. The passionate suitor was followed by detectives, threatened, cursed. But he married Maria anyhow.

The young man was determined to break out of the confines of restoration and to establish a reputation of his own. He painted along Impressionist lines and soon had a one-man show in Hamburg. A few pieces were sold. Maria became the mother of twin girls, but Flag was not destined to be with them for long. He was approached one day after his second solo show by a man named Cellier whom he had known during the war as a French agent.

"You're my contact," Cellier said.

The encounter was embarrassing. In four years Lagrange, who had been paid for his espionage services in advance, had filed only one innocuous report and had then forgotten that his employers even existed. He apologized to the agent.

"You mean that all this time they think you are a spy in Paris and you don't make any reports?"

"I guess that's right. Isn't it absurd?"

Cellier, it turned out, was a double agent, also employed by the Bauers. Three days later Flag was arrested by the Germans and threatened with the firing squad. For two weeks he was interrogated daily. Then suddenly he was escorted to the frontier, expelled from Germany, and warned never to enter the country again or to try to make contact with his wife or his daughters.

He settled in Paris to paint away his frustration and anger. The winter of 1925–1926 was especially cold. He could not turn to his parents for help because they were dead. He moved into a tiny studio, which cost little and did not have much space to heat. He painted a stream of pornographic pictures for a dealer in exchange for canvas. He bought a second-hand easel and sold his overcoat to buy brushes. He made the rounds of the cafés trying to sell his paintings, but "there were more painters in Paris than people." He managed to stay alive by painting smutty illustrations for editions of de Sade.

Life took on a little more cheer when he met Paulette. He never mentions her last name. Although nervous, high-strung, flirtatious, and ill-tempered, she at least warmed the apartment —and continued to warm it even when spring and summer came.

The Swiss government announced an open competition for the design of a postage stamp commemorating the 100th anniversary of the death of Ludwig van Beethoven. Flag entered—and won second prize, 500 Swiss francs, or about $100. He and Paulette were so overjoyed that they blew it all in one night.

A week later Flag was visited by Joel, a small, dapper man with a smooth, round face and a Chaplinesque moustache. Flag reported the conversation in his book:

"Do you wish to remain poor?" Joel [again no last name] asked.

"No."

"Then tell me whether you feel you can actually execute the type of engraving you so skilfully designed in honour of the noted composer."

"The composer?"

"Ludwig van Beethoven. . . . You are an engraver . . . and you have no aversion to money?"

"No."

"Lots and lots of money?"

"The more money the more frivolous the aversion."

Joel proposed that Flag engrave postage stamps. He began ticking off items.

There was a British Guiana 1856 one cent, a pair of Hawaiian Islands 1851 two cents, a Mauritius, a Baden, some United States postmaster issues dating back to 1846, a France 1849 fifteen cents. . . . "We have high hopes of providing collectors with duplicates of a few of these stamps, very excellent duplicates, indistinguishable from the originals. We will supply you with all the materials, including the original stamps."

Flag looked askance. Joel added, "The engraver gets 20 per cent of the selling price."

Flag and Paulette celebrated again. It was a "stroke of incredible good fortune."

Every time Flag had to telephone Joel for something, a different voice answered, but Flag never saw other people, and the relationship between them was strictly business. After Flag had made a perfect duplicate of the Guiana stamp, he wanted to do another.

"Don't be a fool," Joel scolded. "How do you think we could sell two of them in one year? It would be like finding two *Mona Lisas* in the same bed."

Within several months Flag began to branch out. He faked Etruscan coins, broken statuettes, and ancient furniture; he often appeared at galleries as an expert, trading on his father's name, to authenticate his own forgeries. He did a fragment of a frieze ostensibly from the Temple of Athena Nike on the Acropolis, Lucrezia Borgia's chair, a Cézanne sketch, and four or five Van Goghs. He was especially delighted with these assignments, for they brought him immediate flat fees.

One day Joel held a picture before Flag's eyes and shouted "Look at this Van Gogh!"

Flag jokingly replied, "It's authentically artistic."

"You blunderer! You've signed your own name!"

The thunderstruck Flag shrieked with laughter. He had to quit counterfeiting Van Gogh. He felt himself so closely attuned to the Dutch artist that he confused Vincent van Gogh with Francis Lagrange. The next time he carelessly signed his own name, Joel might not notice it.

In his Montmartre studio Flag continued to paint his own stuff, including a suite of tropical nudes, which he adored. Paulette began to develop a distaste for Flag's industry when she saw that he was actually *enjoying* faking Van Goghs. It was all right to counterfeit only as long as he hated doing it. They had a big fight, after which Flag set up a second studio. He painted his own stuff at home, where Paulette could watch him; he did his counterfeiting in the other place, of which Paulette knew nothing.

The scheme worked well until Flag met a girl named Marilyn, "the most beautiful girl I'd ever seen." Again, no last name. She said that she was a chorus girl, but that was only in her dreams. She had absolutely no talent. Flag threatened that unless Joel found Marilyn a job in show business, he would not work for him any more. Joel finally found her a job standing absolutely still, nude, in the Folies Bergère. Flag installed her in the second studio.

Paulette's tastes were simple. But Marilyn wanted everything. As Flag observed in his memoirs, "With Paulette I had had nothing; with Marilyn I owed money." His debts mounted to 500,000 francs. Then Paulette discovered Flag's double life, kissed him gently, and moved out.

Because Joel was slow and methodical and averse to making mistakes, his caution kept turnover at a snail's pace. It would be a long time before Flag could pay his debts. Again an unexpected knock on the door brought a solution to his problems. The caller was a man named Delanoit, who, Flag claimed, was the most feared person in the Paris underworld. He was round-headed, hairless, badly scarred, with a flat nose, heavy jowls, and pale eyes without brows. He wanted Flag to engrave plates and counterfeit foreign currencies.

"What about Joel? I work for him."

"Joel is a nice boy, but he's small time. We'll take care of him. You'll get 20 per cent."

Flag was absorbed into a large and powerful organization and never saw Joel again. Within a few weeks his first fake bills were in circulation, and within a month he was a franc millionaire, though his first half-million went to pay his debts.

There was little risk involved because the French government had no strong penalties for counterfeiting currencies of other nations. It did, however, punish rigorously anyone with the temerity to counterfeit French money.

Six months later Flag was summoned to Delanoit's home, which he found swarming with gunmen. He was introduced to an Amsterdam art dealer who had rashly promised a rich California client that he would find a genuine work by Fra Filippo Lippi—a true rarity. The dealer said: "Creating an original would be extremely risky. The client can't be fooled with a forgery."

In the Cathedral of Notre Dame of Rheims in northern France there was a Lippi triptych with a Madonna in the centre, an Annunciation and Nativity on the sides. It hung in a secluded alcove in a small museum—the old Abbey of Saint Denis—attached to the cathedral. "Can you paint a duplicate of it, Flag?" Delanoit asked.

Flag moved to Rheims. He took a room under his own name in the best hotel, which was near the cathedral, but as George Villard he rented a well-lighted attic room across town. Every day at a different time he strolled, sketchbook in hand, into the museum to study the triptych. Then he went off to his studio to reconstruct what he had sketched. Piece by piece, detaïl by detail, he worked, using a thousand tricks learned from his restorer father.

But, though the restorer must make it *appear* that the work of art has not been restored, he does not have to worry that careful scrutiny will show that it has. The forger, on the other hand, must try to make his hand *undetectable* by any means. He can, if skilled enough, fool the eye and intuition—at least for a while—but the laboratory is another matter. "The variation in physical and optical properties of pigments of varying chemical or physical structure will result in differences," Ralph Mayer says in *The Artist's Handbook* (1957), "even when a general similarity of colour, shade, or tone seems apparent."

Even the matter of support for the painting poses problems. The original Lippi triptych was on wood panelling painted nearly 500 years before Flag's time. The wood selected by fifteenth-century Italians was mostly poplar, in contrast to the oak used in England and the mahogany used in Flanders. Finding old boards, even in Flag's time, was difficult and sometimes hazardous. Abandoned churches were the best source, but even they were not entirely reliable, as there was no way of being certain that the wood found in them was as old as the edifice itself. The origin and age of panels can sometimes be determined merely by the kind of saw marks on the back or by the way that strips of it are joined together—and certainly by radio-carbon dating.

Flag compounded paint from basic materials sent from Amsterdam, "then the art-forging capital of the world." Flag recalled, "The forger's genius, brought to the highest pitch of perfection, is a slightly sinister, almost mystical thing, as if the soul of the original artist were seeking to return to life through it."

Two months later his duplicate was ready for inspection by the Amsterdam dealer. The Dutchman pointed out some minor ornamental flaws, which Flag corrected. The triptych was then perfect, except for ageing. The dealer produced an air-brush and sprayed the painting with a varnish that lent the right appearance. "My client is ready to pay 5 million francs for it," he announced.

"The copy?"

"The original."

"Lagrange," Delanoit announced, "you are about to be hung in the Cathedral of Rheims."

Lagrange returned to Paris, and Delanoit's experts in breaking and entering took over. They took the counterfeit Lippi into the cathedral and came out with the genuine one. Delanoit received a payment of 4 million francs; 800,000 of them went to Flag. But with all Marilyn's demands the money disappeared fast. Flag returned to Delanoit to announce that the only way he could see out of his problem was to begin counterfeiting *French* francs.

A clear warning is printed on every piece of French currency that any counterfeiting of these bills is punishable by a life sentence at hard labour. It is enough to make any counterfeiter think twice. Delanoit finally turned soft-hearted and let Flag resign to go into the counterfeiting business for himself.

But Flag could not keep from returning to Rheims Cathedral to admire his work. One day he bumped into a German pilgrim who admired the Lippi for a long time.

"No one can paint like that today," the German expostulated.

"No. I paint like that."

"You mean you try to paint like that."

"And I succeeded."

"The French cannot paint like Italians. You cannot paint a Lippi."

"I painted that one."

In recalling the incident Flag said, "I had spoken the truth, and I had not been believed."

Delanoit worried about Flag's lingering at the scene of the crime and sent his men to return Lagrange to Paris.

The Lippi theft might have gone undiscovered but for the stock-market crash of 1929. The California collector was wiped out. Eighteen months after purchasing the painting, he was forced to put it up for auction in England. By chance the museum director from Rheims stumbled across an illustration of the triptych in the English auction catalogue. He took the first boat to London to denounce the forgery—only to be confronted by a battery of experts all declaring that the painting offered for sale was genuine. The man rushed back to the cathedral to examine the Lippi there in the dark recesses of the alcove—and quickly called police. Overnight an international investigation embroiled the law-enforcement officials of France, England, Holland, and Germany.

In Rheims police made a complete check of hotels and rooming houses. The landlord of Flag's attic studio rummaged through papers and found a small sketch of a hand with the notation, "Be careful of the second finger and the contrast with the robe at this spot." It had been partially burned, but the landlord had kept it because he thought it quite good. Who had the renter been? George Villard. Police checked Villard's handwriting against hotel registers and came up with Flag's name. A warrant was issued for the arrest of Francis Lagrange.

But Francis Lagrange was already under arrest in Paris, on charges of counterfeiting French currency. He had encountered Paulette, sunk to the lowest depths of prostitution, and he had been overcome with guilt for having driven her out. Contritely he had proposed a ménage à trois in his studio. Marilyn, in a jealous rage, had then denounced to the police the creator of those crisp, almost perfect French francs that she so dearly loved.

For counterfeiting and theft of the painting (he was an accessory) Flag drew ten years on Devil's Island; for counterfeiting money he was sentenced to the same place for life. The sentence was eventually reduced to a total of twenty years and then to fifteen—but Francis Lagrange never returned to France. He painted scenes of prison life, tried to escape several times, and settled in Guiana after he finished his sentence.

Ironically the Lippi Flag duplicated was itself probably a copy. During World War II the cathedral museum was extensively damaged. It has never been reopened, and its treasures have been transferred to the Musée des Beaux Arts. The once-stolen painting is there, but it is stored in the basement, a fate which should never befall a genuine Lippi.

CHAPTER 8

Van Meegeren or Vermeer?

Dr. Abraham Bredius, eyes weakening after eighty-two influential, honour-filled years, hovered between the adulating crowd and the Vermeer masterpiece that they had thronged to Rotterdam's Museum Boymans to see. It was 1937, and behind him lay a lifetime of useful scholarship. In the eyes of many he was the leading authority on Dutch Old Masters; to any detractor who might voice doubts, a series of erudite exhibit catalogues and books would have proved his qualifications. Since the first of them, published in 1885, he had commented on every important piece of art in Holland. The English translation of his monumental work on Rembrandt van Rijn was hardly off the press.

But in 1937 the world was full of Rembrandt paintings, perhaps 700 of them, give or take a hundred, not to mention pictures by his followers. But a work by Jan Vermeer was something else—rarer, and therefore more choice, than Rembrandt. The world knew of only thirty-six authentic Vermeers, and Bredius had just discovered the thirty-seventh, the greatest Vermeer of all: *Christ and the Disciples at Emmaus.*

Emmaus had been revealed to Bredius at Monte Carlo, of all places, by a mysterious lawyer named G. A. Boon, a former member of Holland's lower chamber, but Bredius was the first publicly qualified expert to proclaim the painting. Bredius sensed that this discovery would long outlive his books and perhaps even the many paintings that he had given to Dutch museums. *Emmaus* would establish his name forever in art history, he knew, and of course he was right. Bredius announced his discovery in England's respected *Burlington Magazine.* He harboured no doubts of the painting's authenticity. He called it "a masterpiece," Vermeer's "crowning achievement." But, just to be sure, he had carefully subjected it to the five scientific tests of authenticity then regarded by experts as infallible:

1. Aesthetic considerations
2. Resistance of the paints to alcohol and solvents
3. Evidence of white lead in the white portions
4. X-ray examination of the substratum
5. Microscopic and spectroscopic examination of the principal pigments.

Emmaus had passed with flying colours, and Bredius could truthfully report in *Burlington:*

> It is a wonderful moment in the life of a lover of art when he finds himself suddenly confronted with a hitherto unknown painting by a great master, untouched, on the original canvas, and without any restorative, just as it left the painter's studio! And what a picture! Neither the beautiful signature "I. V. Meer" (I.V.M. in monogram) nor the pointille on the bread which Christ is blessing, is necessary to convince us that we have here a—I am inclined to say—*the* masterpiece of Johannes Vermeer of Delft, and moreover, one of his largest works (1.29 m. by 1.17 m.) quite different from all his other paintings and yet every inch a Vermeer. This subject is *Christ and the Disciples at Emmaus* and the colours are magnificent—and characteristic: Christ in a splendid blue; the disciple on the left, whose face is barely visible, in a fine grey; the other disciple on the left [sic: he was on the right] in yellow—the yellow of the famous Vermeer at Dresden, but subdued so that it remains in perfect harmony with the other colours. The servant is clad in dark brown and dark grey, her expression is wonderful. Expression, indeed, is the most marvellous quality of this unique picture. Outstanding is the head of Christ, serene and sad, as He thinks of all the suffering which He, the Son of God, had to pass through in His life on earth, yet full of goodness. There is something in his head which reminds me of the well-known study in the Brera Gallery at Milan, formerly held to be a sketch by Leonardo for Christ of

> the *Last Supper*. Jesus is about to break the bread at the moment when, as related in the New Testament, the eyes of the disciples were opened and they recognized Christ risen from the dead and seated before them. The disciple on the left seen in profile shows his silent adoration, mingled with astonishment, as he stares at Christ.
>
> In no other picture by the great Master of Delft do we find such sentiment, such a profound understanding of the Bible story—a sentiment so nobly human expressed through the medium of the highest art.
>
> As to the period in which Vermeer painted this masterpiece, I believe it belongs to his earlier phase—about the same time (perhaps a little later) as the well-known *Christ in the House of Martha and Mary* at Edinburgh (formerly in the Coats collection). He had given up painting large compositions because they were difficult to sell, and painters like Dou and Mieris were already getting his prices for their smaller works.
>
> The reproduction . . . can only give a very inadequate idea of the splendid luminous effect of the rare combination of colours of this magnificent painting by one of the greatest artists of the Dutch school.

Bredius' judgement was quickly backed up by the very cream of Dutch experts: Martin and H. Schneider of the Mauritshuis at The Hague, F. Schmidt-Dengerer and Jonkheer Roëll of the Rijksmuseum at Amsterdam, and Van Gelder and Dirk Hannema of the Boymans all testified that *Emmaus* was a masterpiece by Vermeer.

From his first secret look at the long-lost painting, Bredius had resolved that it must not fall into private hands. Although it was being offered to Paris dealers, he felt that it had to be returned to Holland for the Dutch people. He took the case to the rich Rembrandt Association, which, on the basis of approval by so many authorities, lost no time in raising money from its wealthy backers to purchase *Emmaus* as a gift to the Boymans. The price was $286,520. Four-fifths of the sum came from W. Van Der Worm, who a few years later would buy for himself a lesser Vermeer, *Jacob's Blessing*, for nearly twice the price!

When the Boymans staged an exhibition of 450 Dutch masterpieces to celebrate Queen Wilhelmina's Fortieth Jubilee in 1938, *Emmaus* was the piece that every Dutchman—and uncounted foreigners—came to see. Said the monthly *Pantheon*, "few other works of art have ever become so widely known in so short a time." The *Journal of Art History* concluded, "The spiritual focus of the exhibition, despite the distinguished works by Rembrandt, Hals, and Grünewald, is Vermeer's *Emmaus* picture. . . ."

Although the Queen was the most distinguished person to gaze upon *Emmaus*, the humble also passed through the roped-off and newly carpeted area set aside for the Vermeer. One small, slightly bent man made himself inconspicuous. His greying hair was combed straight back. He had a long upper lip, almost completely covered by a triangular moustache. A Dutch expatriate, a portrait painter, he had come up from near Monte Carlo especially to see the Vermeer.

Once inside Han Van Meegeren admired the painting far more than Bredius or the Queen did, for he understood it more profoundly. As a student of seventeenth-century art, he loved the painting, but for Bredius' ability, scholarship, taste, perception, and influence he had only contempt and with some reason.

A decade earlier the portrait painter's best friend, Theo Wijngaarden, had discovered a Frans Hals. At that time both young men had supplemented their meagre earnings by searching for good but unrecognized Dutch paintings in England and Italy and bringing them home to restore and sell in the Netherlands, where they would fetch better prices. Exuberantly, Wijngaarden had called Bredius to see his find. Theo lacked advanced academic degrees, but he had a nose for the authentic—and no doubt about this painting. But he had made a tactical error. In cleaning the Hals, he had used a new solvent, which had an unexpected side effect: it had softened the paint. Naturally, when Bredius had tested the painting for surface hardness, it had failed. Bredius would listen to none of Theo's explanations. The painting was a fake. And without the Bredius imprimatur, the young man could not make the killing that he had anticipated.

Later Wijngaarden had again called Bredius, to see a Rembrandt that he had found. After inspecting the small painting carefully—he later said that the light had been dim—Bredius had glanced up. "It's a pleasure to find you have something obviously genuine for a change. I congratulate you for discovering a genuine Rembrandt."

Before Bredius' eyes Wijngaarden had ripped the canvas with his palette knife. "Fool! This is a genuine Wijngaarden! I painted it last week!"

His curiosity satisfied, Van Meegeren quietly left the Boymans to return to his wife, Jo, at the Villa Primavera in Roquebrune, Cap Martin.

When he reached home he sold Villa Primavera and moved into Villa Estate, a virtual palace in the more fashionable city of Nice. He had, he said, won the equivalent of $60,000 in the national lottery, a prize that he claimed to have carried off on two separate occasions.

During World War II marauding agents for Reichsmarschall Hermann Goering scoured Europe for art. Adhering to *der Führer's* condemnation of modern aesthetics as decadent, Goering specialized in masterpieces sanctified by years of veneration. He amassed paintings and statuary variously valued at $100–$300 million.

By hiding its treasures throughout France, the Louvre prevented the Germans from stealing—by any method—even a single piece from its vast collection. Nor did the Boymans lose its most prized Vermeer, which Goering must have coveted. *Emmaus* and other Dutch treasures were hidden in the great sandstone quarries of Mt. Saint Pieters at Maastricht, near the Belgian border.

Goering had also buried his collection underground, where he hoped that no one would discover it. But he had kept part of it at Karin Hall, his house forty miles from Berlin. As the Allies came closer, he had it piled into boxcars, unprotected against transit damage, and hauled to Berchtesgaden and his home on the Obersalzburg. The paintings were lowered into the Alt Aussee salt mine near beautiful Königsee.

After the Allied victory teams of experts—detectives, art historians, and curators—assisted by tank drivers, armed guards, and muscle men raced on the heels of the front-line troops across the frontier to trace Nazi-plundered art and to prevent its loss or destruction. Following clue upon clue, the armoured detectives found the huge cache, somewhat water damaged, in the mine; the

American 101st Airborne Division found parts of the collection scattered from the mine to the railhead. Within three days every piece found had been moved to the Luftwaffe Rest Centre in Unterstern a mile from Königsee, where the experts methodically checked each painting in an effort to determine its rightful owner and make a reparations appraisal. One of the most fascinating paintings the experts came across was an astounding Vermeer, *Woman Taken in Adultery*, which none of them knew anything about. Why was there no mention of it in any art book? Why had it never been publicly exhibited? Who really owned it? Where had such a masterpiece come from?

Though Alois Miedl, the German banker, who reputedly was Goering's intermediary in these acquisitions, had vanished, a tortuous trail of written records survived. Through this maze the investigators began walking backwards. At its end two Dutch plainclothes detectives knocked quietly on the door of a big house at 321 Keizersgracht, the fashionable street that cuts through the heart of Amsterdam.

In August 1939, when it was obvious that war would soon break across the shoulders of France, Han Van Meegeren and his beautiful raven-haired wife had hastily closed their Nice villa and scrambled back to Holland, which they thought would be spared Hitler's war, which they expected would end quickly.

Holland had not been spared, and once the Low Countries had been invaded Han and Jo had no way of salvaging any of the wealth that they had left on the Riviera. The free-spending, drinking, gambling, speculating Han had been reduced to penury. Yet for much of the war the Van Meegerens had lived in a suburban house in Laren, a house so large that Han had staged bicycle races on the marble ground floor. Then they had decided to move to the Keizersgracht address in town.

And it was no beggar's door on which the two detectives knocked in 1945. In fact, the man who invited the detectives in and offered them drinks owned more than fifty houses and two night clubs in Amsterdam and Laren, from which he received considerable income. All through the war, when delightful things had been so scarce, he had given elaborate parties for his friends.

He was eccentric and reputedly addicted to drugs, but his neighbours liked him.

Jo's patience with her moody husband had been worn away, but though she had divorced him in 1943 she continued to share the same house with him. He gave her 200,000 guldens, money that the Dutch authorities could not subsequently recoup when they attached his property. The couple had shared the most terrible winter in Dutch history, the winter of 1943, when there had been no gas, no electricity, no fuel, and no food, except on the black market, and when people less rich than the Van Meegerens had left the cities each day by the thousands to scavenge for food, often for weeks on end.

The interrogation proceeded civilly, in a low key. The police had carefully prepared their questions, and Van Meegeren had ready answers. He admitted that he derived considerable income from his properties and from buying and selling pictures, though he hated to sell anything that he really admired. As they could see, his house was filled with Dutch paintings, including a number of Ter Borchs.

The questions became progressively more specific. The investigators were trying to find out how a Dutch-owned Vermeer had fallen into the hands of Hermann Goering. Van Meegeren answered with apparent candour. He had sold *Woman Taken in Adultery* to a reputable dealer, Reinstra van Strijvesande. Then the house of Goudstikkers had obtained it. There was no law against that. He had not known at the time that Goudstikkers was partly owned by Alois Miedl, a German who had taken up residence in Holland because of his Jewish wife, or that Miedl would sell the painting to Goering through the Reichsmarschall's agent, Walther Hofer. These affairs were so complicated!

After the sale to Strijvesande vague rumours had reached him that the painting might fall into the hands of the hated Nazi. He had tried to prevent the transfer, but of course, as he no longer owned the painting, he was powerless to do so. Besides, instead of paying in marks or gulden Goering had bartered back to Holland a group of more than 200 Dutch paintings, which were collectively worth far more than one little old Vermeer.

These answers seemed satisfactory. Well, then, where had this mysterious Vermeer come from? It was inconceivable that so important a painting could have reposed anywhere in Holland, where every neighbour knows everything about everyone else, without the art world's knowledge.

Van Meegeren's answer was simplicity itself, a story that with minor variations has had 10,000 true counterparts in the last fifty years. He had discovered the painting in Italy. Originally it had gone from Holland with a rich Flemish family, which had moved south generations before. The family had fallen on hard times, and only a mother and grown daughter survived. Each owned half of a considerable art collection. The mother, who had thought herself in love with Van Meegeren, had sold him the Vermeer on condition that he promise never to divulge the family's name. Public knowledge of her plight would wipe her family out socially.

That had been back in 1931 or 1932.

It was a story that neither side could prove or disprove, but the important fact was that Van Meegeren was safe. He had not broken Dutch law by selling a national treasure like the rare Vermeer to a foreigner. He had demonstrated his innocence in this transaction.

Holland, like the other countries which had endured five years of nightmare and had seen their own peoples torn apart by defeat, distrust, greed, and treason, was undergoing a post-war purge. The German occupation of Amsterdam, Rotterdam, and The Hague had lasted until virtually the end of the European war. As soon as it had ended, the powerful and shadowy individuals who had reaped profits from the war, the collaborators haughty and humble, were being sought for rapid trial and severe punishment.

The Nazi redoubt of Berchtesgaden and the art mine had not fallen until May 4. Van Meegeren's call from the police came on May 29. It is amazing that the Dutch police force could have acted after so brief an interval, but of course its postwar structure had been planned during underground days.

Van Meegeren's complacency after the first interrogation lasted less than twenty-four hours. He had made one terrible blunder: he had blurted out that he had had no way of knowing that the Italian family from which he had acquired *Adultress* was Fascist. "But Herr Van Meegeren, no one has suggested they were."

He had brought a new black cloud on himself by as good as admitting aiding Fascists, which in turn made the suspicion of collaboration with the Germans seem more reasonable: he had wittingly served both Nazis and Fascists. Probably, the reasoning went, the Fascists had given him the Vermeer for some as yet undiscovered services rendered, and he had made his profit by selling it to Goering. He would thus have been a Fascist-Nazi go-between.

The very next day after the police visit Van Meegeren was shocked by a call from two agents of Dutch Field Security. The political police! He was arrested and taken to prison, where the examining magistrate informed him that he was suspected of collaboration with the enemy, which could be a capital offence. Six weeks of custody were enough to break him. He was already in poor health, and he recognized the meagre limits of his own endurance.

For one last, horrid night Han Van Meegeren struggled with his dilemma. Then on July 12, scarcely two months after the German surrender, he capitulated, although some observers said later that it was actually his moment of supreme cunning and that he had invented a story to save his life.

"Fools!" he shouted. "You are fools like the rest of them. I sold no Vermeer to the Germans. I sold no treasure to Goering—only a Van Meegeren painted to look like a Vermeer. I have not collaborated with the Germans. I have only duped them!"

Before he was through, he had confessed to the forgery of fourteen Dutch masterpieces, including *Christ and the Disciples at Emmaus* and *The Woman Taken in Adultery.*

His formal confession began, "Driven by the psychological effect of disappointment in not being acknowledged by my fellow artists and critics, on a fatal day in 1936 I decided upon proving to the world my value as a painter. . . ." Although his confession required verification, in those first few minutes of bitter candour Han Van Meegeren single-handedly shattered the most glorious professional reputations of the Dutch community of connoisseurs—Bredius, Schneider, Schmidt-Dengerer, Van Gelder, Hannema, Martin, Roëll—and of every art critic in the country, the nation's most esteemed picture dealers, two of its most prominent collectors, and a score of lesser lights.

Van Meegeren could not have succeeded better in upsetting the artistic aristocracy if he had planned it all from the first—which is exactly what he had done!

Henri Van Meegeren was born into a strict Deventer schoolmaster's family. There were a brother Herman, a year older, and later three other children. Henri disliked his name, a diminutive of his father's Henricus. So he adopted the still shorter version, Han.

By the time he was ten, drawing had become an obsession. He lacked the concentration to do well in school, but he committed his dreams to paper. He decorated everything with figures, grotesque convolutions, caricatures. His angry father tore up the drawings, declaring that he would do so every time that Han neglected his studies.

Sensitive about his small stature and weak heart, Han was constantly involved in street fights, and he earned himself a lifetime scar on his forehead when he was clouted with a lump of coal in battle with the ruffians from the commercial school.

His contempt for authority and his flair for practical jokes were already manifest by the time he was twelve. The door of the police station at Deventer was opened and closed from the outside with an ancient iron key, which, characteristically in Europe, substituted for a doorknob. Seeing no one on the street one day, Han slammed the door shut, locked it, and threw the key into the nearby canal. He hid where he would be unobserved and roared with laughter as the angry police, most of whom we may fairly assume were fat from the Dutch potatoes and gravy diet, squeezed out through a window, only to discover that they had to shatter the door to get back in. No one in authority suspected Han, a mere boy, but among his peers there never was a doubt as to who had been the hero.

In the same year in which Han locked up the police force, Henricus let him begin art lessons with another schoolmaster, Bartus Korteling. Korteling opened two horizons that influenced Han for the rest of his life. First, Han learned that painting was a way to earn a living, that he might win his bread doing something that he really liked. Second, in four years Korteling trained Han in artistic methods, observation, and meticulous brush work.

Korteling must be blamed, too, for holding the boy to the classics and keeping him out of the twentieth century, where he might have made a substantial name. Under his tutelage Han looked back in time, back to the sixteenth and seventeenth centuries, when Dutch art had been at its zenith. There he lived all his spare moments, reading, studying, painting, trying to re-create the works of the masters. In his police confession forty years later he would say, "My work had to be very exact, very good. Drawing is the art of selection based on knowledge, and I had studied Vermeer analytically. You know, what modernists leave out of their work most of them could not put in anyway."

Although a fundamental command of traditional techniques is an excellent tool for an artist, Han was overtrained in them and prejudiced against anything contemporary.

As his body grew stronger he developed the stamina to keep at his studies and became contemptuous of athletes who had bodies but no brains; he saw that intelligence could beat muscle every time. By the time he was sixteen he was at the head of his class in every endeavour, including drawing. He could continue in school or quit, but he could not enter the University of Delft for a year.

His father drove a hard bargain. He wanted Han to go into architecture, a natural calling for a boy with a gift for drawing. Henricus would pay for the university, but to show his willingness to buckle down Han would have to complete the six-year curriculum in five! It was the best ploy that Henricus could think of to keep his son from wasting all his hours painting. Actually, however, as long as the boy did well in school, Henricus did not care whether he painted or not. Han dropped out of his final year of secondary school, studied for the university exams, passed, and went off to Delft.

Delft had been the home of Vermeer. Another die was cast.

At Delft, Han found a freedom that he had never imagined. He could study, or he could paint. No one was there to see. He did both vigorously, for he fell in love with learning—but mostly with learning about art—and the balance he struck allowed him just barely enough time for architecture.

He painted and offered his works for exhibit and sale. But though he may have been the best in his secondary school, at Delft he was just another boy with an easel. He sold nothing. One day, on the river bank of the Delft Rowing Club he met and sketched Anna de Voogt, the small, brown-skinned daughter of a Dutchman and a Muslim woman from Sumatra. The Sultan of Sumatra had opposed her parents' marriage and had dissolved the union while Anna was still very young. Her mother then married the Sultan's son, and Anna was sent home to her Dutch grandmother.

When Han and Anna met in 1911, she insisted that he was wasting himself on architecture: He should forget what others expected of him and do what he had talent and love for. Besides, she had family that would help. The two were married in 1912 and quickly had a son and daughter. They lived on love and painting.

Every five years The Hague Academy gave a gold medal for the best painting by anyone who had become a student since the last competition. Han decided to try for it, sacrificing everything else. He made this decision at the time when their first child, Jacques, was born. He flunked his Delft exams, but his watercolour of the *Interior of the St. Lawrence Church in Rotterdam* won him the gold medal and $300!

After receiving the gold medal, which he eventually pawned, he began to sell his paintings. But his experiences merely fertilized his contempt for the public, which bought art not because it liked, understood, or wanted paintings but because the artists had become fashionable.

Henricus Van Meegeren offered to keep Han in school for the sixth year, on condition that Han pass the next time and repay his father for the final year's cost. Han agreed. He passed the first part of the exams. On the day of the architecture finals, however, he realized that if he passed he would have to be an architect forever. He was too young to make such an irrevocable decision; he walked away from the exams and never came back.

With no further help from his father but supported economically by Anna's grandmother and spiritually by Anna's faith in his ability, he petitioned The Hague Academy of Art to award him its diploma in art. He claimed that he knew enough to take the exams; he passed the written and part of the practical exam. In portraiture, however, he failed. Then during the final test he was supposed to paint a still life. While he painted the chair, vase, and candlesticks, the judges were ranged across the background, and so he added a portrait of each one as background to the still life on the canvas. It was a tour de force, and they gave him his diploma.

He received his degree on the day in 1914 that England declared war on Germany. Han was twenty-five. Financially he and Anna suffered terrible years again. He had rejected an offer to teach at The Hague Academy. His sales fell off; he insulted his clients; whatever money he earned he spent more; he was in debt to everyone. But Anna's grandmother helped them.

He ran into Korteling, his lifelong mentor, again and was inspired to paint a new collection. Korteling became Van Meegeren's house guest, and huddled like two alchemists they ground and brewed ingredients to duplicate the paints of the ancients.

Anna invited all her rich relatives and their friends to Han's summer show, in an effort to sweeten a marriage that was already going sour. Everything sold. The critics viewed him with favour. One who rushed to his studio to interview him was Karel de Boer, with his actress wife, Jo.

Johanna Van Walraven was a descendant of the dark Spanish conquerors of Holland. She had black hair and was stunning. At first Han thought only of painting her, but before long she was going everywhere with him and Anna.

The five years between 1916 and 1921, which began with Han's first successful show and ended with his second, also an unqualified success—were good financially but disastrous domestically. His sketch of Queen Juliana's deer, executed in nine minutes, became the best-known drawing in Holland. He was elected a member of the Art Circle of The Hague, a weekly conclave of the city's creative people. He used to take both Anna and Jo to these meetings, showering his attention on Jo and ignoring Anna, who often went home in tears, with the sympathy of the rest of the circle but without her husband. When Han and Anna were finally divorced in 1923, she put her children in the hands of a governess and fled to Paris. Han did not marry Jo until 1929, though they had been living together since before Anna's divorce.

He earned considerable sums painting portraits, but much of this money went to Anna and the two children, and he also had to contribute to the support of Jo's offspring. There was scarcely enough left for Han and Jo themselves. It was worst in 1927, when he had to pay a full year's support to Anna in a lump sum so that she could take her children to Sumatra to see their grandmother. When he had first been married to Anna, Han had been lucky to have $100 a week. With Jo he was earning $40 a week from spare-time teaching at the art school and up to $500 apiece for portraits.

At his second show Han had had a traumatic experience. A corrupt critic had offered him a good review for a price. Han had been too stunned to believe it. But it was true: the critic's paper ignored his show completely. This venality, which he began to see on every side, had as severe an effect upon Han as had his first gold medal. His career went to pieces. His dissipation was not easily accepted in Boston-like Hague society. He loved to be the centre of things, to laugh, and to enjoy himself, and he had his own moral code.

Following Theo's lead, he accepted assignments for advertising posters and continued to paint slick, flattering portraits. An American dealer offered him a contract: one year in America, with all expenses paid, during which Han would paint a portrait a week. He stood to net $15,000. But a portrait a week was too much work, too demanding of time that he wanted for other things.

So Han stayed home. But as his income rose his mind and hands could force only hack work from his brush and palette. He worked hurriedly, perhaps trying again for a nine-minute success like the drawing of Juliana's deer, blind to the lesson that he had been sketching the deer for six months before he had dashed off his famous drawing. Legitimate exhibitors refused his work, and the critics carped. Van Meegeren pointedly barred the critics from his parties. He refused to cater to their venality.

To expose the rottenness of the Dutch art community, Han, Theo, and a writer named Jan Ubink founded a monthly journal, *De Jemphaam* (*The Fighting Cock*). This was shortly after Theo had fooled Bredius with the fake Rembrandt. Angry, sarcastic, and libelous, *De Jemphaam* attacked critics, art historians, surrealism, bribery, the incompetence of experts.

Oppressed in the tiny country that offered so many bitter memories and spiteful enemies, Han and Jo elected to abandon Holland. They married in 1929, but it took three years of Jo's skilful saving—and restraint of her husband's spending—before they were able to go. By the summer of 1932 they could afford a car, and they headed south. Van Meegeren told Jo that he would paint the wealthy of the Riviera, and he did, but he went south primarily to find an isolated spot, where he could execute a long-smouldering scheme to make the Dutch art crowd eat bitter crow.

While they were driving along the Mediterranean after a visit in Rome, their car broke down in Roquebrune. There they found the Villa Primavera, one of a cluster of forty-one houses constituting the Domaine du Hameau. They fell in love with it and hurried back to Holland to gather their belongings and acquire some items to make their expatriate life more pleasant—seventeenth-century Dutch accessories for the studio. They took also an ugly unsigned seventeenth-century painting, *The Resurrection of Lazarus*, which Van Meegeren had discovered in Amsterdam after a long search through junk shops. He bought a quantity of badger-hair brushes and two books: one on Vermeer's techniques by A. W. de Wild, the other *Über Fette und Öle* (*On Fats and Oils*) by Alex Eibner.

For their bread and butter, Jo exploited a natural gift, her actress' ability to beguile strangers. She could meet and win over the clientele for her husband's portraiture. She gave the right parties for the right people, and her husband found a life that he loved.

It was a double life. In his public life, he painted a couple of portraits a month, earning an average of $300 for each, though occasionally he received as much as $1,000. This money was enough for his growing appetite for comfort. In his private life, he cut himself off in a room that no one—not even Jo—could enter. There he became scholar and alchemist again, this time without guidance or collaboration with Korteling or Theo Wijngaarden.

One lesson from the latter he had never forgotten. Han had once come back from England with what he was certain was a genuine Pieter de Hooch. Before Wijngaarden had even seen the picture, he had glanced at the back and declared without a second of hesitation: "It's a fake. That's a modern canvas."

The Resurrection of Lazarus was from about 1650. Wijngaarden had innocently verified this date before Van Meegeren had left Holland. In 1650 Vermeer had been in his twenties. The age was just right. After removing the canvas from its stretcher, being careful not to lose the original tacks, Van Meegeren fastened it to a piece of plywood. Methodically, he began to erase the picture with pumice. All the old surface painting had to be removed or else X-rays would reveal it under a new painting. But the ancient ground paint, weathered and cracked, had to be left on, for these cracks were necessary to crack the new surface. In several spots the original lead paint was so thoroughly fused with the canvas that Han could not remove it entirely without damaging the canvas. He would have to incorporate these splotches into his design. He would have to paint white over white, and the white of the new painting would have to conform to the unremovable white of the old.

Paint removal is the easiest part of the forger's tasks. The actual forgery is, of course, the most difficult. Old canvas is easy to find; old-appearing paint must be created. To avoid detection the forger must use only pigments that existed at the time when the picture was supposedly painted. From Korteling, Theo, and de Wild's book Han knew what pigments to use, and he paid enormous sums to obtain some of them. Records indicate that he paid as much as $2,000 a shipment for real lapis lazuli from London. He manufactured his own white lead and used cinnibar to produce his vermilion. Even so, for later fakes he had to stretch out at least one lot of the expensive lapis lazuli by adulterating it with cobalt blue.

Oil paintings may take 100 years to dry thoroughly. Each year they become harder. Van Meegeren could hardly create a seventeenth-century Vermeer and wait around for it to harden naturally. He had to find a medium which would hold pigments as oil does but which could be quickly dried out.

Han Van Meegeren looked for four years before he found his answer: a mixture of phenol and formaldehyde, a synthetic resin used to manufacture Bakelite, which dried so rapidly that he could not mix paints conventionally—he had to dip his brush into the chemical, then into the pigment, and paint immediately. Eventually he evolved a medium of this resin dissolved in alcohol or turpentine and some synthetic lilac oil, and or lavender oil, which, unlike Vermeer's linseed oil, dried rapidly.

To complete the hardening process he intended to bake the canvas, and he experimented to determine the optimum temperature. The hotter the thermometer, the quicker the drying, but there was always the danger of destroying the colours by overheating. How long should the baking period be? Test by test, Han brought the temperature to 105° C. Everything fell into place. He had solved every technical problem blocking his path to the perfect forgery of a Vermeer. Only the æsthetic obstacle—how to paint a painting which would pass unchallenged as a Vermeer—remained.

Exhausted, the Van Meegerens closed the villa and caught a train to the Olympic Games in Berlin and a three-month rest.

Then for six months at the Villa Primavera Han Van Meegeren became Vermeer, a young Vermeer, a Vermeer still under the influence of Caravaggio. Jan Vermeer is one of the most obscure figures in Dutch art. He was forgotten for 200 years because he had quarrelled with an art historian named Houbraker, who cut him out of his *History of Dutch Painters*. For years Vermeer's work was atrributed to another Jan Vermeer, a landscape painter, or to Hooch. Finally he was rehabilitated in

1860 by Thore Burger, but gaps in his life remained, including twelve years when he had supposedly been under the influence of Caravaggio and had painted some of the same religious subjects that had occupied the Italian master. It was postulated that Vermeer had painted religious pictures for an ecclesiastical order with which he was in sympathy. For years art historians had been predicting the discovery of a group of religious Vermeers.

The decision to fill this void was brilliant. Furthermore, religious subject matter appealed to Van Meegeren's own psychological needs. As he dipped his badger-hair brushes—Vermeer had used only badger-hair brushes—into his palette to paint Christ's head, he thought of his brother Herman, who had tried to escape his commitment to the priesthood after eighteen months of study, only to be driven back to the seminary by Henricus; Herman, who had died from melancholy and exhaustion in the seminary in the same year that Han had married Anna. Intellectually, says Lord Kilbracken in his biography of Van Meegeren, *Master Art Forger* (1951), the painter wanted to expel religion from his life but saw in Christ an image of himself. He felt that he, like Christ, had been made a victim of established society. He too had been crushed. But, like Christ, he would rise above his enemies, who ultimately would be forced to call him "Master." As Vermeer painting a religious subject of such great moment—the risen Christ—he found a sustaining power that drove him on.

Finally, his work was done—a perfect Vermeer. He signed to it the name of his first incarnation, the name of the greatest and rarest of all Dutch painters: *Vermeer*! It was a moment of triumph—but he could share it with no one. It was a frustrating plight for a man who needed adulation so much.

Han still faced a nerve-shattering hurdle: the artificial ageing of the paint. With his heart in his mouth he began to bake his big canvas. He had been successful with test pieces—small, meaningless pieces, whose loss would have been no loss at all. Two hours, he decided, two hours in the large electric oven, which he had designed and built himself, would be enough. Each minute added to the pressure on his emotions. When the time was up, he opened the oven, and his Vermeer came out like a perfectly cooked soufflé. But he could let no one taste it yet.

He was still not quite finished. He had to induce additional surface crackling, for the picture still seemed too well preserved. After varnishing the painting, he rolled it, face outward, around a metal tube, unrolled it, rotated the canvas 90°, and rolled it around the tube along the other axis, thus creating a network of fine, almost invisible cracks. He coated the entire surface with India ink, which seeped into the web of fissures. When he cleaned off the ink cover and protecting varnish, a beautifully believable craquelure pattern, apparently blackened by centuries, emerged. To simulate age and abuse still further he flaked away paint from several unimportant places. The machine for his revenge was done!

Eventually he would need some indisputable evidence to prove to the world that *he* had painted the Vermeer. He had already cut off a strip of the canvas to reduce the size before he had started to paint. He hid it for the great and dreadful day of his denunciation. To accommodate the smaller canvas, he had been forced to shorten the original stretcher, and he also hid the leftover pieces of wood.

He then crated the painting and took it to Paris to enlist the support of Boon in reaching Bredius. Because of Van Meegeren's attacks on the critics, he could never have approached any of them directly. He told Boon of a woman named Mavrocke, who had asked him to sell *Emmaus* for her. He said he had smuggled the painting out of Italy but that Boon must not tell Bredius this. Instead he should say that he was representing the estate of someone living in France.

Boon took *Emmaus* to Bredius' retirement villa in Monaco. The scholar was immediately impressed but asked for forty-eight hours to study it carefully. His opinion did not change. The painting was not sold to the Boymans immediately. Theodore Rousseau, chief curator of the Metropolitan Museum of Art, has claimed that, "The [Boymans] museum was pushed into buying it because Van Meegeren floated a rumour that the Rijksmuseum wanted to get it."

Once the painting was in official hands, it was available for constant scrutiny and investigation. But Bredius had called it "the masterpiece." That was enough. Those who had doubted the authenticity of *Emmaus* were drowned out by the Boymans' acquisition of it.

Before the official unveiling, restorers, under H. Luitweiler, laboured for weeks to cover up the paint holes that Han had chipped off and to reline the entire painting with new canvas. None of them—and they were perhaps the real experts—detected anything suspicious. As a matter of fact, after Van Meegeren's confession, Cornelius B. van Bokeman, another of Holland's leading restorers, called him a liar; if *Emmaus* was a forgery, said van Bokeman, it would have been discovered during the relining.

None who handled the picture spoke up against it; it passed into the public domain in an aura of purple praise.

Han Van Meegeren had declared all along that Van Meegerens would someday hang in Holland's best museums. Now one did. Whatever his original intention, he found the profits enjoyable and kept his own counsel. In fact, the money was so enjoyable that he kept right on forging masterpieces. With each one he grew more careless. "They sold anyway," he later said, "so what did it matter?" But he painted *Emmaus* so well that in spite of his confession, many people persisted in declaring it a genuine Vermeer and Van Meegeren a liar, right up until April 1968.

On July 12, 1945, experts rose as one body to declare Van Meegeren a liar. If he wasn't, this one silly man had ruined them all. "To prove your wild tale, Han Van Meegeren, we suggest you paint *Emmaus* all over again," was the official chant.

Van Meegeren replied: "I'll do better. I won't copy anything. I'll paint you a brand new Vermeer."

The Dutch police prepared a large studio in Van Meegeren's own house, put bars on the window and their own lock on the door, and made the Keizersgracht residence Van Meegeren's prison, as the jail had no studio and was crowded with political prisoners. In August, supplied with such materials as the Dutch police would obtain for him, including an old canvas and whatever paints they could find, though probably not any priceless lapis lazuli, Han began work on his last picture, *Young Christ Teaching in the Temple*, before six official witnesses, representing the police, the public prosecutor, and the Ministry of Education. To help the work along they gave him cigarettes, Burgundy, and sleeping tablets daily. They watched, dumbfounded, into October, as a new "Vermeer" grew on the canvas. Unbelievably, Han painted without intensive sketches or models. "If you have painted two to three thousand heads in all lights, you don't need them," he said.

It was a large canvas. The composition was laid out on strict mathematical lines. To preserve a triangular focus he placed a Bible in Jesus' hands; this deliberate anachronism was intended to forestall anyone's attributing the picture to Vermeer at some future time.

Kilbracken has called the painting "one of his best," but Jean Decoen, about whom we shall have much to say, called it "butchery," an obvious forgery. Deprived of his full chemical arsenal and with so many eyes upon him, it is a wonder that Han could paint at all. But he declared that he had never enjoyed painting any picture more, for as he worked he lectured and twitted his captive audience.

Van Meegeren did not bake *Young Christ*, and perhaps he did not even finish the actual brush work, for he learned that in view of his impressive demonstration, the collaboration charge was to be dropped and some other charge substituted—no one quite knew what, for the case was unprecedented—and he quit abruptly. When the charge was changed, the Dutchman in the street quit hating him for being a collaborator and joined the world in admiring him for having duped Goering and confounded the experts.

There was worldwide sympathy for Van Meegeren and delight at the embarrassment of the experts, the men who had helped to establish the ridiculous system by which value lay in the signature of a painting rather than in the painting itself.

Goering was still alive, though in custody, and when he was informed that he had bought a fake Vermeer, he still had enough spirit to rage: "That's impossible! That picture was old, so old I had to have it restored!"

Decoen boasted in *La Lanterne* (November 1945):

> If Van Meegeren is the author of *Disciples*, I'll eat my hat. . . . All these qualities that this work possessed and that everyone saw and discovered [in 1937], do they no longer exist? Everything that makes a masterpiece, do they then exist only in the spirit of man and not repose in any reality? Everything changes because the name of the artist or the period changes? Then it is the name and not the issue that possesses the power of evocation!

It was a touchy issue. National treasures were at stake. There were political implications too: the museum experts were employees of the Dutch state and held a public trust; the private purchasers of the Vermeers were wealthy, powerful, and influential men who had lost a lot of money and a lot of the lustre from their own collections if Van Meegeren's tale was true. For two whole incredible years Han Van Meegeren lived at his home on Keizersgracht and waited while a panel of experts and the Dutch court sorted things out. French investigators came into the act too. If *Emmaus* and *Supper* had come from France into Holland, then they had been French national treasures first, and France wanted them back.

Police poked into every crevice of the big house at Laren. The Frans Hals and the much larger Jacob Maris over the window, not to mention the Oriental rugs, one of which went up to the ceiling behind the Hals, all turned out to be genuine. In the loft they discovered a secret studio that could be reached only by a ladder, which was not there. From below the outlines of the trapdoor were concealed by the massive ceiling beams. The loft itself was triangular in vertical cross section. It sat under the roof beams, each of which was fully a foot square. The concealment of the place was complete: there was not even a window. Van Meegeren had used powerful daylight lamps. There he had painted five forgeries.

Altogether the following paintings were attributed to Van Meegeren:

1. *Christ and His Disciples at Emmaus* (Vermeer), purportedly painted in 1936–1937 in Roquebrune and sold through Boon and the Amsterdam art dealer D. A. Hoogendijk (who had the highest reputation in Holland) to the Boymans for $286,520.

2. *Interior with Drinking Party* (Hooch), painted in 1937–1938 in Roquebrune and sold to D. G. van Beuningen for $117,360.

3. *Interior with Card Players* (Hooch), probably painted in 1938 in Nice and sold to W. Van Der Worm for $97,680.

4. *Head of Christ* (Vermeer), painted in Holland in 1940 as a test piece for Van Meegeren's oven. When it turned out satisfactorily he decided that he would sell it as a study ostensibly for a still-undiscovered larger Vermeer. Through Strijbis (a runner) the painting was sold to Hoogendijk, who sold it to Van Beuningen for $191,663.

5. *The Last Supper* (Vermeer), three times larger than *Emmaus*, purportedly painted in 1940–1941 in Holland and supposedly the great painting, miraculously discovered, for which *Head of Christ* had been a study. It was also offered through Strijbis to Hoogendijk, who sold it to Van Beuningen for $645,600. To pay for it, Van Beuningen returned *Head of Christ* to Hoogendijk and sold twenty-one presumably authentic paintings from his collection, which was the finest private collection in the Netherlands and one of the ten best in the world.

6. *Isaac Blessing Jacob* (Vermeer), painted in Holland in 1941–1942 and sold through Strijbis and Hoogendijk to Van Der Worm, probably for $512,445. Strijbis claimed that he could not recall the amount and had kept no record of the sale! He had also failed to declare his income on any of the Van Meegeren sales and was subsequently thrown into bankruptcy because of unpaid taxes.

7. *The Woman Taken in Adultery* (Vermeer), painted in Holland in 1941–1942 and passed through the hands of Reinstra van Strijvesande to Goudstikker, Meidl, Hofer, and Goering for $665,775.

8. *The Washing of the Feet of Christ* (Vermeer), painted in Holland in 1942–1943 and sold to the Dutch government for the Rijksmuseum through Jan Koh, a friend of Van Meegeren, and dealer P. de Boer, for $524,550.

9. *Young Christ Teaching in the Temple* (also called *Jesus Among the Doctors*) (Vermeer), painted in 1945 under the scrutiny of the Dutch Field Security. Of course this painting would never figure in any complaint.

Four unsigned paintings were discovered in the villa in Nice, all of them, according to Belgian scientist Paul G. Coremans, painted before *Emmaus*: two Vermeers (*Woman Reading Music* and *Woman Playing Music*), one Hals (*Woman Drinking*), and one Ter Borch (*Portrait of a Man*).

Van Meegeren claimed to have painted and hidden one other

painting. He alluded to it on his deathbed and was beginning to whisper its secret to his son when an intruding nurse cut off the conversation. Another Van Meegeren forgery. In what style? By what artist? Where hidden? There have been no reliable answers ever.

The eight pictures sold had fetched $3,041,593, of which Van Meegeren is (according to official Dutch dispatches) believed to have received $2,800,000.

For more than two years then Han Van Meegeren lived at home in a sort of never-never land while the examination continued. Directing the inquest was J. W. Kallenborn, chief of investigation of the Criminal Bureau at The Hague; D. C. J. Wooning of the police did much of the field work. Han was not charged, nor was he freed. While awaiting trial he was declared bankrupt. This judgement froze his assets and left him unable to carry on in his accustomed grand style. His excesses had long since ruined his health. He roamed the streets of Amsterdam buying drinks for "hundreds" of workingmen and singing beer songs with them. An attack of angina pectoris hospitalized him, but as soon as he was discharged he returned to the bottle and to the many friends to whom he was a hero.

He was the darling of journalists, and dealers wanted him to paint pictures—not Vermeers but Van Meegerens done in classic style. A Manhattan gallery was reportedly willing to pay him $6,000 apiece for portraits. He did not paint, except to give lessons to his son Jacques, who before long brightened the art world with his own brand of mischief. He saw Jo daily, and perhaps there was consolation in that.

Meanwhile the artistic investigation dragged on under the direction of Justice G. J. Wiarda, a professor at the University of Utrecht. It took until June 11, 1946—nearly a year after Van Meegeren's confession—for a panel of impartial experts to be sworn in. It consisted of Dr. J. Q. van Regteren Altena, an art historian at the University of Amsterdam; Dr. H. Schneider, former director of the State Department for the History of Art records; Dr. W. Froentjes, adviser on chemistry to the Dutch Ministry of Justice; Dr. A. M. de Wild, picture expert at The Hague (the same de Wild whose book on Vermeer's technique had proved indispensable to Van Meegeren and who had testified in the Otto Wacker trials); and Paul G. Coremans, director of the Central Laboratory of the Belgian Museum, the inquiry to be under the chairmanship of Judge G. J. Wiarda.

Two British technicians, H. J. Plenderleith, keeper of the British Museum Research Laboratory, and F. I. G. Rawlins, head of the National Gallery Laboratory, came to Brussels for a week in January 1947 to re-examine the physical and chemical findings. Coremans gives no indication that these men did any more than read his report and discuss it with the panel. He also acknowledged the help of a dozen other men from Holland, England, and the United States (from Harvard University's Fogg Museum), "who placed their knowledge and experience at our disposal," but this assistance seems to have been mere window dressing.

When this panel had its time in court it declared unanimously that the paintings, as far as visible images were concerned, were contemporary, and that they could have been the work of Han Van Meegeren.

The scientific basis consisted of the following points:

1. Although the æsthetic quality of the seven other pictures was not as good as that of *Emmaus*, the colours and paints were comparable, the modelling of the figures and working techniques were similar, and so the general impression was that all had been painted by the same hand.

2. The craquelure appeared to have been faked because the dirt in the cracks was homogeneous, whereas there would have been an uneven mixture of dirt accumulated over the centuries had the work been authentic. Also the crackle in the white-lead ground did not always match the surface crackle; cracks visible in black-and-white photographs of an authentic painting's surface should match exactly the X-rays of substratum cracks when the two are superimposed.

3. The islands of paint caused by crackling were flat (there had been no moisture penetration underneath) and therefore suspicious; the paint should have been curled slightly along the cracks.

4. X-ray examination showed all the canvases to be old, as Van Meegeren had said. The threads had been distorted by tension around the nails holding the canvases to the stretchers, but there was no distortion at the end of the *Emmaus* canvas, which Van Meegeren said he had shortened.

5. The old canvas and stretchers used for *Emmaus* had been shortened by more than a foot on the left side, as Van Meegeren had claimed.

6. Although the canvas that had been cut off and hidden in the Nice villa had not been found, one piece of the stretcher had been, and it matched the original with perfect alignment of the wood's age rings. The saw cut also had passed through a worm hole which marked both and helped to match the stretcher and the Nice fragment.

7. In July 1946, in the presence of the examining magistrate, Van Meegeren made a rough sketch of the original painting on the *Emmaus* canvas. This sketch corresponded to traces disclosed by X-ray, traces which the painter had declared that he had not been able to eradicate. Several of his other statements about the underpainting also proved out.

8. X-rays indicated that a white-lead paint never used by Vermeer had been applied in modelling of faces in these pieces.

9. Spectroscopic examination revealed the presence of minute quantities of cobalt blue in *Woman Taken in Adultery* and *Woman Reading Music.*

10. The original paint layer on each of the eight pictures resisted water and ethyl alcohol just as did genuine seventeenth-century paintings but reacted differently to strong acids and alkalies. "No old picture reacts in this manner," Coremans said.

11. Various paint layers were as hard as those of old paintings but possessed uncharacteristic porosity and dullness. These paints contained no fatty medium, as they would have if genuine.

12. The medium used was classified as an artificial resin of the phenolformaldehyde group. The relevant testing on this point had been largely the work of Froentjes, and comparative tests run on the resins found in Van Meegeren's studio had yielded identical results. (Some inconclusive testing was also reported.)

13. De Wild reported that his examination of pigments revealed that Van Meegeren had used only seventeenth-century materials, except for the small amounts of cobalt blue noted in several later pictures.

14. Modern resin-based layers on the surface were easily separated from the ancient white-lead, oil-based layers underneath. Examination of the layers revealed aspects that were not typical of genuine paintings. Van Meegeren's working technique was reconstructed in the laboratory and proved out.

The trial of Han Van Meegeren in the Fourth Chamber of the District Assize Court lasted only one day, October 29, 1947. The charge: forging signatures. On the back wall hung Van Meegeren's best, *Christ and the Disciples at Emmaus* and *The Last Supper*, if indeed they were his! The other paintings hung about the courtroom. A projection screen was set up on the left. A few feet in front of the judge was a short balustrade at which the attorneys stood, and six feet from it was an oblong box in which Van Meegeren sat alone, with his hands folded. His crumpled collar was tied with its usual Windsor knot, and he held his head high.

Coremans carefully explained the findings of his committee. Replying to Court President V. G. A. Boll, Han eagerly acknowledged Coremans' evidence and declared; "I find this work excellent. Indeed it is phenomenal. It will never be possible to get away with forgery again. To me, such work seems much more clever than—for example—the painting of the *Emmaus*."

The public prosecutor asked de Wild how the experts had been fooled by the painting acquired by the Rijksmuseum.

"Because de Boer would not let us take X-rays of his pictures!"

Why had de Boer refused? Why had the purchasers gone ahead anyway? Those questions were neither asked nor answered.

Strijbis and Hoogendijk testified that they had been deceived. Said Hoogendijk: "It's difficult to explain. It is unbelievable that it fooled me. But we all slid downwards—from the *Emmaus* to the *Last Supper*, from the *Last Supper* to the *Blessing of Jacob*. When I look at them now, I do not understand how it could possibly have happened: a psychologist could explain it better than I can. But the atmosphere of war contributed to our blindness."

Hannema of the Boymans admitted that the Rijkmuseum had asked him to come to Amsterdam to pass judgement on a new Vermeer that the state was considering purchasing and that he had recommended purchase. "But," he admitted in court, "none of us liked it much but we were afraid it would go to Germany."

"Why did you buy it?"

"After all, Vermeers are scarce." So they had finally paid $525,000 for a painting that they disliked!

Han was having his day.

"You agree that you painted these forgeries?"

"Yes, Mr. President."

"And you sold them at a very high price?"

"I had no alternative. If I had sold them at a low price, it would have been an *a priori* indication that they were false."

"But you continued, did you not, after the first forgery?"

"I found the process so beautiful. I came to a condition in which I was no longer my own master. I became without will, powerless. I was forced to continue."

"At least you made a considerable profit."

"I had to, Mr. President. I had been so belittled by the critics that I could no longer exhibit my work. I was systematically and maliciously damaged by the critics, who don't know the first thing about painting."

"Perhaps the financial side had some influence on your actions?"

"It made little difference. . . ."

"Did you act from a desire to benefit?"

"Only from a desire to paint. I decided to carry on, not primarily from a wish to paint forgeries, but to make the best use of a technique which I discovered."

The trial ended abruptly. It could have gone on to endless probing of the unanswered questions, but this would have been truly devastating for the whole Dutch art community.

Han Van Meegeren was judged guilty, exactly as he had wished to be. But he became deeply concerned about his pictures. By Dutch law, fake art works must be destroyed to prevent their re-entry into commerce. If his "Vermeers" were burned, the only art which gave Han Van Meegeren any lasting importance would be gone, and no tangible evidence of his work would survive for posterity. All his brilliance would indeed have been in vain. To his immense relief no burning order was handed down, the judge instead instructed that all the forgeries be returned to their owners.

Sentencing required reflection, and Van Meegeren was therefore sent home. Two weeks later he appeared before the court to be sentenced to one year in prison. But the prison was not ready to take him yet, and he went home again to wait for the police to come for him. Another heart attack sent him back to the hospital. Six weeks after his sentencing, Han Van Meegeren was dead.

The Van Meegeren story was far from over, however. The court had acted, the legal decision had been made, and most of the world was willing to give Van Meegeren his due. But Decoen, Van Beuningen, painters like André Lhote, and many others were not. No one doubted that Han had forged Vermeers, but many people were not willing to grant that he had done *Emmaus* or *The Last Supper*. These paintings were much better than the others. Aesthetically, to these people, they *were* Vermeers. So another explanation had somehow to be found and justified.

The dissidents hit upon the explanation that Van Meegeren had discovered and purchased these two authentic paintings years before. Being a man of enormous ego and little talent, he had repainted and restored them—badly. After he had sold *Emmaus*, he had realized that *The Last Supper* was the last of his assets. So he had begun to paint fakes to sell, using the genuine pieces as models. The story had some plausibility, since the later paintings were not as good.

But before this tale could be swallowed, even by its own proponents, Coremans' testimony, which *had been accepted in court*, would have to be demolished.

In 1949, two years after the trial, the hue and cry against his panel had become so loud that Coremans wrote a summary of the technical evidence—forty pages of text with seventy-six plates—which was published in English, probably for the same reasons that Bredius had published in *Burlington Magazine*. But Decoen found in this a deliberate effort to keep data from ready access by the Dutch.

Decoen, a sculptor and painter of some talent and a connoisseur of old paintings, became Coremans' most articulate adversary. Just as Coremans had made himself the spokesman for the experts who fully accepted Van Meegeren, Decoen spoke for those who could not reject the authenticity of *Emmaus* and *The Last Supper*.

Both Decoen's attitude and his persistent carelessness can be illustrated by this brief post-trial exchange, which he himself related:

> Decoen: "How did you make the craquelure?"
>
> Van Meegeren: "I repainted an old canvas, and these are the cracks of the old painting, which formed those which are visible today."
>
> "Is there still an old picture below?" someone asked.
>
> Van Meegeren: "No. I scraped it away completely."

Decoen's comment: "Upon this flagrant contradiction I terminated my interview."

There was no contradiction. When Van Meegeren spoke of the "picture" that he had completely scraped away he was referring only to the surface image and not to the underpainting which had fused with the ancient canvas.

Decoen cried, "How many times have we seen mediocre paintings sold for enormous prices because of illustrious provenance or good certificates, while works of real value, even masterpieces, coming from who knows where, are carried off for little money by some real connoisseur?" Decoen claimed that Van Meegeren had found the two Vermeers in some church or monastery in Italy and swindled them away for almost nothing.

Turning on Coremans, Decoen lectured disdainfully, "The physicochemists [sic], having but a very small knowledge of the restoration of antique paintings and especially of the possibilities that this offers a forger like Van Meegeren, are not visibly able to discern true from false."

Decoen's cry fell on the sensitive ears of Van Beuningen, he who had cashed in twenty-one paintings from his collection to acquire *The Last Supper*. Of his genuine affection for the painting or his devotion to art there can be no doubt. A shipping tycoon and financier, he was constantly upgrading his collection. Of 5,000 paintings that he had owned at one time or another, he had kept about 500. They eventually went to Rotterdam, and his name was added to that of the museum, which became the Boymans-Van Beuningen.

On matters of opinion, sincere contradictory witnesses can be found overnight. But the very tenets of science demand that identical results come from identical procedures and that those results be unique to the prescribed situations. Science also demands admission of error and discarding of false doctrine.

Early in the battle, while Decoen was still groping on the basis of only his intuition, he met with Coremans and Van Beuningen in Rotterdam. Five other experts, consultants to the Boymans Foundation, were also present. Coremans summarized his views as a chemical investigator. He detached flakes of paint from four alleged Van Meegerens, including *Emmaus* and *The Last Supper*, treated them with caustic soda, and let each man look into the microscope to see how the flakes decomposed into pebble-like pieces. Then he took flakes from several authentic seventeenth-century paintings that had been brought by Decoen himself and let the men all peer into the microscope again. These pieces saponified and formed an emulsion, just as Coremans had predicted.

When Van Beuningen observed that all the samples from the Decoen paintings were coloured, whereas Coremans had selected only white from the Vermeers, the good doctor replied that he had selected white particles only because they would be more visible to people unaccustomed to chemical procedures. Van Beuningen, "having unlimited confidence in the loyalty," of Coremans, accepted the evidence, as did Henri Lavachery, Coremans' superior at the Belgian museum laboratories.

A few days later a furious Decoen telephoned Van Beuningen from Brussels. He had bought a microscope and had repeated Coremans' procedures on a long series of seventeenth-century paintings from the whole school of Delft to Rubens—and had obtained exactly the results that Coremans had on the four Vermeers! Van Beuningen was furious, believing that Coremans had deliberately hoodwinked him. There is ample reason to believe that thereafter the wealthy Van Beuningen encouraged and probably subsidized Decoen's efforts to discredit Coremans and to establish the authenticity of the two Vermeers.

Decoen set out to become a chemical expert or to find one, and in 1951 he published simultaneously in French, English, and Dutch—again probably with Van Beuningen's financing—a much bigger book than Coremans had done: *Return to the Truth—Two Authentic Vermeers*. It ran 60 *Life*-size pages of text plus 201 plates. But in his zeal to marshal every possible piece of evidence, Decoen himself made careless assertions. To defend the Boymans, for instance, he made the indefensible statement that no major museum anywhere in the world during the past fifty years had hung a forged painting!

But what was the truth? Both sides accused each other of

deliberate lying and falsification of evidence. As to *Disciples at Emmaus*, Coremans' book contains a picture showing how the piece of stretcher found in the villa at Nice matched the *Emmaus* stretcher right down to the worm hole, as Han had said it would. Yet Decoen's book has photographs that purportedly show that the wood did *not* match!

Coremans thundered that someone had disfigured the pieces so that they would no longer match, and he predicted that very soon the *whole stretcher* would disappear. (It did not.)

Through all this controversy there was no mention of sophisticated chemical tests of the two pieces of wood, just of a visual matching.

Coremans pointed out that in the presence of a magistrate Van Meegeren had made a large sketch of the painting *The Resurrection of Lazarus*, which he had almost entirely cleaned off before painting *Emmaus*. This sketch had shown where the parts lay that he had not been able to remove. Coremans showed an X-ray picture of the painting, which coincided with the sketch. Decoen accused Coremans of having shown Van Meegeren the X-ray in advance of the demonstration and declared, "It is impossible to admit this evidence."

The controversy over *The Last Supper* was even greater. Van Meegeren had declared that he had painted it on top of a Hondius. In September 1948 A. Van Schendel, curator of the Rijksmuseum, informed Coremans that he had found a sales record in Amsterdam showing that in May 1940 Van Meegeren had purchased a large Hondius from Douwe's antique shop for 1,000 guldens. Van Schendel had also found a photograph of the Hondius. Radiology revealed the original picture in great detail, for Han had erased little of it. Decoen claimed that Vermeer himself could have painted over another picture. But the photograph coincided with the X-ray. It would have been impossible, obviously, for there to be a photograph of a Hondius which had been painted over by Vermeer.

But, according to the bill of sale, the Hondius had been a few inches larger than *The Last Supper*. Decoen jumped on this discrepancy. Coremans replied that the size specified in the bill of sale included the frame and that there really was no discrepancy.

Decoen then charged that the photograph could *not* have been made from a Hondius oil. Instead, someone had used the X-ray as a guide to paint on paper a replica of the Hondius, which had then been photographed before the paper painting was destroyed.

Decoen came up with a letter dated 1939 from Van Meegeren to lawyer Boon, describing a great masterpiece *Last Supper* that he had seen:

> Last Monday Mavrocke stood suddenly before me bearing letters from her daughter. . . . She wrote that Mavrocke's cousin, Germaine, who lives in the Midi, wanted to see her because he is dying with cancer (86 years); Mavrocke is one of his heirs. The daughter wrote that she had seen a photograph of the *Emmaus* [probably in the newspapers] and wanted to sell something from her own collection (as I think I told you before). She remembered seeing at Germaine's—whose collection had the same provenance as the pictures that her father brought with him when he arrived—a similar biblical painting, but much bigger and with far more saints. On Tuesday I went to one place with Mavrocke: we spent two days searching—found no saints—only pictures from later periods—until on Saturday one of the servants told us of some rolled-up canvases in our attic.
>
> There we discovered a painting, which is the finest and most important ever made. It is a *Last Supper* painted by—Johannes [Vermeer], much bigger and more beautiful than the Rotterdam picture. It is stirring in its composition, venerable and dramatic, more sublime than all his other paintings. It is perhaps his last work and is signed. . . . After rolling it up we walked into the mountains like a couple of idiots. What to do. . . . [It is a] symphony of our most lovely character, such as was never painted before by Leonardo, by Rembrandt, by Velázquez, by any other master who painted one *Last Supper*.

Was the letter authentic? If so, had Han been trying to drum up business for a painting that he *intended* to paint, or did he have a (the) *Last Supper* already?

Coremans needed an explanation of the Van Meegeren letter, which he evidently believed authentic. He found his explanation and revealed it on December 5, 1949, at a press conference in the chambers of the Musées Royaux d'Art et d'Histoire in Brussels: Under blinding lights he unveiled a new Van Meegeren *Last Supper*!

On September 26, he said, he had made a thorough search of the Nice villa, ruining three shirts and two suits in the process, and had discovered hidden between two pieces of plywood—the second *Last Supper*! Van Meegeren had painted his subject—"a masterpiece"—in Nice, had been forced to abandon it because of the war, and had painted a second version in Holland. Van Beuningen had bought the second one.

Decoen cried foul. Just four days before Coremans' search—that is, on September 22, 1949—Decoen and a Dutch consular official had themselves combed every corner of the villa, including the two huge basement rooms, and had found nothing. The plywood sheets that Coremans claimed to have found were 58 x 105 inches, much too big for Decoen or anyone else to have missed! Decoen and the other man had returned for a second search on September 27, but of course they had found nothing then, either. Was that because Coremans had just been there and walked off with the prize? Decoen pointed out that Inspector W. J. Wooning of the Bureau of Criminal Investigation in The Hague had thoroughly searched and inventoried the entire villa on October 25, 1945, and again in 1946. No such painting had been found. Decoen also produced affidavits from the old gardener who had moved everything into the cellars after Han and Jo had fled and the Italian army had moved into the villa; the gardener had known of no such object.

Several days *before* Coremans' "discovery," Decoen had written in a Belgian newspaper, *La Lanterne*, that just such a painting was being fabricated and that he expected it to be found in Nice. He had rushed to the villa expressly to preclude its being found there! Van Beuningen subsequently declared that he had known in *July* that someone in Holland was painting a *Last Supper*, a forgery of a forgery! Decoen believed that Jo Van Meegeren had paid to have the new *Last Supper* painted under Coremans' tutelage. She had allegedly completed the purchase on September 8, but the supposed painter was never identified. Decoen openly accused Coremans of being "the author of a fraudulent comedy."

According to one Belgian art publication, guests at the press conference who were familiar with Van Beuningen's *Last Supper* were "petrified by the mediocrity of this canvas." But Coremans argued that it was an uncorrected version. If Meegeren had been able to age it artificially, it might have been even better than that owned by Van Beuningen. With equal alacrity Coremans produced a photograph of a painting by Dutch artist Govaert Flinck and a receipt from a dealer who had purportedly sold the Flinck to Van Meegeren in 1938. This Flinck, Coremans asserted, had been the base canvas for the new *Last Supper*.

That would have been a play on canvas difficult for the technical prowess of even Van Meegeren. The dimensions of the Flinck were 87 x 79 inches, the dimensions of *The Last Supper*, 57 x 105 inches. Yet Coremans would have had the world believe that Van Meegeren had cut some of the canvas off the height and had added it to the width. Technically this procedure would have been possible, but the seam could not have been disguised, and it would have been an immediate tipoff that something was not quite right. Van Meegeren would have known better, Decoen was quick to point out.

The Nice version of *The Last Supper* disappeared more quickly than one could say abracadabra—and permanently. No amount of pressure from either journalists or officials could make Coremans bring it out again. It had been spirited back across the French frontier and hidden in the vaults of a Lille museum! No one could gain access to it, even though, if Han had painted it, it belonged neither to Lille, Coremans, nor Jo but to the Dutch state, which had confiscated all the forger's property.

Decoen then attacked the æsthetic mediocrity of the painting as shown in the photograph.

To add still another dimension to the brouhaha, J. M. Charlier, a government restorer working for Coremans, charged that one M. Oudenberg had reported to police that he had been offered $10,000 to declare that he had painted the Nice *Last Supper*. This revelation was not made until 1956, however; whether Oudenberg or Charlier had delayed the news until then is not known.

Decoen came up with an elaborate tale of how in 1939, a month after war had broken out, a forwarding company in Paris had received a shipment of four cases from Nice in Van Meegeren's name. Two cases had contained paintings. One was large enough to have held Van Beuningen's *Last Supper*. Tailleur Fils, the forwarder, had kept the cases until May 1941, when they had been picked up by a German military truck and carried to the rail station in Hilversum, Holland. There they had been received by Strijbis and Van Meegeren. The big case had been put on a train to Amsterdam, with Strijbis accompanying it, in fact, sitting on it in the baggage car. Strijbis had taken the case to Hoogendijk's, where it was opened.

Since 1941 had been the birth date of *The Last Supper*, according to Van Meegeren's confession to police, was Strijbis in cahoots with him in the elaborate charade to make it appear that the painting had come from France? Had Van Meegeren lied when he claimed he had done the painting? Or had some unknown party forged the documentation for this transaction and dropped it into Decoen's unsuspecting lap?

My own hypothesis is that there *were* two *Last Suppers*. On his deathbed Van Meegeren was about to tell his son of a missing picture when he was interrupted. No one has proved that the Van Meegeren letter produced by Decoen was not authentic. Six weeks after Van Meegeren had written it to Boon from Nice, he and Jo returned to Holland. Van Meegeren may have delivered the oil to Boon before leaving France. Boon was to sell it, but the war broke out immediately, and Boon, a Jew, was never heard from again. He simply disappeared and could not be found. One rumour says that he went to Canada, but if so he apparently went under a different name. He may have been killed in an air raid or in a German gas chamber. He either took the painting with him or hid it—whether in trust for Van Meegeren or for his own profit, who knows? If he was still alive when Van Meegeren confessed, it would have done him no good to come forward. His own participation in the sale of *Emmaus* might have put him in danger of prosecution. This *Last Supper* may have been destroyed by now, or it may yet turn up, a final monument to Van Meegeren.

One by one other scientists filed their testimony against Coremans' chemical analyses. They were egged on by questions put to them by Decoen and Van Beuningen, who attacked not only Coremans but also Froentjes ("incompetent") and de Wild (who "proved that *Washing of Feet* was authentic in 1943 and false in 1946").

E. Bontinck led off in 1950 with an attack in a chemical publication. Charles Meurice of the Meurice Chemical Institute and the University of Brussels then supported Decoen in detail, declaring that it was impossible to claim the presence of a synthetic resin in *Emmaus*. Cyril Grob of the Institute for Organic Chemical Research and the university of Basel added that not only was there no proof of synthetic resins but there was also evidence of the natural resins found in authentic antiques. In Graz, Austria, and in London, two more important voices were raised against the scientific competence of the Coremans panel.

By December 1954 Coremans' findings—and his adamance—had become so discredited that Henri Lavachery, honorary chief conservator of the Musées Royaux and a professor at the Free University of Brussels, according to Belgian sources "one of the high consciences of the world of archaeology and art history," held a conference in the museum on *Vermeer and Van Meegeren: False and Authentic*. Lavachery had made a special trip to Holland to look at the two disputed paintings, and had been overwhelmed.

Lavachery, who was technically Coremans' superior and who had regarded himself as a close friend of the chemist, reviewed Van Meegeren's claims, Coremans' research, and his own efforts to persuade Coremans to produce the Nice *Last Supper* for public scrutiny—or to offer new evidence and admit any of his procedural errors, or at least in some way to break his self-imposed five-year silence.

At the end of the conference, Lavachery declared *Emmaus* and *The Last Supper* to be genuine Vermeers.

In Paris even the respected and sober *Le Monde* came out against Van Meegeren and for Vermeer.

In 1952 Van Beuningen had filed suit against Coremans in Brussels, claiming that the chemist's testimony was false and had done him great damage. Coremans had filed a countersuit.

Although the litigation was between two private individuals, the Belgian state, urged by the Minister of Public Instruction, entered the case on Coremans' side. There were insuperable delays, and Van Beuningen died in 1955. His heirs offered to pay court costs and to drop the matter, but the government would not accept.

The Belgian court based its decision entirely on the findings of the Dutch court in the trial of Van Meegeren, even though substantial parts of the evidence from that trial were obviously faulty. Coremans won, and the Van Beuningen estate was forced to pay him a judgement and costs! Coremans compelled the losers to pay for printed retractions in publications of his choice. He also won $15,000, although he had asked for $20,000.

The decision was legal, but it had settled nothing.

Then, to everyone's consternation, Van Meegeren's son, Jacques, started visiting European museums, examining Dutch Old Masters, and declaring them actually to be the works of his father!

Had Han Van Meegeren forged all six of the Vermeers that he had sold, or had he possessed two authentic Vermeers, which he had used as models for the four that he unquestionably had painted? His reputation as a forger—as a painter—hangs on the answer to this question, and so does the future of the two paintings.

More than a dozen years have passed since the decision against Van Beuningen, more than twenty since Van Meegeren's own trial. But only now there has finally come a definitive, apparently incontestable scientific answer—and it has come not from European laboratories but from American.

For several years the Mellon Institute (Carnegie-Mellon University, Pittsburgh), which is the scientific investigative body for the National Gallery in Washington, D.C., has been developing a method for determining the age of paint pigments through measurement of residual radioactivity.

For centuries artists have used white lead, a major pigment. Natural lead ore contains uranium, which slowly decays to produce radioactive lead, Pb^{210}, and radium, Ra^{226}. In deposits which have been undisturbed for thousands of years the rates of radioactive emission for these three chemical species are precisely equal. In the refining process almost all the radium and its family are separated from the lead. The minute quantity of radioactive lead which remains is then out of balance with the residual radium that has survived the refining process and begins to decay; it has a half-life of twenty-two years. In each successive twenty-two-year period after the time of smelting the "excess" radio-lead in white-lead paint will lose one-half its radioactivity. This decay continues until the lead has reached a new equilibrium with the very minute quantity of radium, which has a half-life of more than 1,000 years and so is nearly a constant. Thus, after 44 years, the Pb^{210} would have lost 75 per cent of its imbalance, and after 132 years, more than 98 per cent. Solid-state detectors and modern methods of radio-chemistry make it possible to meter the amount of radioactive lead, radium and polonium (Po^{210}, which is actually measured to determine the amount of Pb^{210}) in any sample of white lead obtained from a painting. From these readings it is possible to calculate the approximate age of a work of art. In the comparison of old works (150 years old or older) with modern pieces, the measurable difference is extremely wide, for the Pb^{210}–Ra^{226} ratio will be way out of balance for a new painting but approaching virtual equilibrium for an old one.

In the April 26, 1968, issue of *Science*, Bernard Keisch, radiation expert at the Institute, reported the application of this method to five Van Meegeren–Vermeer paintings, including *Emmaus* but not *The Last Supper*. For control two genuine Vermeers from the National Gallery were tested simultaneously. The results were decisive. To use Keisch's words: "There remain to this time some persons who still believe *Disciples at Emmaus*, 'discovered' in 1937, to be a genuine Vermeer. My results, however, conclusively confirm that all five of these paintings are modern, and hence, probably correctly attributed to Van Meegeren."

CHAPTER 9

The Frescoes on the Postage Stamps

One thousand and twenty years ago missionary priests of Otto I, King of Germany and soon to be Holy Roman Emperor, moved into Danish territory and established in Schleswig the northernmost of the early German bishoprics. Because Schleswig was the bishop's see, the small trading community began to build a cathedral, St. Peter's. It grew with typical medieval speed: it had a Romanesque transept by the end of the twelfth century, an early Gothic nave in the thirteenth century, a late Gothic choir by the end of the fourteenth, a divided nave in the fifteenth—and finally in the nineteenth century a hastily erected afterthought of a belfry.

The princes of Schleswig chose to be buried in St. Peter's, which was the town's only artistic focus. The cathedral's greatest, though sometimes neglected, glories were its Gothic fresco cycles in the choir and cloister. In time they became recognized throughout Germany as national treasures.

Over the centuries dust and the damp Baltic fogs gradually blackened the unsigned frescoes. In 1888 they were cleaned and restored by August Olbers, but fifty years later they needed cleaning again. Authorities turned to Professor Ernst Fey and his son Dietrich, who had been retouching and preserving tattered frescoes in Silesia for several years; they were asked to restore the Schleswig works to their original condition.

Professor Fey had gilt-edged academic titles and a reputation based on his remarkable success in the restoration of churches in Oppeln and Neisse. He was not about to downgrade his own fame by admitting that his best work had been done since he had hired a young painter from Königsberg.

Once inside St. Peter's Cathedral, Fey lost no time in asserting his authority. To get down to the original fresco, he decreed that August Olbers' incompetent overpainting be peeled off. But, when this crude upper layer had been gingerly removed from one figure, nothing was left on the walls except mouse-coloured plaster. The Gothic masterpieces, the priceless treasures of the German people, had vanished!

Formal penalties for such carelessness or incompetence would not have been grave: there would have been no onerous fines, no jail sentences. But the dishonour, the damage to self-esteem, and the loss of future contracts were penalties quite beyond what Fey and his son were prepared to accept. They turned to their young but versatile employee, who had demonstrated his prowess in Oppeln and Neisse, and implored him to repaint a Gothic figure there.

When the figure had been restored, the Feys could have announced to the authorities that the rest of the frescoes were beyond restoration. But they had said the job could be done, and it was a lucrative commission. Prestige and money over-rode professional integrity.

There are as many philosophies of restoration as there are restorers. At one extreme stand those technicians who maintain that only the artist's original work, however badly deteriorated, should be preserved. This position was formulated in 1926 by Otto H. Forster during restoration of paintings in the Cathedral of Cologne: "There must be no element of addition, completion, or other conjectured reconstitution of any supposed original state."

At the other stand equally skilled technicians who hold that their mandate is to make a painting look as it probably did when it was new. To accomplish this aim the restorer generously replaces missing areas (often more in accord with his fancy than with researched fact) and overpaints to simulate original colours.

At work in St. Peter's Fey followed neither of these positions or any intermediate point. The work done under his direction was bald-faced counterfeiting!

For week after week during 1937 the walls of St. Peter's were methodically scraped bare. The bricks were then replastered with a new ground consisting of several layers of lime muddied with grey pigment to simulate age. Then Fey's Königsberg artist sketched and painted a cycle of Gothic figures of his own concocting: "Gothic," therefore Teutonic and readily extollable by leaders of the Third Reich. Virtually no effort was made to discover what the original frescoes had been like. Nothing was restored.

In decorating the walls with pre-Columbian twelfth-, thirteenth-, and fourteenth-century frescoes, the Königsberg, painter perpetrated one of the most famous anachronisms in the history of art forgery. Among the animals in *Massacre of the Innocents* he included an American turkey!

When all the frescoes had been completed, the restoration was hailed far and wide throughout the Fatherland. Professor Fey was declared a genius. Dr. Alfred Stange, then on his way to recognition as, in the words of a European collector, "the world's foremost authority on the work of Van Eyck," stepped out of his specialty to edit a large book, *Schleswig Cathedral and Its Mural Paintings*. He praised paintings "that have been restored to us by cleaning and treatment as restrained as it was careful." He waxed ecstatic over the frieze of animal medallions: "Some are imaginary animals commonly found in medieval art, but others are taken from real life and . . . are portrayed so faithfully and with such animation that this frieze appears to be unique in its period. . . . The portrayals . . . are based on a high degree of personal observation."

He did not say which long-dead Gothic artist had observed turkeys. He *had* noticed the turkey, however, and he had recognized that turkeys had been introduced into Europe by the Spaniards only about 1550, at least 200 years after the supposed execution of the fresco. His explanation: long before the Spaniards Nordic sailors had discovered America and had brought the turkey back to Germanic lands in Viking ships. It was a tidy theory that no one bothered to challenge.

All Germany was willing to praise the author of these paintings, whom Stange lavishly called "one of the greats in the realm of art." It was a pity that no one knew his name. But two people *did* know his name. The Feys knew, and they were not about to tell.

Years and a terrible war passed before the rest of the world heard of Lothar Malskat.

Malskat was born May 3, 1913, in Königsberg, East Prussia, and began his professional life apprenticed as a house painter. But whitewashing kitchen walls was beneath his obvious talent, and he was permitted to withdraw from his apprenticeship and to enter art school. There a Professor Marten was impressed by his "almost uncanny productivity and versatility." And a Professor Wolf prophesied, "A lot more will be heard of Lothar Malskat."

As might be expected of any beginner, his work consisted of both original, imaginative drawings and eclectic, derivative renderings. He was especially good at portraits. In time, he had a one-man show. It was so successful that Königsberg became too small for him, and he hurried off to Germany's supermagnet, Berlin, carrying the blessings of Professors Marten, Wolf, and Gruen and a letter of recommendation to Fey, who was already doing church restoration.

Malskat demonstrated the variety and quality of his work to substantiate his teachers' recommendations. Fey was impressed. The young man could be exploited. Fey started him on rough manual work: mixing plaster, cleaning walls, sweeping up debris. He also gave him illustrated books on stylistic criticism of early ecclesiastical painting. Fey's confidence was rapidly vindicated when Malskat began his work on the Oppeln and Neisse churches. For his creative labours on these churches and the Cathedral of Schleswig Fey paid him 25 cents an hour. As praise for the frescoes in St. Peter's came showering down from the experts, however, Malskat grew unhappy. The praise was fine, but the lack of recognition rankled. Yet the timid painter could find courage neither to break with Fey nor to denounce him. Presently escape came from another source.

Malskat, who was able-bodied and intelligent, was soon inducted into the Wehrmacht and went with the occupation forces to Norway. He was as much a painter as a soldier, however, and spent time sketching Norwegian landscapes, his fellow soldiers, and—when he could persuade them to pose—Norway's beauties.

After the war Malskat drifted back to Lübeck, the Baltic port south of Schleswig, which was much bigger than the provincial capital. There he found stop-gap employment as a window dresser. Nearby was the ancient Marienkirche (the Evangelical Lutheran Church of Saint Mary), which had been gutted by fire in the Palm Sunday air raid of March 29, 1942. Under the intense heat, layers of whitewash had peeled off the interior walls, revealing forgotten medieval frescoes under the high windows of the nave and on pillars and vaulting. These frescoes were photographed and sketched. Officials of government and church had managed to collect sufficient material to reconstruct the nave and roof to protect the ancient structure from further deterioration. There was talk of eventual interior restoration.

As quickly as he was able Malskat used his modest income from window dressing to buy new brushes and paints, so that he could do a portfolio of heavy-breasted commercial nudes. These he took to bomb-gutted Hamburg, where any kind of beauty was much in demand. The paintings were snapped up. The choice of Hamburg could not have been an accident: Malskat knew that Dietrich Fey lived there.

The elder Fey had disappeared from the scene, but Malskat found Dietrich. In *Three Thousand Years of Deception* (1961), Frank Arnau says that the meeting was by chance, but chance seems improbable. Since the days in Schleswig, Malskat had nursed resentment of the Feys. But in the post-war disorganization he decided that his best chance of rising above menial labour was through re-establishment of some sort of collaboration with Dietrich Fey.

Soon the two were operating a picture factory. Fey was the pusher: he made contacts, closed sales, took care of incidental paper work. Malskat, forsaking ecclesiastical frescoes, began to turn out canvases and watercolours by Ernst Barlach, Marc Chagall, Rembrandt van Rijn, Max Liebermann, Edgar Degas, Jean Baptiste Camille Corot, Jean Antoine Watteau, Maurice Utrillo, Edvard Munch, Paul Gauguin, Henri Pascin, Henri Rousseau, Ferdinand Hodler, Max Beckmann, Max Pechstein, and other German Expressionists. The two men sold 600 of them!

The picture dealers whom they encountered in Germany wanted assurance only that the paintings had not been looted. Malskat reassured his dealers that they were his legitimate property. Fey and Malskat prospered, even though Bremen police arrested and released Malskat for forgery in 1949. Details on this affair are lacking because nothing came of the arrest.

Again in Germany paper money was not trusted, and people preferred to convert excess currency into art, which would not lose value. Then abruptly Ludwig Erhardt imposed currency reform. The drying up of surplus currency was an immediate blow to shady operators of all kinds. The Fey-Malskat factory supposedly went out of business, but the two men stayed together long enough to take a gigantic step backward.

Relying heavily upon his father's ill-deserved reputation as a restorer, Dietrich Fey won the contract to restore the blackened frescoes of the Marienkirche in Lübeck. He did not obtain the work without opposition. The provincial curator, Dr. Hirschfeld, had sent a secret report to church authorities in Lübeck, the Ministry of Culture in Kiel, the Municipal Board of Works, the administrators of the Lübeck Museum, and the West German Association for the Preservation of Ancient Monuments, saying:

> The restoration of defective medieval mural paintings is, in the final analysis, a question of trust. Dietrich Fey will not guarantee that he has

> never done any overpainting in an unguarded moment. I therefore declare that I dissociate myself from the working methods of the restorer Dietrich Fey. If Lübeck's monuments are to be properly preserved, work can continue only under a restorer who is absolutely trustworthy at all times and never carries out secret overpainting or amplification. I decline all further responsibility.

The West German Association for the Preservation of Ancient Monuments was disturbed by the report but nevertheless appropriated $50,000 to assist the work.

Hirschfeld's protest was duly filed in the public-records office, and the provincial curator repeatedly demanded that there be no overpainting; Deckert and Scheper, the latter a Berlin museum curator, came out against Fey. But their efforts were to no avail. In the aftermath of the war lines of responsibility had been blurred, and jurisdictional fog confounded federal, provincial, municipal, and ecclesiastical authority. Besides, the figures in the choir began seventy feet above the ground and could be examined closely only with the aid of scaffolding or telescopes.

Fey and Malskat allowed no one to come close enough to the work area to see what was going on. Entrance to the church was barricaded and forbidden. Notices of danger from falling masonry were conspicuous. Art historians, inspectors, and public officials were all barred. A trusted workman was always on duty where intruders might enter, and his hard hammering was a signal to warn of unwelcome visitors. Later visitors were permitted to see completed work with a guide, but sliding wood partitions screened off the areas where Malskat was still plying his craft.

Malskat drew inspiration from illustrations in Bernath's *History of Fresco Painting* and portraits of Coptic saints preserved in the Kaiser Friedrich Museum in Berlin.

On September 2, 1951, the Marienkirche celebrated its 700th anniversary. The restoration was complete, and the birthday party became a gala rejoicing for the whole nation. High ecclesiastical dignitaries made the pilgrimage to the Marienkirche from all Germany; a few came from abroad. They were joined by professors, city and municipal officials, high federal dignitaries and ambassadors from Bonn, and Chancellor Konrad Adenauer himself.

Adenauer asked to see the "unique frescoes," and a bubbling Dietrich Fey, in his role as restorer, personally escorted the Chancellor from fresco to fresco and described the difficulties inherent in the restoration.

Three days before the celebration the West German Federal Post Office had issued two commemorative semipostal (part postage, part contribution to charity) stamps (a 10p — 5p green, Minkus No. 1358; and a 20p — 5p lake, Minkus No. 1359). Both portrayed Malskat's frescoes in the choir.

Praise flowed for the frescoes—but not for Lothar Malskat. Berthil Berthelsson, Sweden's National Curator, said, with more truth than he realized, "Entirely unique, [such frescoes] are to be found nowhere else in the world."

The Institute of Art History at the University of Kiel issued a formal declaration:

> There is so little "prettiness" about the splendid Madonna that we can only assume that the author of this masterpiece was a German. The whole group was executed by one brilliant artist. The sacred figures seem to be gazing westward towards the Last Judgement. Two styles are in evidence at St. Mary's. In the elder style, flesh and draperies are uniformly outlined in black, whereas the younger naturalistically reserved the red subcontours for flesh and modelled only the draperies with black lines.

H. A. Grabke, director of the Lübeck Museum, wrote a book extolling the murals, and even Dr. Hirschfeld greeted them as "The most important and extensive ever discovered in Germany, in fact one of the finest intact sets of frescoes of the thirteenth and fourteenth centuries extant throughout western Europe." In a meeting of the National Trust Fey's work was unanimously approved.

In a colour-illustrated Swiss treatise in 1952 Hans Jurgen Hansen declared:

> After the fire, the frescoes were very badly exposed to the elements. However, it proved possible to save them by careful restoration which added nothing new but merely preserved what had survived. The Virgin

> and Child from the central figure in one of the triple groups of murals. . . . The painting dates from circa 1300. The brilliance of its colours has survived with unusual freshness because until their discovery after the incendiary-bomb raid in the year 1942 the murals had lain hidden under a layer of white plaster for almost 500 years.
>
> Most impressive are the triple groups of saints. . . . They stand . . . beneath the windows of the central aisle. Above the high altar is a portrayal of the Virgin together with St. Anne and St. John, the two copatrons of the church, and in other parts of the choir are triple groups of Apostles, patriarchs, and monks. These exhibit a severe style, Byzantine-influenced and still almost Romanesque, and undoubtedly originated a few years earlier than the figures in the main aisle. The latter are more animated, softer, entirely Gothic, comparable in character with the celebrated illustrations in the *Manessische Liderhandschrift*, to which they also correspond in date.

The countenances of Mary and the angels were described elsewhere as "celestial beauty, detached from earthly worries." These radiant countenances, showing some Byzantine influence and supposedly painted from medieval models by an unknown genius of A.D. 1300, were actually based on some 1951 models: Lothar Malskat's sister Frieda, his close friend Kurt Meiser, film actress Hansi Knoteck, and, apparently, Marlene Dietrich!

While Hans Hansen was preparing his eulogy to the Marienkirche for publication in Switzerland, Malskat—like Israel Rouchomovsky, Giovanni Bastianini, and Alceo Dossena before him—was preparing for battle to obtain his deserved recognition. He continued to let himself be employed by Dietrich Fey, and he busied himself with very creative restoration of Malskat-discovered Gothic murals in the Lübeck Rathaus.

But on May 10, 1952, the postman handed Dietrich Fey a registered letter. In it, Malskat demanded that Fey "inform all interested parties that new paintings, not discoveries, are involved."

Fey failed to comply. Malskat then wrote to church authorities in Lübeck and told them the sordid details of the fraud. There was no immediate response, for the authorities knew that the two men had had a falling-out.

Then Malskat began to tell other people. The press called him a painter gone crazy. A commission was hastily called to interrogate the self-accused culprit. The authorities produced sworn affidavits from bricklayers and their foremen to refute his claims.

Malskat responded by producing a roll of Leica film showing identifiable bare walls where his murals now glistened. Yet on August 20, 1952, a joint statement was issued by the church architect, Dr. Bruno Fendrick; the retired director of municipal building, Dr. Munter; the senior public surveyor and curator of public monuments, Herr Blunck; Dr. Grabke; and Bishop Gobel: "Any charges at present being levelled at the restorer Dietrich Fey are as yet insufficient to arouse our misgivings. The work of preservation will therefore continue under the restorer Dietrich Fey."

Frustrated by the scorn of officials, Malskat instructed his attorney to file charges against himself and Dietrich Fey. These charges went beyond the stories of what had happened in Schleswig and Lübeck. They laid bare similar work done in the cathedrals of Ratzeburg and Lübeck, the Hospital of the Holy Spirit, the Church of St. Catherine, and the work in Oppeln and Neisse—not to mention the counterfeiting of 600 paintings and drawings. Malskat declared that he had done everything—innocently of course—on instructions from Fey.

Dr. Flottrong, the attorney, filed the charges on October 7, 1952. Fey was arrested at Travemunde on a Lübeck police-court warrant. His house was searched, and twenty-one drawings and seven paintings were discovered.

Within the incredibly brief period of thirteen days, a distinguished committee examined the Lübeck murals. Its chairman was Graundmann of Hamburg, who was also chairman of the Association for the Preservation of Provincial Monuments, which had contributed so generously to the Lübeck project. Other members of the committee included a legal consultant, Dr. Scheefe, a senior county-court judge from Hamburg; and Professor Stois of the Munich Institute of Chemistry and Physics. Stois, a colour analyst and expert on pigments, demonstrated that the frescoes had been done on modern plaster and could not be originals. X-ray examination supported his conclusion: there were no medieval remains. The committee declared categorically that the Marienkirche frescoes were modern freehand renderings by Lothar Malskat. But the accusation did not register very clearly in some quarters.

Within the hour statements were released by the Lübeck public prosecutor and Bishop D. Johannes Pautke. Pautke explained, "the restorer Dietrich Fey has fraudulently succeeded in getting his work recognized as faithful restoration. . . ."

Once again Fey had appropriated Malskat's credit!

Malskat was not arrested until three months later, on January 23, 1953. He was enjoined to stop talking about his Gothic painting, but the press continued to bristle with fresh details. Officials still refused to believe him, and a preliminary hearing was not held until a full year after Fey's original arrest. The main proceedings did not begin until August 9, 1954; they lasted sixty-six days!

Malskat became something of a public hero, for again the experts had been hoodwinked!

Not until January 25, 1955, were Fey and Malskat sentenced. Fey received twenty months and Malskat eighteen months.

Robert Aries, founder of the International Institute for Scientific Expertise for Works of Art, Monaco, has declared, "All the best works of Malskat's facile brush would still be hanging and enjoying admiration if he had not himself denounced the deceit that fooled the world."

Through these deliberations the intrinsic nature of Malskat's Gothic murals had changed not one whit. If they had been beautiful before, they were beautiful still. But in the eyes of the beholders they had changed. Germans, already wretched from disclosures of a decade of hideous crimes, could not tolerate reminders of another, even a mere crime of æsthetics.

If a rose window in a cathedral had been destroyed, a new one—not just ugly window panes—would eventually have been installed. Malskat's work could have been viewed in this way, as new decorations—replacements—in the antique manner. After all, the church walls had been blackened, and except for a few isolated places there had been nothing to restore. But this rationale was too simple.

Hirschfeld had his vindication. He demanded:

> The forgeries should first be plastered over so as to obtain a clear surface free from all theoretical preconceptions and thus enable careful plans to be laid for an ideal solution of the problem by substituting true works of art for forgery, honesty for insincerity, with consequent obliteration of the stain upon morality. It should be considered the duty of any truly Christian community to carry out this task.

Malskat's paintings were stripped from the church walls, which were left naked and ugly.

Malskat himself fled to Sweden, where he found ample honest employment for his talent. He imitated fourteenth-century decorations for the Tre Kronor restaurant in Stockholm, designed a turkey for the entrance of the Royal Tennis Courts, and continued to paint in the Gothic, Romantic, and Byzantine styles.

His paintings did not bring premium prices, and yet Lothar Malskat is the only art forger in all history whose fakery has been immortalized on postage stamps. The supreme irony is that these stamps—which once sold for as little as 5 cents each—are now valued far more highly than are Malskat's paintings. A block of 100 is already worth $2,500!

CHAPTER 10

The Hoax That Fooled the Met

About 1860 fragments of two magnificent Etruscan sarcophagi were unearthed twenty-two miles northwest of Rome on the ancient site of Caere, once one of the wealthiest cities of Etruria. There so many tombs had been cut into the porous limestone that the interiors were laid out along regular routes like houses on a street.

The task of assembling the jigsaw pieces correctly demanded considerable patience and skill, more than that possessed by the ordinary stoneworker. So Pietro and Enrico Pinelli were called in, thereby setting motion to a sequence of art frauds that were not fully exposed until a century later and that escalated into the most grandiose hoax that ever caught the Metropolitan Museum of Art.

The Pinelli brothers measured up to their assignment. One sarcophagus that they assembled found a permanent shrine in the Louvre; the other remained in the museum of Rome's Museo Nazionale di Villa Giulia.

After this double achievement the Pinellis thought of themselves—correctly—as the world's experts on the reconstruction of such caskets. No one else had ever done any. But, they reasoned, if we can reconstruct, why can we not just as easily construct?

By 1873 they had finished and aged a new Etruscan tomb, which became known as the *Castellani Sarcophagus*. A pair of connubial figures reclines on the lid. He is nude, his bearded head shaped much like that of an Easter Island tiki. He leans against a couple of pillows, while she leans, with one knee bent, upon his thigh and points her hand towards his face in a gesture more appropriate to a Bali dancer.

For sixty years (until 1936) this masterpiece of Etruscan funerary art graced the treasure rooms of the British Museum. The sarcophagus had been sold through Domenico Fuschini, who had built up a thriving business in reconstructed vases. Great quantities of broken majolica had begun turning up in long-abandoned wells at Orvieto. Often, however, the necessary pieces could not be found to complete the vessels; so replacement fragments were manufactured to fill the gaps.

Either the Pinellis could not keep pace with Fuschini's volume, they died, or there was a falling-out. The record is not clear. At any rate Fuschini hired Pio and Alfonso Riccardi to glue his majolica fragments back together. These two brothers had left their ancestral home in Trevi del Lazio near Assisi and established a workshop in Rome.

Pio Riccardi had four sons: Riccardo, Amedeo, Gino, and Fausto. Riccardo, born in 1888, was the most gifted. He and the two sons of Alfonso—Teodoro and Virgilio Angelino—followed the family business, which had progressed from the mere manufacture of missing shards to fabrication of complete vases and other objects.

When Riccardo was about twelve he became good friends with Alfredo Adolfo Fioravanti, who was a few months younger. Fioravanti was apprenticed as a tailor, but he had an artisan's taste and skill with sculpture, and he finally persuaded Ricardo's father to take him on.

For 800 years Etruria had dominated Italy from Po to Tiber. The loose confederation of states had, however, been crushed by the Romans in the first century B.C. Numerous unexcavated Etruscan tombs still await examination in Italy even today.

Pliny recorded that the art of modelling in clay had been introduced early in Etruria and had developed during ensuing generations. He wrote that in 509 B.C. an Etruscan sculptor named Vulca had been summoned by Tarquinius Priscus from Veii to Rome, where he had made a statue of Jupiter for the temple on the Capitoline Hill and a Hercules, both in clay. By Roman times the colossal scale of these statues had become legendary. Plutarch added:

> When Tarquin was still king and had all but completed the Temple of Jupiter Capitolinus . . . he commissioned certain Tuscan craftsmen of Veii to place upon its roof a chariot of terracotta. Soon afterwards he was driven from his throne. The Tuscans, however, modelled the chariot and put it in a furnace for firing, but the clay did not contract and shrink in the fire, as it usually does when moisture evaporates. Instead it expanded and swelled and took on such size, strength, and hardness, that it could with difficulty be removed, even after the roof of the furnace had been taken off and its sides torn away.

Rome was accused of taking the city of Volsinii to obtain its 2,000 Etruscan terra-cotta and bronze statues. Volsinii—the Etruscan name and town disappeared centuries ago. But on top of the necropolis had grown a Roman town—Orvieto!

Archaeologists and collectors expected Etruscan artifacts to be discovered abundantly in the environs of Orvieto, and Italian enterprise would not permit these scholars to be disappointed. So Pio and Alfonso Riccardi and their young sons earned their daily bread filling the demand for small, quickly produced articles, especially majolica ware and revetment plaques. They were careful to consult many books and photographs and to scrutinize objects actually excavated in the environs of Orvieto. But, harkening to the call of Pliny, they decided that the time had come to produce an entire bronze chariot.

In December 1908 a biga, a two-horse chariot, was discovered in the vicinity of Prodo, on the road from Orvieto to Todi. After its supposed 2,500 years of burial it needed cleaning and restoration. This work had been undertaken, so the British Museum was told, by Pio Riccardi of Rome. The museum purchased the chariot from Fuschini, and the acquisition was announced in 1912.

In the meantime other museums had begun to acquire the terra-cotta plaques. The first sale—of three pieces about 17 inches square decorated with rows of palmettes, lotuses, and scrolls—was to the National Museum in Copenhagen in 1910. Doctor Angelo Signorelli began collecting them the next year. Samples were acquired by the Villa Giulia and the Antiquarium of the Palazzo dei Conservatori in Rome, the Städtische Kunsthalle in Mannheim, and the Metropolitan. Except for the examples at the Met, this architectural tile all came from Elio and Ugo Jandolo, but the Jandolos had acquired them from Fuschini (unless there had been still another intermediary). The Metropolitan's seven plaques were all purchased from Pietro Stettiner by John Marshall.

From 1906 until 1928 Marshall served as European purchasing agent for the Met. As reported in Chapter 4, he has been credited with building up the museum's outstanding inventory of antiquities: in the Met's own appraisal the collection is a monument to his labours and judgement. Marshall was an English architect, but he made his headquarters in Rome. He drew a salary from the museum, and he had an annual acquisitions budget that he was permitted to spend at his discretion. Unusually expensive items that demanded more than the budget allowed were referred to the director and trustees in New York for decision.

Marshall also checked on attributions, dates, and provenances and occasionally performed services for the museum in fields outside the boundaries of classical antiquity. On those occasions when they were not competing for the same objects Marshall worked closely with Edward P. Warren, an American who chose to live in England and who performed similar services for the Boston Museum of Fine Arts. (Marshall, Warren, and Harold W. Parsons—who served the Cleveland Museum of Art and Kansas City's William Rockhill Nelson Gallery—formed a potent triumvirate of American museum purchasing agents.)

Marshall's activities have been documented in diaries and letters. Stettiner, on the other hand, is a more mysterious figure. In 1911 he published a book, *Roma nei suoi monumenti*, which brought him some personal recognition. Years later he was identified as a high official of the post office and a collector. Marshall first met him on October 24, 1913, in the latter's house at 68 via del Boschetto. He noted in his diary that day: "Stettiner's bust of a goddess seemed to me false—Helbig came: told him that I thought Stettiner's head false. Jacobsen had, it seems, expressed doubts about it."

Helbig was then the purchasing agent for the Ny Carlsberg Glyptotek in Copenhagen, which had been founded by Jacobsen. Both men and Marshall were, however, destined to buy major items of false Riccardi art from Stettiner. Marshall's first purchases were the architectural plaques, which he acquired the next year.

Even before then Fuschini had ordered Pio Riccardi and his family to move to Orvieto, where they would be nearer the scene of the purported excavations. Pio had set up his workshop on the via San Paolo. Then in 1912 he had died, and Riccardo Riccardi, his two cousins Teodoro and Virgilio, and Fioravanti decided to bring Pliny's history to life on grander proportions than even Pio had done when he created the British Museum's biga.

They began with an *Old Warrior*. No precise model is known for it, but the elongated shape is vaguely reminiscent of the reclining male figure on the *Castellani Sarcophagus* fashioned by the Pinelli brothers. If so then the forgery was, ironically, fashioned after a forgery!

The *Old Warrior* stands 6 feet 7½ inches high, and in modern times would not have seemed a warrior but a skinny basketball player or a Giacometti. He wears a plumed helmet, a sleeveless cuirass to the top of his hips, and armour on his calves. From knees to pullover he is naked. His left foot is extended forwards in a giant stride, emphasized by his upward-swinging left arm. The top of the left thumb is missing, as is the entire right arm. He wears an Attic-style headpiece with upturned cheek guards. He had a moustache and beard, the hair indicated by wavy black lines. His eyeballs are white, and a large black spot marks each iris. The lips have a trace of brilliant red. The ornamentation on his uniform is painted white, red, and black.

To begin the *Old Warrior*, the four conspirators put a large slab of clay two to three inches thick together piecemeal (instead of beating out a single ball). Upon this base they roughly modelled the lower parts of widely spaced legs. These parts were solid, but from the knees up the legs and torso were fashioned with rolls of clay. Soft clay was smeared abundantly inside the members to cement the rolls together and to stiffen the outer walls. The hollow inside the body was of small diameter. As the clay dried and hardened sufficiently to bear additional weight, the structure was gradually built up. The elongated symmetry was unusual, and it disturbed some scholars. Gisela Richter wrote later, "Perhaps there was an Italian tradition—which now eludes us—to account for the unusual proportions."

The four conspirators argued heatedly about the pose and placement of the right arm. Logically it should have held a shield, but a shield added too much weight to be supported. They solved the problem with an equally logical decision: they agreed to discard the arm.

They also had a disagreement about the shape of the left side of the torso. "You're making it too thin," Fioravanti warned, but the Riccardis kept scraping away the clay until the thickness had been reduced to ½ inch, in contrast with 1½ inches on the right side. This fragility was particularly dangerous because the left side bore the weight of the remaining arm. After the statue had come to New York this thin wall did crack.

The modelling mixture consisted of a fine-grained clay, sand, and grog. The grog was made from broken pieces of old pottery. With the sand it gave porosity to the mixture. Because the grog was made from already-seasoned dry pottery, it did not contract or lose moisture during firing, and it thus served to stabilize dimensions. Without it the drying figure would have contracted enormously—as much as 33 per cent—and the sculpture would undoubtedly have developed perilous cracks and perhaps broken to pieces.

On November 15, 1915, Marshall wrote to Gisela Richter, who was then assistant curator of classical art but who would soon rise to curator, a position that she held for twenty-three of her nearly forty years of distinguished staffwork at the Metropolitan:

> One thing I have arranged for, if a permisso for it can be obtained. It will make you groan to hear of it: the biggest T.C. [terra-cotta] you or any reasonable being ever saw. Milani's *Atlante* Tav. XXX will give you an idea of it, but you must multiply the height by 7 (seven!). . . .

Stettiner was the seller.

Ten weeks later the pieces of the *Old Warrior* had arrived in New York—the purchase having been financed by the Rogers Fund—and Miss Richter was able to write: "The Etruscan terra-cotta has arrived safely and is at present being put together. I think it is quite exciting and will be one of the most dramatic things in the museum. How beautifully the painted patterns are preserved. Do you know anything of the provenance?"

Marshall and Warren must have been working closely on the provenance problem, for soon after Marshall received Miss Richter's letter, he had Warren cable her from London: "Please delay publication of large terracotta."

There was another reason for delaying publication. Marshall had scented another piece. It would not do to bring other museums and collectors swooping down to push up the price and perhaps make off with the prize. The coveted terra-cotta *Apollo of Veii* had just been discovered, and Italy swarmed with agents and informers.

As far as is known the *Old Warrior* was the first monumental sculpture produced by the Riccardi ring. If there had been earlier attempts they had failed and been destroyed, perhaps serving as grog for the next attempt. Though the *Old Warrior* was tall, it seemed a far cry from Pliny's description of the terra-cotta Jupiter and Hercules created by Vulca for the temple on the Capitoline. Such a figure could conceivably have been twenty-five feet high! That size was too much for Riccardi and Fioravanti, with all their skills. But they could create the head of such a figure!

For inspiration the Riccardis used terra-cotta aryballôs, helmet-shaped Greek vases scarcely three inches high; the magnification was thus nearly twenty times. The sculptors probably also consulted a large stone head in the Orvieto museum.

On July 25, 1916, four large cases of terra-cotta fragments

arrived on the New York docks. It was the middle of the war and German U-boats were taking their toll of trans-Atlantic merchantmen. One wonders that Marshall risked shipping absolutely unique, irreplaceable treasures during such a period, but as Italy was also in the war perhaps he thought they were as safe at sea as in Rome.

The four cases contained 178 fragments. Again the purchase was financed from the Rogers Fund, and the seller was Stettiner. The *Colossal Head* was not assembled and cemented together until October. Miss Richter eventually wrote, "The broken edges at the bottom of the neck and of the crest presumably indicate that the head formed part of a colossal statue of a warrior." With the crest, the head stood four feet seven inches high, and she calculated that the original figure, if it had been standing rather than sitting, had been no less than twenty-three feet high. "No wonder," she said, "that centuries later there were still stories current of Etruscan sculptures which had expanded to a huge size in the kiln." Pliny himself had described having seen an Apollo that measured fifty feet from the toes! So perhaps the Riccardis were warming up for something bigger still.

Miss Richter and Charles F. Binns, then director of the New York State School of Clay Working and Ceramics at Alfred University and, according to *Art News*, "the leading ceramic expert in the country," calculated that the figures had been fired in one piece, the kilns having been erected around the figures after the modelling had been completed. Binns estimated that firing had been done at 960° C., that the variation in temperature between the top and bottom of the huge makeshift kiln had been at most an incredible 20°, and that the firing had had to be maintained at a continuously diminishing temperature for several months so that the terra-cotta mass would cool slowly.

Encouraged by the success of the *Old Warrior* and the *Colossal Head* Fioravanti then produced single-handedly—if his later claim is to be believed—a beautiful full-length kore in the Etruscan style. He modelled her in clay, polychromed her, dried her, fired her, and mutilated her. In the various stages he photographed her for his own records. The kore went through the hands of a number of unsuspecting dealers and thus picked up affidavits of authenticity from distinguished archaeologists. Eventually she entered the marbled halls of the Ny Carlsberg Glyptotek and became known as the *Copenhagen Kore*. Helbig and Jacobsen had joined Marshall in the ranks of the grandiosely seduced.

Communication between Italy and America was difficult because of the war. Marshall went to England to attend the auction of the Hope collection at Christie's. While there he mailed a twenty-two-page report to Edward Robinson, director of the Met, on August 3, 1917:

"That head was found at Boccaporco," a site not on modern maps but supposedly located about five crow-flight miles south of Orvieto.

> The men have found large tiles coming from a big temple: they have found the two terracottas of Mars which you have [*Old Warrior* and *Colossal Head*]: a couple of fragments of vases of excellent date, circ. 500 Attic: and great blocks of a base on which your great T.C. "undoubtedly" stood. This base (which I haven't seen) is in *solid* terracotta: rectangular and about a metre high.
>
> The whole place which was being excavated had to be covered up and sown over with wheat. Nothing can be done till the harvest here is over: but I expect news of some sort when I get back.

Marshall had spent much time in the Orvieto neighbourhood but had not located the Boccaporco site itself. He explained that it was quite unknown on official records. The discoverers of his terra-cottas had no desire to take him to the site, of course, as there was none. By then Marshall must have come to know the Riccardis personally, but an Italian professor, Pico Cellini, subsequently declared that Marshall's intermediary was the Orvieto chief of police. That Marshall was also in direct contact is, however, clear from his complaint that "there are two small fragments of the beard which I am trying to get from one of the excavators."

The likelihood of the Boccaporco site was stronger in Marshall's mind because of the discovery about a mile north of there only a few years earlier of an apparently genuine fourth-century B.C. sarcophagus. (Although the sarcophagus had been in excellent condition at the time of its disinterment, a dispute over acquisition had arisen between Orvieto and Florence. The relic had been packed in cotton wool but left outside in the rain; most of the paint had peeled off. Orvieto had won, and Marshall was thus able to study the sarcophagus in the museum.) Adding to the excitement of the new find was the fact that a peasant named Campanella, who had discovered the sarcophagus, had also apparently discovered the two warriors that Marshall had found.

After complaining that the countryside, though rich in Etruscan relics, seemed too rugged for an Etruscan temple, Marshall declared:

> At any rate your head is pure Ionic work of about the period to which tradition assigns the Jupiter Capitolinus of the Tarquins. I can find nothing approaching it in importance. There is nothing known of the Jupiter Capitolinus, though it is generally "supposed" to have been gigantic. The discovery of your head simply demolishes whole volumes of Paio's History of Rome.
>
> The business has occupied most of my time. The excavators imagine that they are going to find a whole figure 25 feet high of terracotta, and they will not listen to me when I suggest that the body was of wood.

Riccardo Riccardi and Fioravanti, however, found their careers temporarily interrupted. While Marshall tramped around Orvieto looking for clues, they were taken into the army. They were privileged to serve together in the same regiment, and there can be no doubt that they used their spare time to plan their next move against Marshall.

No sooner was the Armistice signed in 1918 than they began work on their largest project, a big warrior.

In Berlin's Old Museum is a small bronze Etruscan statue of a standing warrior from Dodona. It is barely five inches tall. None of the Riccardis had ever been to Berlin to see it. They did not even possess a model, though models existed, but they had a photograph. From this photograph they decided to create an Etruscan warrior so imposing that it would have pleased even Pliny.

They built it by the same method that they had used for the *Old Warrior*: solid lower legs, with upper legs and torso of clay rolls copiously smeared inside with clay to strengthen them. Inside the torso two stout walls were built from front to back to brace the head. The crotch joint was strengthened by a large internal buttress of clay.

The arms were constructed separately and attached to the torso with a rod, which was withdrawn after the clay hardened. The torso was modelled with a conical depression at the tip for attaching the head, which in turn was built up as a hollow oval. At the top a peg was inserted where the material was moulded together to form a crown. It was later removed, and the hole was mistakenly interpreted as a vent to facilitate evaporation during firing. No inner skeletal armature was used to support the heavy figure, which must have weighed 1,000 pounds before drying.

The figure was modelled and fired on the ground floor of a rented house on the via dei Magoni in Orvieto. Among the members of the Riccardi ring there was no mathematician. By the time that the sculptors had built the figure to waist height it became obvious to them that the ceiling of the room was too low to permit the elegant proportions of the Dodona model. They could not—or would not—tear the figure down and start over; so adjustments had to be made from the waist up, and the figure developed stocky proportions.

The room was so small that no one could step back for perspective on the growing statue. Even if there had been room, not much could have been seen, for it had been necessary to swaddle the lower part of the body with wet rags, in order to keep the clay from drying too fast. The body was further hidden by a scaffolding of slats and rods. It was difficult, then, for the men to judge the interrelation of parts of the body, and the left arm was made too long.

In both æsthetics and techniques, Etruscan potters followed Greek leadership. Genuine Greek and Etruscan terra-cottas were subjected to single firings. Any paint or decoration therefore had to be put on before the piece went to the fire. In the manufacture later of majolica, a term not used until the fifteenth century, black was obtained from manganese dioxide. Its properties were known to the Riccardis, who ordered the material from a supply house in Milan. They did not know that this method was *not* the one used to obtain Attic black colouration, but at that time neither did anyone else.

Not only did the Riccardis use manganese dioxide for decoration, but they also added quantities to the body clay of the *Big Warrior* so that interior fractures of the terra-cotta would have the characteristic grey tones of the genuine article.

Glaze and colouration were painted on the figure while it was standing. They waited patiently as the clay figure dried in the air and developed cracks. Then they toppled the heavy mass to the floor and broke it.

This process was exactly the one used previously on *Old Warrior* and *Colossal Head*. The Riccardis had no giant kilns; none larger than 3 x 3 x 4 feet existed in Orvieto. They fired the warrior piece by piece. The job took two nights and a day.

The kiln had no open doors but an open front, which was bricked up during firings. They had to tear this front down and put it up for every new batch of *Big Warrior* fragments. The fuel was wood, probably heated to 800–900° C. Through peepholes the men could judge temperature by the colour of the kiln or by drawing out test pieces connected to long pokers.

Because of the use of sand and pottery grog and the relatively low temperature, there was very little shrinkage. As the pieces were of unequal mass and shape, shrinkage would have caused a disastrous problem, for the fragments had to fit back together again perfectly and give the appearance that the warrior had been fired in one piece. Sand prints were made on the bottom of the plinth to strengthen the impression that a kiln had been erected around the whole figure. (A large kiln would have been erected on a sand floor, and the figure would have been modelled on top of the sand, which would have left its imprint on the bottom.) During firing the pieces did warp some, however, and where the edges did not quite match the men chipped them off so that the mismatching did not show.

Acceptable crackling of the glaze developed during firing because the coefficients of expansion of the clay body and the decorative slip (which was made from a finer, purified clay) were slightly different.

As the work progressed, Riccardo Riccardi felt a need to get away from it briefly. He went horseback riding and was thrown and killed. Under Fioravanti's direction the work continued, but it was the last of the big projects. Fioravanti would direct the final seduction of Marshall, but without Riccardo (the two cousins were fools) the ring could not survive.

Marshall still counselled against publishing the acquisition of the *Old Warrior* and the *Colossal Head*. On February 28, 1919, C. Densmore Curtis of the American Academy in Rome wrote to Robinson (again on behalf of Marshall, who had a predilection for having other people handle his correspondence) to report the discovery of additional terra-cottas, notably a high-relief slab of 6½ x 20 feet with about twenty figures in combat, some said to be carrying round and oval shields. Also reported was another huge head whose helmet crest alone was nearly a metre high. But neither Marshall nor Curtis had seen so much as a snapshot of any of these finds. The head was that of the *Big Warrior*. Marshall could best be tantalized if the head was recovered piece by piece.

In the meantime (April 15, 1919) Marshall acquired a corroded eleven-inch bronze statuette of a male warrior from Stettiner. Tall and thin, it echoed aspects of the *Old Warrior* but had some elements (for example, the Corinthian helmet) of the *Colossal Head*. It was meant to underline the authenticity of Marshall's two major purchases. Actually—and this fact was not discovered until more than forty years later, when the piece was thoroughly cleaned—the figure was an extraordinary assembly of old and modern pieces: the upper part was that of a woman, the lower part that of a man, and the entire figure was elongated by a bronze midsection attached with a copper rivet. The head had been rechased, the shanks contoured to form greaves, and an alien bronze crest added, as well as a nosepiece, a beard, and cheek pieces. It had then been covered with a thick, obscuring patina of paint, wax, and gesso.

As the year wore on, rumours floated everywhere, rumours

that had probably been deliberately set loose to whet Marshall's appetite. On August 1 Curtis reported:

> Marshall himself was leaving for Bagni di Lucca, but had left word that his agents (presumably including the chief of police) were to telegraph for him in case of anything of importance required his presence. They have a huge terra-cotta statue all excavated, but it is so carefully guarded we could not see it. . . . All we could find out about the statue is that it is of a different type than the one in New York, of very heavy build, and that the helmet has a huge well-preserved crest which is modelled but not painted, and reaches far down the back. The site is being worked by three brothers of whom the capable one died in an accident last winter. The one with whom we deal is apparently half crazy, so you can imagine negotiations are difficult and will take a long time.

On August 11, 1919, Warren cabled Robinson, "John Marshall requested us to telegraph you as follows: Have seen the new find Mars fighting 260 or 270 centimetres high Wonderful preservation Same artist as big head Most important thing ever offered us Cannot get photograph Price asked quite fantastic."

Still the sellers kept Marshall dangling. After a quick Christmas visit to the United States he returned to Italy and did not dare leave again during the entire following year. In July 1920 he wrote to Miss Richter, "I am nailed to this spot waiting for a big matter."

Finally in early 1921 he took possession of the *Big Warrior*, which was in fragments, and shipped it to New York. The Met's purchasing committee met on February 26, 1921, and allocated money (from the Kennedy Fund) for the acquisition. For the *Old Warrior* and the *Colossal Head* the ring had been paid only a few hundred dollars by Stettiner. For the *Big Warrior* Fioravanti and the two Riccardis extorted $40,000, a fortune.

All three major works of the Riccardis and Fioravanti had fallen into Metropolitan hands, and the museum had no way of knowing that there would be no more. No doubt Marshall hoped to obtain the huge relief that Curtis had written about. Hope for it alone would have explained his reluctance to publish. But even without such self-interest, the Met did not intend to put the acquisitions on view until the completion of scholarly analysis and investigation.

Binns was called in to examine the new find, and Robinson drafted an article explaining how the *Big Warrior* had been reconstructed, but the article went into the files. In the meantime Marshall continued to study every large-scale Etruscan terra-cotta that he could find between Rome and London. He doubted the authenticity of the *Castellani Sarcophagus* in the British Museum but did not recognize in it an antecedent of his *Old Warrior*. He repeatedly attempted to visit the dig near Orvieto, but every time the excavators were either sick or had some other excuse. Month after month, and finally years, dragged by. During all that time Marshall continued to buy small items from Amedeo Riccardi and Stettiner. In 1924 he found additional cause to grumble when his "friends" (as he called them) sold a large collection of vases, bronzes, and terra-cottas to Ny Carlsberg Glyptotek behind his back. He complained, "I have lost touch with the rogues."

In 1926, eleven years after the purchase of *Old Warrior*, he still had not seen the site. Professor Roberto Paribeni, an Italian archaeologist, warned him against buying anything from the Riccardis. They were being watched by the government because they evidently knew the Etruscan sites very well and were making excavations without a permit.

Then the chief of police, who was Marshall's contact, was transferred from Orvieto to Genoa. Marshall's patience was finally exhausted, and he "cut all my relations with my Orvietans for good." Quite probably the Riccardis were grave robbers as well as forgers. After the police chief left, the ring began to feel the heat. One brother moved to Florence and the other to Siena. Fioravanti went to Rome.

Soon after Marshall was assigned another problem by the Met: investigation of the fake sculptures that had been done by Alceo Dossena. While thus engaged he died quite suddenly in Rome. Three years later, in 1931, Robinson, then busy with installations in the museum's new south wing (which would have an Etruscan room), also died. Installation of the room fell to Miss Richter. She was anxious to obtain further information about some Attic vase fragments which supposedly had been found with the warriors. She called for help from Annie Rivier, who had been Marshall's secretary in Rome. Miss Rivier tracked down Amedeo Riccardi, who had apparently not followed quite so closely the family businesss. He claimed to remember nothing about the shards.

The three big Etruscan pieces finally went on exhibition in February 1933. Although the museum's *Bulletin* described the pieces, this report was incomplete, entirely preliminary, and the museum considered the pieces still unpublished.

For three years the public admired the warriors, and Miss Richter and her associates studied them and prepared the definitive paper. The Met refused to publish this paper until its entire staff became absolutely convinced of the authenticity of the pieces. In April 1936 Piero Tozzi, the sleuth who had tracked down Dossena for Marshall and had since become an art dealer in New York and Florence, dropped Miss Richter a note from his New York gallery, asking her to come around and talk to him. He had just returned from Rome, and the market there was alive with stories. He scribbled across the bottom of his note, "Fioravanti—Riccardi Bros. Teodoro."

Miss Richter wrote to Miss Rivier:

> There is an absurd story going around that our t.c. dollies are modern and the work of Fioravanti. Aldo [Jandolo] told Tozzi about it, who told it to me. It is easy to see why such a story should be told, as it makes it more comfortable for many people. And I don't propose to pay any attention to it except to ask you to find out who this Fioravanti is and what kind of things he makes, so that if I am confronted with such a theory I may know about this man.

Miss Rivier's reply (in May 1936) was that Fioravanti had begun as a tailor, become a chauffeur, sold old furniture, returned to cars, and for many years drove a taxi in Rome. "It does not sound much like an artist." Rumours did say that he had made clothes and chauffeured for art dealer Alfredo Barsanti.

Reassured, Miss Richter went ahead and completed her monograph, and the statues finally received definitive publication in 1937, more than twenty years after she had first wanted to publish them. Her *Etruscan Terracotta Warriors in the Metropolitan Museum of Art* was only the sixth in a series of papers so authoritative that the museum can produce them only rarely.

Publication brought Miss Richter acclaim in the *Journal of Hellenic Studies*, *Latomus II*, *American Journal of Archaeology*, *Berliner Philologische Wochenschrift*, and *Gnomon XV*. She was hailed in the United States, Germany, and Denmark. This publication was neither her first nor her last but one of many that marked a distinguished career. Her first book (of thirty-six), *Greek, Etruscan, and Roman Bronzes*, had been published in 1915 when she was twenty-seven. Her last was *Korai—Archaic Greek Maidens*, published in 1968 when she was eighty. Her handbooks on Classical art are still used as study texts.

The Met had made a mistake, as every museum of any consequence does occasionally. Publication brought a simmering conflict into the open. There were plenty of people willing to pounce on what they claimed was the Met's error, and most of the pouncers were Italians.

During the affair of Otto Wacker Dutch experts had whined that they were the only people capable of judging the authenticity of work attributed to Van Gogh, who had been Dutch. Now a group of Italian scholars proclaimed Italian preeminence in matters Etruscan. Some did so rather foolishly. Professor Giulio Emanuele Rizzo declared the *Colossal Warrior* to be of indisputable authenticity. Young archaeologist Massimo Pallottino (whom Parsons called "the foremost Etruscologist of Europe" fourteen years later) dismissed all three pieces as forgeries. For his temerity he was summoned to Rizzo's apartment for an angry tongue-lashing.

World War II muffled the outcries from Italy, but the dispute burst out anew afterwards. In 1950 Michelangelo Cagiano de Azevedo theorized that the craquelure of the glaze had been created by use of a drying element in the varnish. Cagiano had not seen the statues—they had no varnish! In 1955 Cellini claimed that the statues were fakes and that the clay grog contained ground glass from Peroni beer bottles! Met technicians quickly demolished this absurdity.

Marco Modestini, a restorer, advanced the theory (in 1958–1959) that the black glaze on the warriors was only casein paint. This theory was also quickly disposed of by scientific testing.

In 1955 Christine Alexander, Miss Richter's successor, visited Amedeo Riccardi, the last survivor of the Riccardi brothers and cousins, in Florence. He had been notably unhelpful to Miss Richter and was not about to change. He sketched a map of the Boccaporco area and identified the owners of the land where the warriors had supposedly been found. The roads were so bad, he said, that the area could not be reached by car. Since his family had not had anything to do with the warriors—and certainly had not made them!—the best that he could do would be to ask other people from Orvieto who might still be alive if they knew anything. He promised that he would consider the matter, and for five more years he was in occasional touch with Miss Richter, who was living in Rome, but nothing helpful came from his "considering." Occasionally he dragged a red herring across the trail; for example, there was a letter he brought to Rome in 1959 from an Orvietan named Menchinelli. As a youth Menchinelli had seen a peasant carrying volcanic stone mixed with terra-cotta and clay slabs to fill a ditch. Riccardi proposed obtaining a permit to dig out the ditch.

In the fall of 1959 Dietrich von Bothmer, who had succeeded Miss Alexander as curator of Greek and Roman art, took Cagiano on a rush tour through the museum. Cagiano, smarting perhaps because of his foolish assertions about varnish, refused to take even a second glance at the warriors.

"How can I," he asked, "when I know the man who made them?"

Clearly the time had come for the Metropolitan to make a new investigation.

The burden of the investigation fell upon von Bothmer and Joseph Veach Noble, administrative head of the Metropolitan. Although they worked closely together, von Bothmer concentrated upon æsthetics, historical data, and provenance, while Noble took care of scientific analysis. Although not himself a curator, Noble is a self-taught expert on Greek vases who had at that time been attempting to make indistinguishable replicas in a potter's studio in his home. It was his insatiable curiosity about discovering the lost techniques of ancient Attic craftsmen that had led to his employment by the Met.

Among the many lost techniques of ancient craftsmen was the means by which the Greeks (and by extension the Etruscans) had obtained the colours for decorating their ceramic ware. During World War II this problem had been attacked by a German scientist, Theodor Schumann. Although Schumann's findings had been published in 1942, they had not become generally available until after the war. Schumann had died before he could pursue his studies to their conclusion.

Schumann had discovered that the iron oxide present in Attic clay turned red if fired in an atmosphere permitting abundant oxygen but black in an atmosphere which was oxygen-starved.

Noble brought Attic clay, which contains ferric oxide, from Greece. From portions of it he extracted the finest particles, which he used with water as a slip, the smooth material painted for glaze and decoration on the body of the vases he made. When he allowed plenty of air into the kiln during the firing of a completed vase, the kiln became filled with inactive carbon dioxide, CO_2. Because of the ferric oxide both body and glaze stayed red.

But if Noble threw green wood or moist sawdust on the fire and closed the kiln to outside air, the resulting incomplete combustion filled the kiln with highly active carbon monoxide, CO. Carbon monoxide exerts such a strong pull for oxygen atoms that it takes them right out of the clay. The chemical composition of the clay changes, from ferric oxide (Fe_2O_3) to ferrous oxide (FeO), and so does the colour of the clay, from red to black.

If the firing is halted at this point, all the clay stays black. But Attic and Etruscan vases have red bodies and black decoration. Noble discovered that if he then opened a hole in the kiln and let fresh air come rushing back, the body of the vase—but only the body—would turn red again. This fresh air gave oxygen atoms back to the clay, which once again became ferric oxide. But wherever the vase had been painted with the slip, the fine particles of quartz in the clay had fused; the glazed areas had become impervious, and the fresh oxygen atoms could not penetrate. These areas remained black, providing care was taken to keep the firing temperature below 1000° C.

That is the secret of Attic black, and none of the Riccardis or Fioravanti or anyone else living knew it when the warriors were fabricated. The forgers had used an anachronistic process, and modern science eventually unmasked it.

As Noble has declared, "In order to detect a forgery, it is best to remember that every object made by man carries within it the evidence of the time and place of its manufacture."

In a meeting of the Archaeological Institute of America in 1959, Noble pointed out that, "The black glaze of forgeries made before Schumann's discovery of the ancient technique would have been coloured by an added mineral." In January 1960 Noble took samples from the warriors to the laboratory of Lucius Pitkin, Inc., in New York City; subjected the clay bodies and glazes to spectrographic analysis; and found the presence of manganese, a colouring agent unknown in Etruscan times.

In 1960 von Bothmer and Noble, travelling separately, examined authentic large-scale terra-cottas from Greece, Cyprus, and Etruria, in Cyprus, Greece, Italy, France, England, and Denmark. They observed that vents had always been made to allow proper airing of the clay mass in firing and drying. The Met's warriors had no such holes—for even the one hole in the *Big Warrior* would have been inadequate for the job—and could never have been fired in one piece. Had they been, they would have exploded!

So on the basis of technical analysis the three Etruscan figures were definitely proved to be fakes. But where had they come from?

While Noble was doing his spectrographic investigation, von Bothmer learned that Harold Parsons, who had been living in Rome since 1953, was gathering evidence on the modern origins of the terra-cottas. For twenty years Parsons had made no secret of his doubts about the warriors. He had already identified Fioravanti as the forger of the *Copenhagen Kore* but had not connected him with the warriors. On December 12, 1960, Parsons wrote that he had seen the missing thumb of the *Old Warrior*. Then on January 5, 1961, Parsons brought Fioravanti to the American Consul in Rome, before whom the old man made and signed a full confession. On February 6 von Bothmer arrived in Rome to interview Fioravanti and go over the ground at Orvieto.

Von Bothmer brought with him a plaster cast of the hand of the *Old Warrior*. Without hesitation Fioravanti fitted to the cast the thumb that he had kept for nearly fifty years. Of course, the fit was perfect. This fact did not in itself prove that the warrior was fake. Fioravanti, or someone else, could have found or stolen the authentic thumb, but the old faker filled in so many details that there was no doubting his story.

On Valentine's Day 1961 New Yorkers (and others around the world) picked up their morning papers and learned that the Metropolitan's astounding Etruscan warriors were fabulous frauds.

CHAPTER II

Temptations on the Modern Scene

By trade Casper Caspersen was a cabinetmaker. Brought up in the vital tradition of Scandinavian craftsmanship, he was probably a good one. But he was not a creative cabinetmaker: he worked from other men's designs or copied traditional pieces.

Away from his workbench Caspersen was a painter, but again an imitator. His idol was another Norwegian who had also worked with his hands, painter Edvard Munch. In privacy Caspersen imitated Munch, Munch, Munch—like the French copyist who painted 1,000 replicas of the *Mona Lisa*.

Munch was not the easiest artist to copy. The greatest Scandinavian painter of all time, he achieved this standing because his work expressed the tumult and power of his unique emotional nature. He had begun his formal training at the royal school of drawing in Oslo but had rebelled against the academic preoccupation with physical reality.

When he was still only eighteen (in 1892) Munch had been invited to show fifty-five of his works as part of the Verein Berliner Kunstler exposition in the gallery of the Berlin Artists Association. He had been acclaimed by painters throughout

Germany, but the public had reacted so adversely, particularly to his *Vampire*, that the association had been forced to close the exposition. Two years later Munch's genius had been lauded in a monograph to which Julius Meier-Graefe, whom we have met in conjunction with the Otto Wacker scandal (see Chapter 5), had contributed. Through Munch, the German art world had been introduced to the brusque æsthetic of Vincent van Gogh and Paul Gauguin, and the influence of all three had encouraged the flowering of German Expressionism.

Long before Munch's death at eighty was announced by Oslo radio in 1944, he had become one of Norway's most admired sons, and his work had found ample place in the Oslo Nasjonalgalleriet, the University Festival Hall, and countless private collections. In 1944 Caspersen himself was forty years old.

Oslo is not a large metropolis. Although it is unlikely that Munch had ever had anything to do with Caspersen, the latter may have seen the painter. More significantly, Caspersen worked in the Nasjonalgalleriet and had the opportunity to study and copy Munch's works. He felt a kinship for the painter—so much so that he was able to quit making copies and to begin painting Munch-like subjects.

A travelling exhibition of Munch's works made the rounds of American museums in 1950–1951. Soon afterwards bogus Munchs began to appear in American collections. A number of them had come through Oslo dealers. About the same time the City of Oslo acquired the remaining works in the Munch estate. Several of these paintings were so badly damaged that museum conservators decided that they could be saved only by removing the paint itself from the old canvases and transferring it to new linen.

Transferring, as described by F. Schmidt-Degener of the Amsterdam Rijksmuseum, is a slow and delicate process. The original canvas is removed from its stretcher and laid face up on a hard, flat surface. Strips of paper 10 inches or more wide are pasted around the edge of the painting, like a frame, with only about a one-inch overlap on the canvas itself. The back of this wide, exposed paper border is then glued to a flat wooden frame. The strips of paper are soaked with water, which makes them shrink, thus stretching the old canvas flat and taut. Plain newsprint or layers of tissue paper are glued over the face of the old painting, and any irregularities that might be caused by overlapping sheets, wrinkles, or minute glue bumps are sandpapered away. The whole assemblage is then turned over and laid face down on the flat table and weighted. Because the wooden frame is open, the technician has free access to the back of the painting, which he dampens so that the bond between the canvas and its original first layer of sizing weakens. The sizing is dissolved. The canvas is carefully peeled off. What remains on the table under the massive flat frame is a thin layer of paint (in this case Munch's oil painting) backside up. After this back surface has been cleaned of old sizing and treated with a relining glue, a new linen or canvas support, mounted on a new stretcher, is laid and bonded to the paint. Finally the paper frame is cut away and the painting's facial paper cleaned off.

The restorers asked Caspersen to make new stretchers for the paintings which were to be transferred. He had to study the originals and take measurements.

The skill of the restorers was such that the old canvases were peeled from the Munch paintings intact. The curators were not interested in the old canvases or stretchers, even though they had Munch's markings on them. When Caspersen asked if he might have the debris, they gave it to him.

Caspersen put the Munch canvases and stretchers together again. Then he painted new "Munchs" on them. If he had hung these paintings in his own living room, there would have been no problem, no crime. But he had become Munch, and therefore he had to play the whole role. He dropped in on Oslo art dealer Arnstein Berntsen.

"We knew Caspersen as a capable, honest, and dependable man," Berntsen later explained. "He worked with curator Martin Haug [of the Nasjonalgalleriet] on University Street. We had no reason to believe he was selling false or stolen Munch paintings. When he told us he was selling paintings for an old lady we took him at his word."

According to *Nå*, a Norwegian weekly, when Berntsen was asked why he had not requested the name of the old lady, he replied: "As art dealers we have the duty to keep names of buyer and seller unknown to each other. We considered Caspersen a reliable contact—if an old lady wished to be anonymous, we respected this."

Berntsen bought *Summer*, apparently for 22,000 kroner, and passed it on to a well-known collector for 47,000. *Road at Sunset* was acquired for 17,000 kroner by dealer Rolph Hause of the Modern Art Gallery. These transactions occurred in 1959, more than three years after Johan H. Langaard, director of the Oslo Municipal Art Collection, had expressed his opinion in the Oslo *Dagblader* (*Daily News*) that paintings in the Albright-Knox Art Gallery in Buffalo; the Phillips collection in Washington, D.C.; the G. David Thompson collection in Pittsburgh; and elsewhere in the United States and Scandinavia were not by Munch at all. Langaard had seen *Summer* and *Road at Sunset* fleetingly and had had no misgivings. Later he had an opportunity to study both paintings more closely, and he became suspicious not only of them but of other so-called "Munchs."

His investigative path led back through the dealers to Caspersen.

Police demanded to know where the cabinetmaker had obtained the paintings. "Why, I painted them!" Caspersen replied. Then he tried to cover himself by declaring that he had sold the paintings as his own works—a claim hard to support, considering that both paintings were signed and dated (*Road at Sunset* bore the inscription "Edv. Munch 1899–98" [sic]) and that he had been paid so munificently for them.

The police and public response was classic: no mere carpenter could ever have forged a Munch! So Caspersen proceeded to demolish the challenge in equally classic fashion: under supervision of police and art experts in police headquarters, he painted a new *Summer Landscape* in only three hours.

The resulting scandal was a new experience for descendants of the Vikings. Norway's *Arbeiderbladet* (*Daily Worker*) editorialized: "To forge a piece of art is a crime, but only against the artist. The person who is left with the painting has in any case the work of art he bought. Nobody will feel sorry for him if he has bought it out of motives other than to obtain a work of art he likes. We laugh at him."

An indignant painter, Hakon Stenstadvold, grumbled that the two dealers involved either were not experts or had conspired with Caspersen. There was no evidence Caspersen was responsible for wholesale forgery; the case against him was dropped and he receded into his pre-Munich oblivion.

Jean Pierre Schecroun was born thousands of miles from any consequential art centre—in Tananarive, Madagascar, in 1929. He did not reach Paris until 1949.

Before him, the first man of art to conquer Paris from the islands of the Indian Ocean had been dealer Ambroise Vollard from Réunion. Schecroun was determined to be the second and—because he was a painter rather than a dealer—far more luminous star.

He had genuine talent. At the École des Beaux Arts he was recognized instantly as a brilliant student. Fernand Léger was impressed and took him on as an assistant. Working under Léger Schecroun did more than dirty jobs around the studio: he learned the master's style and methods. As part of his training he also studied the styles, touches, and techniques of other established painters around Paris, picking up their traits with amazing rapidity and fidelity. He was a natural mimic with the bush.

When Léger died, Schecroun went on his own. But the transition from brilliant student able to assimilate and ape others' styles to brilliant original artist was one that he failed to make. As a painter he could not earn a living.

But one day in a bar his luck changed: he met several men who were willing to listen as he bewailed his fate. They were not only sympathetic; they were also practical. They suggested ways in which Schecroun could use his talent to make them all very rich. Thus was hatched a confidence ring that included Francis Manlay (seven years younger than Schecroun), Serge and Frederic Botton, and Jean Jais, all from respectable families. Of the five men only Schecroun was a producer. The rest were pushers, who operated like today's market researchers making sure Schecroun fabricated only what the market demanded.

They did not confine their plot to Paris but travelled from city to city. They would hit a town like Geneva, and, while

Schecroun stayed out of sight (setting up his production line in the bathroom), would systematically canvass dealers and known collectors. If a prospect said "Braque," the salesman would return to the hotel and tell Schecroun to paint a "Braque." Schecroun could produce an excellent "Braque" within the hour.

In such a short time, of course, he could not do an oil painting, but he wanted nothing to do with oils. They took too much time to paint, required years to dry properly, and were the most likely to be detected. He concentrated instead on water-colours, drawings, and pastels, all forms which could be done quickly but would not easily betray their freshness. He usually did small pieces, almost like studio sweepings: the kind of works that every artist makes by the dozen in preparation for major paintings. They are sought by collectors who dote on the creator's name but cannot afford masterpieces.

What a *Who's Who* Schecroun sketched out! Jean Bazaine, Georges Braque, Robert Delaunay, Hans Hartung, Vassily Kandinsky, Frank Kupka, Léger (another case of the master being cuckolded by the apprentice), André Lhote, Alfred Manessier, Joan Miró, Francis Picabia, Pablo Picasso, Jackson Pollack, Pierre Soulages, Nicolaes de Stael, Wols, and still others. Schecroun later acknowledged seventy-four pieces, forty-one of them "Picassos." Probably the number was even larger. His associates, working in France, England, Germany, and Switzerland, sold them for a total of $200,000.

Their most notable victim was Jacques Dubourg, an expert accredited to the Court of Appeals and the Supreme Tribunal and member of the Chambre Syndicale of art experts. He purchased what he judged a superb de Staël "Composition" dated 1944. Dubourg made the purchase in 1962, when Schecroun's work was already being investigated.

In 1961 a cautious client had attempted to verify the cachet of the Gallery Maeght of Paris. The cachet, stamped on an invoice for a "Picasso," turned out to be as false as the invoice. Then the director of London's O'Hana Gallery had asked French experts to authenticate a Braque that had been questioned by a customer. The verdict had been fraud. O'Hana actually had two bogus Braques and therefore laid plans to file a civil suit against the supplier. Investigations began in earnest.

Schecroun benefited only briefly from his share of the $200,000. He was skiing in the mountains when he was arrested. "My trial will be that of the picture dealers," he boasted. This boast became the theme of his defence. He divulged that some of his pieces had been sold to the very art galleries that served as exclusive official agents of the painters whom he had forged!

Schecroun was sentenced to a brief term, part of which was suspended. In all he served but ten months.

He was allowed to paint while in prison, and he spun out a series of works signed with his own name and ennobled with the legend "Painted in a prison cell." He was subsequently lionized in the press and on television. He had a London show and then one at La Palette Bleue on Rue de Seine in Paris, with café society, Françoise Sagan included, in attendance. For Schecroun, it was *la Gloire*. But café society found new fads, and the part of the art world that mattered did not take him to its bosom. Schecroun's limelight burned out.

David Stein was born in Alexandria when Egypt was still a British protectorate. His father, a British doctor sent there to do medical research, also collected paintings. David Stein cut his teeth on art. His mother was French, and David was sent to the Sorbonne to take his *baccalauréat* in French literature. He also studied music at the Paris Conservatory before going on to England to major in English at Westminster College. In 1955—when he was nineteen—he took a minor job reporting for *L'Intransigeant*, a Paris daily. Then he became assistant to the newspaper's literary and art editor. This position opened the doors to a whole new intellectual community, a world into which he glided easily thanks to his charm and a talent for the piano.

By that time Stein was also doing public-relations legwork for American film companies. He now bought every book on Picasso he could afford and went from museum to museum and gallery to gallery, studying the artist's work. He made a point of meeting Picasso's friends, of learning about and imitating

Picasso's life style, of grasping as best he could the Picasso spirit.

"After I managed to make a refined copy of a Picasso work of the '30s, I took it to an art dealer. He immediately bought it for $5,000 as a genuine Picasso," news reports later quoted him. The sale was made so easily that the temptation to continue making fakes was more than Stein could resist.

Once he had mastered Picasso's style he applied the same approach to other contemporary masters. "If a painter I was copying was left-handed," Stein later boasted to a *Newsweek* reporter, "I had to use my left hand. Braque was a lefty. If an artist like Picasso painted at night and daylight was not important to him, I had to know it."

Stein worked methodically. Three years later, in 1964, he had developed enough confidence in his ability to handle Marc Chagall's style to offer two gouaches to a major London gallery, which bought them for $4,000 each.

In 1965 Stein entered the United States through Canada. He brought with him a few genuine paintings, bought with profits from his fakes. He found an office in the Empire State Building and from there began to hawk art. His business prospered, for he was a supersalesman. He opened the Galerie Trianon at 525 Park Avenue and established a branch in Palm Beach, where he cultivated rich women.

One way to make it big in the field of pretence is to look big. The handsome Stein began tooling around in a chauffeured Rolls-Royce. In five years he painted—by his own claim—200 bogus Matisses, Dufys, Van Dongens, Mirós, Picassos, Derains, and Chagalls. By his own estimate he made up to $30,000 for a painting and took in nearly $1 million altogether. He sold to the public and dealers alike. He sold at least nine pieces to Abraham Lublin for a total of $22,400; two to E. J. Korvette for a total of $7,000; and nine to Irving Yamet for a total of $25,400. These figures represent only sales of fake Picassos and Chagalls.

When Stein required capital to stock art books and original graphics for the Galerie Trianon, he borrowed the money from French & European Publications Inc., of 610 Fifth Avenue, pledging his paintings as security.

When Chagall came to New York to do two murals for the new Metropolitan Opera House at Lincoln Centre, as Stein tells it, Chagall bumped into a Stein-Chagall in a Manhattan gallery—and questioned it because the price was too low.

Soon afterwards Yamet appeared in the office of the New York County Assistant District Attorney Joseph Stone, who was then in charge of the Criminal Court Bureau. The scholarly and thorough Stone had for years been a specialist in all forms of consumer fraud. More than a decade before he had published "The Prosecution of Trademark Counterfeiting and Mislabelling." At that time art fraud had not been much of a problem in New York, but as its incidence increased all such cases within the Manhattan jurisdiction came to Stone. He has since become probably America's leading authority on investigation and prosecution of art forgery. Yamet should have been suspicious the first time he was able to buy an original "Chagall" from Stein for as little as $2,000, but he had continued to deal with Stein for so long that he later admitted, "I imagine I have more information on David Stein than any other single person."

In Stone's office Chagall was shown several questionable pieces. The aging master was furious: "They are all very poor fakes!"

"He was on the verge of tearing one of them up," reported Stone, "but we were able to talk him out of it because we needed it for evidence."

In September 1966 detectives raided the Galerie Trianon. They found two spurious Picassos, one false Chagall, and—more intriguing—a photograph of Stein, stripped to the waist and painting a new "Chagall." Detectives called at Stein's apartment, but the dark, handsome con man fled through the back door and disappeared.

The Trianon premises also yielded a scrapbook containing other photographs of Stein and many of his victims—the kind of testimonial photographs one finds in restaurants catering to celebrities.

Stone characterized the Stein case as "one of the biggest art fraud cases we've ever had," and he pursued the forger relentlessly. Police across the country were put on the lookout for Stein. Other victims of the forger were ferreted out. But, as usual, many did not want it known that they had been victimized and preferred to take their losses in anonymity.

Photographs of suspect Picassos were sent to Vence in France, where Picasso studied each and then scrawled across the face either "vrai" or "faux" ("true" or false").

In January 1967 Stein was finally arrested in Los Angeles. Los Angeles authorities were preparing charges against him for selling fake Dufys in California, but they were willing to give Stone first crack. Stein waived extradition and was returned to Manhattan, where bail was set at $10,000. He could not raise it.

The initial case against Stein was limited to his fakery of Chagall and Picasso, for these two men were alive and could personally testify to the authenticity of any painting or drawing that had passed through Stein's hands. An attempt to prosecute Stein for alleged forgeries of Raoul Dufy, André Derain, Cocteau, Henri Matisse, or Kees van Dongen would have required importing experts from Europe and would have been excessively drawn out and costly.

Consequently, when a grand jury handed down its indictment of Stein, all ninety-seven counts involved works by Picasso or Chagall—forty-one works altogether, which had brought Stein $168,000. Stein was charged with first-degree larceny—for having stolen money by false and fraudulent pretences from Lublin, Yamet, Korvette, Fanny Niviau, John Marqusee, Charles DuBoise, Louis D. Cohen, and several other collectors.

Arraigned before Justice George M. Carney of the New York State Supreme Court, Stein found his bail reset at $7,500, which he still could not make. He was taken to "the Tombs," the New York County jail. By then Stone's office had become a virtual warehouse of Stein-made art, including all the pieces cited in the indictment.

Meanwhile Stein's creditors began to take action against him. French & European Publications Inc. wanted to recoup the $25,000 that it had loaned to Galerie Trianon. Stein's pictures had been the security for the loan, but was the security worth anything? A forced sale of art books had previously realized

$8,000. On May 24 seventy people crowded into a small room of Surrogate's Court at 31 Chambers Street for a sheriff's auction of the paintings.

Perspiring under television lights, H. Kehl, undersheriff in charge of the sale, declared, "We assume these works are good, but we make no representation or warranty." Any buyer who paid more than $150 for a piece was given a ten-day grace period in which to ask for his money back if he could prove that he had purchased a fake. A Utrillo and a Rodin had been authenticated by "one of New York's outstanding dealers." The Utrillo went to Bernard Danenberg, owner of the ACA Heritage Galleries, for $9,250; Mrs. Gertrude Jarvis of Jarvis Carriage House bought the Rodin for $6,000. The offerings included etchings by Braque, Alexander Calder, Derain, Gauguin, and Édouard Manet, plus "a lot of junk." The total came to $17,500.

Stone's investigation disclosed that Stein had forged certificates of authenticity, including experts' signatures and seals. Stein had persuaded a doctor's doorman to go to Brooklyn to procure the counterfeit rubber stamps for the seals. Stone found the studio where Stein's fakes had been photographed in such a way that they had appeared to be on exhibition in a respectable gallery.

Stone's case against Stein grew stronger every day. Expert testimony and pieces of circumstantial evidence piled up. Stein remained in the Tombs, where pressure, worry, and loneliness finally broke him. He decided to tell Stone all that he knew about art forgery and to confess to having painted bogus pictures.

Stone produced paper and paints, and in his office before witnesses Stein made new fakes, which were annotated and added to the evidence. According to Stone, "Stein developed a fixation like a child who has learned to imitate a certain kind of drawing and does it over and over again." Stein's Chagalls, and Picassos—most of them imitative pastiches rather than direct copies—were well done. "Stein has learned to imitate the simple, the childish," Stone says. With Matisse, "Stein is out of his element."

Stein was allowed to plead guilty on six counts: three felonies (falsely representing a Chagall, a Picasso, and a Matisse) and three misdemeanours (counterfeiting trademarks, that is, the signatures of the three painters). The other charges were dropped. Sentencing was set for September. Once Stein had confessed, some friends put up bail, and he was temporarily freed.

He immediately began to paint again, still in borrowed styles. He wisely signed these new works with his own name. Meanwhile he sought all the publicity possible. He urged NBC to rerun a *New York Illustrated* programme on his life. He even made *Reader's Digest:*

> David Stein, the confessed art forger, told TV director Don Luftig about the time he refused a bid $4,000 lower than his $18,000 asking price for one of his homemade Chagalls. Luftig asked why he hadn't taken the $14,000, since the picture cost him $10 to make. "It's the principle of the thing," said Stein. "I couldn't do that to Chagall's reputation."

Ever the manipulator, Stein worked his way into a small New Jersey community. In the role of reformed forger eager to succeed honourably, he persuaded the Ocean Side Surf Club in Seabright to give him a one-man show featuring twenty-five works done both in Stein style and in the styles of his former victims. He also managed to wangle a two-column gush in the art-review section of *Newsweek:*

> His new paintings are a posh potpourri of the best of modern art, a combined legacy of everything from Nolde to Derain, from Braque to van Dongen. Guernica-like Picasso figures twist and turn against brilliant colour-filled Dufy backgrounds while men and women appear to float effortlessly through space in a Chagallesque defiance of gravity. Seaside fantasy monsters recall the witty, whimsical hybrids of the surrealists, and luxuriant vegetations in sun-drenched landscapes beg kinship with Matisse and Derain. Despite their genealogical debt, the ex-forger's paintings do come alive on their own as explosive colour decoration.

The *Newsweek* article said that Stein had served six months in jail for trademark forgery (he had not yet done so) and that he had been freed; it also implied that he would be at the public opening of the Surf Club show. He never made it.

On the Friday before the opening the friends who had posted Stein's bail enticed him back to New York, where they promptly revoked their bail. When his show opened in Seabright, he was again sitting in the Tombs.

On January 23, 1969, Judge Gerald P. Culkin fined him $6,000 and sentenced him to two and a half to five years in Sing Sing. There he persuaded the warden to let him continue painting.

David Hepburn, the London gallery owner, lost little time in asking Stone for permission to mount a sale of Stein's prison paintings. Stone warned, "You better sell them as Steins and not Chagalls, or you'll be joining Stein inside." Hepburn negotiated a two-year contract with Stein, and on April 29, 1969, the London show was in full swing. Of forty paintings labelled "Chagall," "Braque," "Picasso," and "Matisse"—but all clearly signed by Stein—twenty-one were sold. The difference was in the price tags: Stein's imitations brought only about $125 to $500 apiece, less gallery commissions.

Said the flamboyant Hepburn: "After all, he's made it in the art world, hasn't he? Stein never would have sold this well otherwise. We're going to have another show in New York as soon as he gets out of prison. He's painting away there now. Just right for the start of the New York art season. We're going to pick him up with a car at the gates of Sing Sing and drive him right to the gallery on East 60th Street."

Just how freely David Stein will be allowed to move for the next few years is open to conjecture. He is still facing charges in California and possible deportation by the U.S. Immigration and Naturalization Service. He also has some worries about the reception awaiting him in England should he decide to return there, and there are also warrants against him in France and Switzerland.

CHAPTER 12

Judging Fakes

In 1965 Robert Aries declared—in a mimeographed publication whose French title can be translated *Fakery in Painting and Scientific Expertise*—that the world art market had reached an annual volume of $300 million. Of this sum, he claimed, $30 million had been realized from the sale of fake art. The book was published in Monte Carlo, where Aries, a chemical engineer and former professor at the Polytechnic Institute of Brooklyn and the University of Geneva, had established—at least on paper—the International Institute of Scientific Expertise for Works of Art, called ISART.

Aries (who held 50 industrial patents and had written more than 200 scientific papers and books) gave neither explanation nor source for his statistics. During the 1968–1969 season, however, the combined annual sales of Sotheby's (including Parke-Bernet Galleries) and Christie's reached $133,408,804. It does not seem unreasonable that total art sales would be about three times these auction-house figures. A total figure of $300–$400 million would thus be plausible.

More debatable is Aries' opinion that 10 per cent of this total volume is realized from fake art. If he meant that many old pieces are mistakenly attributed, his 10 per cent figure is more credible, but, if he meant that 10 per cent are counterfeits sold fraudulently, he has, in my opinion, exaggerated the situation. The sales of works by the better-known forgers like Jean Pierre Schecroun, and David Stein amounted to only a few hundred pieces in any year, whereas tens of thousands of authentic pieces changed hands in the same period. Millet and Cazot are credited with having passed 3,600 counterfeits but over a ten-year period. There are, admittedly, hundreds of art forgers whose names and adventures have not been mentioned in this book, but most of their fakes, like the great bulk of the Millet-Cazot output, have been spotted and taken out of circulation.

My own estimate is that art fraud accounts at most for 1 per cent of the market. It is possible that some unknown latter-day Giovanni Bastianini has turned out quantities of excellent fakes which have not yet been detected, and no doubt there are many new Schecrouns and Steins plying their craft. But whether the figure for fake art is $3 million or $30 million, the legitimate art community is anxious to stamp out counterfeiting, which, even in small quantities, is poisonous.

The whole purpose of Aries' book was to drum up patronage for ISART, whose laboratory was to be open to anyone seeking scientific appraisal of a work of art. In Aries' opinion, the best art laboratory in Europe was at Brussels—the Coremans Laboratory, named by the Belgian government after the expert who had played so controversial a role in the Van Meegeren affair. But, Aries lamented, the best European laboratories are all government-operated and charged with the restoration and analysis of museum properties. Private individuals have no access to their facilities. By creating ISART Aries proposed to make available to all—individuals, governments, and institutions—the finest in specialized laboratory facilities, as well as the judgement of experts the world over. Presumably charges for these services would have been based upon hourly rates and not upon a percentage of the appraised or selling value of an authenticated painting, a dangerous practice all too frequent among individual experts. But apparently Aries' brave idea died in infancy. No one speaks of ISART, and letters addressed to him at Monte Carlo go unanswered—a pity. The need remains, but probably no such enterprise can exist merely on fees; a rich endowment is necessary and desirable.

A somewhat similar, though more restricted, mechanism has been proposed by Paul Renoir, a grandson of the illustrious painter Pierre Auguste Renoir. He claims there are still many uncatalogued Renoirs in existence—but not as many as there seem to be. He has established the Maison de Renoir foundation at Cagnes-sur-Mer, also on the Côte d'Azur, whose purposes are to preserve the home and possessions of Renoir and to authenticate his works as they are brought forward. The latter objective is still more a dream than a reality, and Renoir lobbies vigorously for the necessary cooperation and financial support.

The idea is to accumulate complete documentation on every Renoir in the world and to maintain files of data and photographs of fake pieces. Authentication would be entrusted to a committee of experts, some of them selected by the Maison de Renoir foundation, some by government appointment, and some by French art dealers. The panel would consider itself the supreme court in matters of Renoir attribution. But the whole scheme, according to Renoir, is vigorously opposed by the art-dealer "establishment." No dealer, he claims, wants to risk having something that he wants to sell declared a fake.

Whatever system is used to authenticate it, any work of art must pass four general tests:

Style. Did the artist paint this way? Does the painting reveal the personality and handling characteristic of his other works?

Content. Is everything portrayed in harmony with its time and free of anachronisms?

Provenance. What is the history of ownership, public exposure, and documentation of the work?

Technological Considerations. Does the work stand up to the most advanced scientific examination possible?

The first test, an æsthetic one, is the most debatable way to judge authenticity. Yet it is still sometimes the only test upon which ultimate judgement can be based. German Impressionist painter Max Liebermann, who helped to introduce French Impressionism and post-Impressionism to his countrymen and to nudge German artists into a modern vision, acknowledged wryly that "Art historians are not so superfluous after all. If they didn't exist, who would be there to explain, when we are dead, that our bad pictures are forgeries?"

The critic who relies on æsthetics claims that, even when a forgery cannot be detected technically, its lack of stylistic logic will offend a connoisseur. This claim is a little vague, but it amounts to the same thing as Klaus Perls' "ringing bells": intuition! *Art News* quoted Joseph Duveen as having said during the Hahn-Duveen trial over the authenticity of a da Vinci painting in 1929, "When Berenson speaks of a 'sixth sense' he defines as nearly as can be the foundation of criticism. A sense of æsthetic values which has been developed through years of study and comparison is indefinable but nonetheless real."

Aries, on the other hand, wanted to base the judgement of ISART largely on laboratory analysis. Metropolitan Museum expert Joseph V. Noble has written:

> In order to detect a forgery, it is best to remember that every object made by man carries within it the evidence of the time and place of its manufacture. It is a challenge to the trained eye of the art historian and to the technical examination of the scientific analyst to penetrate beneath the surface appearance and to discover the truth.

Noble argues for a balanced four-test attack; he used it well on one of the Metropolitan's prized possessions—a small bronze Greek horse, considered to be 2,400 years old and originally placed on exhibition in 1923. For some years Noble passed it in the museum's Greek galleries several times a week. Suddenly one day in July 1961

> I did a double-take. For the first time I paid attention to a line—it can be seen in all the photos in all the books—that runs from the top of the mane down to the tip of his nose. I examined it through the glass showcase and followed the line, a very thin line across his back, down his leg, under his stomach, back up the legs to his head. I knew as sure as I was standing there that the piece was a fraud. I had seen the piece a

> thousand times before and the lines had not registered. This time the lines did. The lines were mould marks that had been filed off. This indicated that the horse was cast in the sandmould process, which was not invented until about the 14th century, and that it was not cast in the ancient lost-war process, which we had thought all along.

The fifteen-inch horse was withdrawn from exhibition and an investigation undertaken; it lasted six years. "I knew it was a fake," Noble said, "but I knew I had to prove it."

The horse had been purchased as an archaeological find. There was no information on provenance other than the name of the Paris dealer who had sold it. Provenance could not substantiate the horse's antiquity. Noble had spotted a technical anachronism, but his judgement had to be backed up with additional proof. In January 1962 Noble and Dietrich von Bothmer, his partner in the investigation of the Etruscan *Warrior*, took the horse to the Bedi Rassy Foundry in Brooklyn and asked how to make a sand-cast duplicate. Part of the process involves placing a sand core inside the mould, which is held in position with iron wires. The wire ends pierce the surface, and are covered with bronze plugs. There are fifteen bronze plugs in the Met's horse, but curators had always assumed that the ancient Greeks had used them to cover up bubbles and similar minor imperfections in the casting, a common practice. When Met officials held tiny magnets to the plugs, however, the magnets stuck, this indicating that there was iron just inside the bronze plugs: magnets do not stick to bronze.

The investigators were still not totally convinced, and for the next five years they continued stylistic investigation in England, France, Germany, and Italy. Then Noble heard about a Woodbridge, New Jersey, company which had developed a gamma-ray device to search for flaws in the hulls of atomic submarines. It was capable of penetrating up to nine inches of steel. A machine containing radioactive iridium 192 was aimed at the horse, and a gamma-ray shadowgraph was taken. "They held up the film dripping wet and for the first time I could see inside the horse," Noble recalled. "I could see the sand core, the iron wire, and the iron points. That was it."

The age of the horse was sliced from 2,400 years to about 50 years—discovered thanks to considerations of æsthetics, anachronisms, provenance, and technical aspects.

Paul Eudel told a story years ago that has since been repeated in many versions; it cannot be documented, but some version of it probably did happen. Towards the turn of the century an English art runner supposedly commissioned a painter to make a copy of a Flemish-school painting that hung in a Rotterdam museum. At that time the United States had a 20 per cent duty on imported paintings. The copyist made a faultless rendering, right down to the original artist's name and date: Jan Steen, 1672. After examining the painting the merchant declared himself satisfied. "You've painted it so well, why don't you sign it yourself? Here, take your brush and paint right over the original."

Three weeks later the painting was on a boat headed for New York and an address that the merchant habitually used. In the meantime an anonymous letter was on its way to customs officials in Manhattan warning that they were about to be the victims of a fraud. A certain painting—a Dutch masterpiece—was coming through with the name of an unknown painter superimposed upon it.

One forewarned appraiser is worth ten innocents. The painting was found and the top signature removed. There was the real signature, Jan Steen! The painting was appraised at $40,000.

The merchant had to pay a 50 per cent fine—$20,000—plus the 20 per cent duty, $28,000 in all. But he received official papers from American customs reporting the action and certifying that the painting was done by Steen. With this endorsement he sold the painting within three days for $50,000!

Today a twentieth-century Steen would go down to crashing defeat in the laboratory. As Salvador Dali has observed, "Being a modern painter is the only thing, no matter what you do, that you cannot avoid being."

The scientist has armed himself with chemistry, X-rays, ultraviolet light, infrared light, electron microscopes, and spectroscopes. X-rays reveal otherwise invisible layers of paint, exposing structural coatings and supplementary colour. Luminescent photographs taken in ultraviolet light from quartz-tube lamps reveal retouching and restorations in almost every kind of material. Infrared prints isolate various stages of construction. Spectroscopy is used in chemical analysis of colour pigments.

But forgers can make science work for them too. A forger can render a spectroscopic examination difficult and sometimes impossible by adding metallic salts to his paint. X-ray photos can be scrambled if the painted substructure is treated with metallic substances. It is for such reasons that Sherman E. Lee, director of the Cleveland Museum of Art, has told the International Academy of Law and Science that not even the combination of artistic expertise, modern physics, and chemistry can always foil the clever art forger.

Nonetheless, the technological gap between the forger and the scientist continues to widen, as the scientist keeps inventing new tools. Thermoluminescent dating is among the latest techniques. With it a scientist can determine the age of such ceramic objects as pottery and terra-cotta sculpture from the nineteenth century back. Most mineral substances absorb the natural radiation from uranium, potassium, and thorium in the earth. Although the rate of radiation has been constant since art began, all absorbed radiation is released when a substance is heated. When a piece of clay is fired, its radioactivity—as measured by devices like those used in atomic reactors and hospital radiotherapy rooms—is reduced to zero. Then the object again begins to absorb radiation at the constant rate. By reheating the object and measuring the radiation given off, scientists can determine the length of time since the previous firing.

Dating through radioactivity of lead (see Chapter 8) and thermoluminescence makes it impossible for today's counterfeiter to pass anything off as being, say, more than 100 years old—provided, of course, that the prospective buyer can afford the expense of analysis.

Expense is one of the problems with laboratory procedures, even those not involving atomic technology. In 1953 the Boston Museum of Fine Arts reported an investigation of the subsurface structure of glazes on certain old Chinese ceramics. The investigators had taken more than 1,500 photomicrographs of surfaces and sections—obviously a very expensive procedure—to discover that the air bubble structure in the clay of genuine Kuan articles is quite different from that of Kuan-like fakes produced in the eighteenth century.

Every examination of a work of art for authenticity must follow the law of economy of means: the cheapest and easiest tests to administer must come first. If a piece of art fails at a lower level, there is no need to put it through more sophisticated procedures. The first tests, then, will be esthetic and historical. Recourse can be made to archives for references and documentation. Difficult cases that could not be resolved by the æsthetician and the archivist would be referred for appropriate laboratory examination. But the laboratory cannot help much in unmasking a forgery of an Old Master done during the lifetime of that Old Master. Radioactive examination of a 350-year-old duplicate of a 350-year-old Rubens can settle nothing.

Different art forms pose different problems, and science has not yet turned its full armoury on more than a few areas. In 1968 the National Gallery of Art in Washington, D.C., and the U.S. Atomic Energy Commission each contributed $25,000 for a three-year project at the Mellon Institute to perfect the process of atomic fingerprinting of the Old Masters: bombarding flecks of paint with neutrons in a reactor to measure the exact nature of their chemical impurities. The Institute hopes eventually to compile a library of precise chemical analyses of the different types of paint used by a dozen famous artists—or at least the types of paint prevalent in the period and country of each. But twelve painters hardly cover the field.

As for Oriental art, the prestigious *Encyclopedia of World Art* says, "It is the work of copyists which largely fills the museums and collections of the world." Oriental art is only one of many areas of study that have not received as much scientific attention as that given to Western painting.

Still, for the moment at least, there seem to be no more Bastianinis, Dossenas, Van Meegerens, or Fioravantis but only Steins, Caspersens, and Schecrouns. Successful forgery of *old* works could be a dying art. Increasingly the forger is being forced to concentrate on modern works. The laboratory has made it impossible to succeed with forging very old works if the would-be buyer investigates, but it has not yet provided answers to the problem of forgery of modern masters.

A perfect forgery has been defined as one that corresponds perfectly to the degree of our knowledge and understanding of the original. A theoretically perfect forgery could be spotted only by the perfect expert. If there ever was a perfect expert, it would seem to be the artist who supposedly painted the picture, yet even this expertise has its pitfalls.

In 1930 Giorgio de Chirico disowned his friends and everything that he had previously painted, declaring all such paintings to be forgeries. In 1947 a dealer hauled de Chirico into court in a dispute over one of these pictures, which the dealer had sold. The court found de Chirico guilty of fraud and fined him 330,000 lire. The painter's attitude gave rise to a good many disputes over other works.

More than 1,000 bastard Utrillos have been catalogued. An accusation was once made in a Paris court that a bogus Utrillo was sold at auction every week at the Hôtel Drouot. In 1947 *Elle*, a French women's magazine, claimed that there were 100,000 fake Utrillos in the world; yet in that same year, during a trial brought against some forgers, Maurice Utrillo himself admitted that he could not always distinguish the genuine from the spurious. When Madame Utrillo made a bonfire in her backyard of a mass of fakes which had been seized on her say-so since her husband's death, she muttered all the while, "I'm not sure they're all fakes."

In an earlier trial (1910) Maurice de Vlaminck had declared himself incapable of certifying that certain works were not his own. Under cross-examination he admitted that once, for fun, he had painted a picture in the style of his friend, Paul Cézanne. It had been put on the market with a forged signature—and Cézanne had declared it his own.

Some customers will not believe even the perfect expert. The English painter Laurence Stephen Lowry was called upon by an acquaintance, who had bought a Lowry for £100. It was signed only "L", whereas the artist always signed "L. S. Lowry." The purchaser asked Lowry when he had painted it. Lowry replied that it was not his picture. "Are you certain it isn't yours? Isn't there some expert I could take it to for an opinion?" Lowry exploded!

As the dealer's opinions have diminished in influence, he has passed the burden of judgement to the expert. Commerce has thus become based on certificates. Many people will believe a certificate signed by someone whom they do not know far more readily than they will trust their own judgement and their own eyes.

Paul Eudel complained sixty years ago in *Trucs et Truquers* that in the twentieth century anyone can call himself an expert: "Every merchant is an expert and all experts are merchants."

Obviously there are experts who *really are* expert, but it is unlikely that any individual can be truly qualified to judge more than a few painters or one period. Usually some individual emerges as *the* expert for a given subject, a monopoly which can be powerful and lucrative. A few years ago one could not sell a Rubens without a certificate from Jakob C. Burckhardt, a Van Eyck without one from Friedländer, an Italian primitive without one from Longhi, a Guardi without one from Fioco, a Corot without one from Schoeller, or a Cézanne without one from Lionello Venturi. In more recent times, a painter's dealer has most often been considered by the art community as the pre-eminent expert on that artist, and next in line is someone who has written a book about him, preferably a catalogue raisonné, or has organized a major museum exhibition of his works. Yet Friedländer cited a Hamburg gentleman who called himself an art scholar and who, for an hourly fee, wrote authentications for pictures that he had never seen and even for pictures that had not yet been painted.

Friedländer himself has been counterfeited. Legal action was taken in Zurich in 1957 against a dentist named Richard Friedländer, who added Maria to his name so that he could sign papers "M. Friedländer." He issued certificates of authenticity, and the similarity of names persuaded many victims that the documents had come from Max the famous German expert. The ingenious Swiss formed the Swiss Art Dealers and Experts

Association, a dummy group composed entirely of himself. He put the association forward as a neutral body and did a thriving business certifying paintings brought to him by prospective buyers who had obtained the works from three touts in collaboration with him. On a typical certificate was a very brief declaration of authenticity signed "M. Friedländer." This declaration was endorsed and framed as if it had been confirmed by the association, and gaudy seals and ribbons added to the authentic air.

Baiting the experts has become public sport. In November 1968 stories broke in the European press about the extraordinary luck that Hans Kiesel, a West German businessman, had had in the Paris flea market. Kiesel had found a grimy oil painting of a couple of nudes. He had paid $40 and taken it away to be cleaned. The nudes had dissolved to uncover one of Monet's *Gare St. Lazare* paintings, which was then restored and authenticated by experts of the Herzog Anton Ulrich Museum in Braunschweig. The painting, dated 1877, was appraised for as high as $1 million. In December Kiesel confessed that the picture was a hoax. The canvas had originally been of two nudes sunbathing. An artist friend of Kiesel's had removed them, faked Monet's scene, aged it in front of a gas oven and in the sun, and repainted the nudes on top. Kiesel explained happily: "We wanted to protest against the middle-class stock-certificate-on-the-wall concept of art. And we wanted to demonstrate against the 'experts' who are a little too quick to 'authenticate' a picture."

Most of the examples in this book have involved museums—the Metropolitan, the Louvre, the Boymans, and many smaller institutions. But museums are no more vulnerable than are individuals. They simply have larger collections, as well as greater facilities for continual investigation and evaluation of what they already own. The private individual, when he discovers that he has been duped, can quietly hide the evidence (or sometimes give it to charity) and forget it. The museum, being at least a quasi-public institution, must usually explain why it has removed a popular piece from exhibition. If there is evidence of fraud the museum must, as part of its public duty, take appropriate action. The fabulous frauds which have fooled museums tend to become known, whereas private mistakes remain unexposed. The fight against counterfeit art is not furthered by those victims who hide from publicity.

Dealers, in particular, do not like to have their names associated with scandal. The confidence of their clients is their life's blood, and anything that might damage this dangerous. Usually, when a dealer finds that he has sold a fake, he offers quiet reimbursement to his client and avoids litigation if at all possible; he will then seek a refund from the person who sold it to him, but he will not often start a lawsuit, even when that is the only way he himself can achieve redress.

The public is apt to judge a gallery—in fact any part of the art world—by sensational stories. Hilton Kramer wrote in *The New York Times* (January 7, 1968):

> Such stories are themselves a part—certainly the most comic part—of the secondary culture that has grown up around the modern interest in, and consumption of, works of art. This secondary culture, with its elaborate publications and vivid personalities, its myths and fashions and ubiquitous spokesmen, can itself be consumed and enjoyed—one can even become expert in it—without the actual experience of original works of art ever trespassing upon one's consciousness. To turn from the products of this culture, which is essentially a branch of the communications industry, to original works of art is often, alas, a distinct disappointment. You cannot *do* anything with a work of art; you can only stand there. The action, clearly, is elsewhere, where art is talked about, reproduced, debated, exalted, sold, and—best of all—exposed.

To put it more succinctly: art forgery is a child of commerce, and the general public looks upon the unmasking of the faker and the victim's fall from grace as a branch of entertainment!

The reputable dealers, though they usually work quietly, carry on an endless vigil against counterfeit paintings and sculpture. When clients have bought fakes from other sources, the dealers frequently have urged them to take legal action that will, it is hoped, put the counterfeiters out of business.

One dealer who has followed the advice that he gives to clients is Frank Perls of Beverly Hills. A Berlin dealer had written to Perls offering him a Giacometti statuette, a fourteen-inch rough-cut bronze of a long-armed nude. It was described as the last of six casts made from the original. Perls checked out the offer before telephoning the Berlin dealer to ship the bronze to California. "I compared it very carefully with a photo of the statuette in a book on Giacometti's works," Perls said later. "I was satisfied that it was a Giacometti, and I sent the dealer a cheque for $7,600."

Perls later encountered Alberto Giacometti's widow in Paris. She and the Paris foundry that had cast the sculptor's works had recently asked French authorities to confiscate several counterfeits that had come from a foundry in Rome. Madame Giacometti herself owned the genuine sixth casting of Perls' nude. When Perls asked the Berlin dealer for a refund, the dealer insisted that the nude was genuine and refused. Besides, the dealer said, he had been acting merely on behalf of a client, had received only a small commission, and could therefore not make the refund.

Perls brought his bronze back to Paris and placed it beside the true sixth casting. "Then it became really beautifully evident how bad the fake is and how blind one can be if one trusts a work of art implicitly." Having failed in the quiet approach, Frank gave the story to the press, declaring that he had surrendered "the little monster" to authorities for ultimate destruction and had filed a police complaint against the Berlin dealer and a man connected with the foundry in Rome.

The jet plane has radically internationalized the marketing of fraudulent art by making American wealth more accessible to European forgers. It is significant that, whereas Stein, an Egyptian, and de Hory, a Hungarian, both achieved their greatest commercial success on American shores, America has never turned out a really first-class art forger. But it will. In the past art forgery demanded great technical skill, and many of the best forgers spent long years doing picture restoration. This was simply not an American vocation. The future American art-fraud genius will not need these long painful years of apprenticeship, for he will not be faking Rembrandts or Goyas, not even Monets or Rouaults. Instead he will be doing American Minimal

Painting and Pop Art and international Op Art. The best of Abstract Expressionism may turn out to be too personal, too individual, and he will have to take extreme care with Jackson Pollack, Franz Kline, and Willem de Kooning if he wishes to escape visual detection, but technically he will be able to feast on certain periods of Ad Reinhardt, Josef Albers, Andy Warhol, Roy Lichtenstein, Jim Dine, Gene Davis, Frank Stella, Richard Mortensen, and Victor Vasarely. Chances are, though, that he will meet some frustration because contemporary painters are documenting their work better and the Archives of American Art, now part of the Smithsonian complex, will be of immeasurable service to a prospective purchaser willing to do a little researching before he spends his money.

A plethora of counterfeits is bound to affect a painter's prices, if for no other reason than that a painter who is widely imitated on every side soon becomes so commonplace that the public tires of him. When *Elle* said that there were 100,000 fake Utrillos in the world, its editor must have meant paintings done in the style of Utrillo but not necessarily being sold as actual Utrillos. If there were that many, the market would have become too depressed to make forging Utrillos worthwhile.

In Oslo, on April 23, 1968, Reidae Revold, chief curator of the Edvard Munch Museum, was charged with selling abroad 100 of the museum's paintings and graphics for his personal profit. Revold had closed most of his transactions directly with dealers in West Germany and Switzerland, to whom he had written on official museum stationery.

Original Munch lithographs are extremely valuable, for the artist had wanted them to have a rarity approaching that of his paintings and had printed only a few strikes of each rendering. When Munch died, some of his drawings were still on the stones, which remained in the hands of Munch's printer until Revold obtained them, apparently in exchange for prints belonging to the museum. Police suspected that Revold had made and sold new impressions from these stones. If so, the value of all Munch prints would have dropped drastically, as no one could be sure which pulls were made under his own supervision. Not until the Norwegian government had made a complete investigation and determined that no fraudulent impressions had been made did the Munch lithograph market regain its stability.

The market is the key to art fraud. A shortage of genuine pieces begets imitation. Soaring prices stimulate greed. Most paintings bought by individuals eventually come back on the market, but once a painting has gone to an institution it rarely re-enters commeree. The supply of paintings by a given artist of growing reputation thus becomes progressively smaller while the demand for his work—and the number of museums and individuals interested and able to purchase it—becomes ever larger. The spiral seems endless, and even painters who drop out of fashion eventually come back.

"The forger is a thief," according to Guy Isnard, a senior officer of the Sûreté Nationale and probably the world's number-one expert on art forgers. "He is a reproducer of someone else's thought. He does not counterfeit that which is especially beautiful but that which is worth a lot of money."

Isnard was referring only partly to the financial loss of a collector or dealer who is innocently stuck with a fake; he is more deeply concerned that the forger *steals from the original artist*, even though the artist may be dead. "His plagiarisms," Isnard continued, "which can show talent but never genius, are always distinguished by the uneasiness that they evoke, by [Georges Rouault's words in a catalogue to an exposition of fakes] 'The sentiment of a dead thing that they arouse among those who are able to commune with an authentic work.'"

The forger can never see what the original artist saw. He can never feel what the artist felt. He can never paint or sculpt with the spontaneity of the original artist, and so his pieces are always a little dead. If these pieces are not recognized as forgeries, if they pass into hallowed halls as true works of the imitated artist, they throw our understanding of that artist and the body of his work out of focus. Inevitably that artist's reputation must suffer. Short of being forgotten, this is the greatest catastrophe that can befall a creative human being.

The forger is an adventurer, and all of us who are merely spectators are apt to feel excitement when he tricks the establishment. We tend to sympathize more with the forger than with his victim, for the crime is one of cunning, not of violence. Yet the art forger deserves none of our sympathy. However clever he may be, the forger's masquerade cheapens, demeans, and robs someone whom society needs most to encourage—the creative artist, who is able to give us new worlds and new visions of ourselves. But as long as buyers compete for names, fakers will enjoy a seller's market.

Acknowledgments

In 1950 the Special Libraries Association in New York City published *Fakes and Forgeries in the Fine Arts*, a bibliography by Robert George Reisner, containing more than fourteen hundred entries, including books published in many languages; magazine articles in English, French, German, Italian, and Russian; and articles in *The New York Times* since 1897. This bibliography has been enormously helpful during my months of research through written sources found in the Library of Congress. The Library's card catalogues, *Readers' Guide to Periodical Literature*, *International Index—Social Sciences and Humanities Index*, *Art Index*, *Public Affairs Index*, *The New York Times Index*, *London Times Index*, and *The Wall Street Journal Index* have added hundreds of items published since 1950 to my list of sources. Besides written materials I have made use of interviews with dealers, law enforcement officials, museum curators, collectors, and attorneys; and field research which has taken me as far away as the cathedral and museum of Reims.

The majority of recent books on art fraud and authentication have been written by Germans or Frenchmen, and most of the books appearing in English have been translated from German.

Of the hundreds of written sources I have consulted I am particularly indebted to three general books, one legal case study, and one autobiography. Frank Arnau's thoughtful *Three Thousand Years of Deception in Art and Antiques* treats only four forgers in detail but is equally indispensable for its general chapters and its seven chapters on forgers' methods, from paintings to textiles and furniture. Dr. Hans Cülis' account of how he filmed Alceo Dossena at work can be found in a number of places, but I have used the somewhat more detailed translation found in Arnau's book.

When it comes to forgers instead of forgery, no book in any language can equal *Faux et Imitations dans l'Art* by Guy Isnard, chief commissioner of the Sûreté Nationale, Paris. Beginning with prehistory and ending with the twentieth century, Isnard takes major and minor artists and catalogues the names of their imitators and forgers. His pages on Rubens, for example, refer to dozens of painters. The volumes are filled with incidents, but they explore no forger to any depth. Isnard does offer hundreds of footnotes, particularly to articles in French periodicals, and in most cases these have not been catalogued in any of the American indices; for the most part, unfortunately, they are accessible neither in the Library of Congress nor the Bibliothèque Nationale in Paris. Isnard's books would be infinitely more valuable to scholars if they were indexed, a common failing in French books. (Arnaud's book is carefully indexed in English translation and unindexed in the French.)

Another book has been a rich fund of information: Sepp Schüller's *Forgers, Dealers, Experts: Strange Chapters in the History of Art.* Curiously Schüller, conservator of the Marienkirche at Lübeck, in which Lothar Malskat painted fake frescoes, devotes less space to Malskat than does Arnau. I am indebted to Schüller for the reconstruction of the newspaper exchange which took place between Bastianini and Lequesne.

The legal study is *The Rosso Case* by Abraham Kaplan, Samuel Berger, and George I. Gross. Of course the Rosso case is thoroughly documented in court histories, but this book was so complete that there was no need to seek out these old archives. I am indebted to my friend J. Carroll Bateman, general manager of the Insurance Information Institute, for suggesting this chapter.

The chapter on Francis Lagrange rests largely on his autobiography, *Flag on Devil's Island*; the dialogue I have used is, of course, taken from the first chapters of the book, most of which is devoted to his experiences in the penal colony.

From as many sources as possible I have tried to corroborate facts and incidents, but the Valfierno role in the theft of the *Mona Lisa* defies positive verification. I have chosen to tell it because it is part of the legend of art forgery, a tale still heard in art salon chatter, and I have used as my source a *Saturday Evening Post* article by Carl Decker, who claimed to have been a friend of Valfierno, or whatever his real name was. Information on Han Van Meegeren is available from hundreds of sources, but the most complete biography of his personal life has been written by an English lord, John Kilbracken. This book, *Master Art Forger*, was published in 1951 under a pseudonym; a second book, *Van Meegeren, Master Forger*, written with more technical information, appeared in 1968. By then my chapter was completed, and I was not unhappy to discover that Kilbracken and I had reached a number of similar conclusions.

When I've had a question regarding the Metropolitan's Etruscan Warriors, I've usually fallen back on the museum's official report by Joseph Noble and Dietrich von Bothmer, *An Inquiry into the Forgery of the Etruscan Warriors in the Metropolitan Museum of Art*. For the most part quotations of letters are from this source. I am also indebted to Joseph Noble for the preamble to this book. To the many people who have answered questions, provided information, and made suggestions, my deepest thanks.

Selected Bibliography

Aarons, Leroy F. "That Kid Michelangelo Set a Bad Example." *Washington Post*, May 21, 1967.

Aitken, Martin J. "Thermoluminescence." *Science Journal*, June 1965.

Anderson, David. "Old Masters Made to Order: Forgery as Fine Art." *New York Times Magazine*, December 23, 1945.

Aries, Robert. *Les Faux dans la Peinture et l'Expertise Scientifique*. Monaco, 1965.

Arnau, Frank [Heinrich Schmitt]. *Three Thousand Years of Deception in Art and Antiques*. Translated from the German. London: 1961.

Ballo, Guido. *Vero e Falso nell'arte Moderna*. Turin, 1962.

Barstow, Nina. "The Forgeries of Bastianini." *Magazine of Art*, no. 9, 1886.

Basham, William. "Grand Jury Investigating Art Gallery." *Washington Star*, December 20, 1967.

Beauford, Thomas R. *Pictures and How to Clean Them*. London, 1926.

Bloch, Vitale. "Van Meegeren, Faussaire de Vermeer." *L'Amour de l'Art*, January 1946.

Boswell, Helen. "Berlin Newsletter." *Art Digest*, February 15, 1948.

Brandi, Cesare. "The Nature of Falsification." *Encyclopedia of World Art*, New York, 1961.

Bredius, Abraham. *Amsterdam-Rijks-Museum*. Amsterdam, 1886.

———. *Catalogue Raisonne des Tableaux et Sculpture*. The Hague, 1914.

———. *Paintings of Rembrandt*. Vienna and New York, 1937 and 1942.

———. "A New Vermeer." *Burlington Magazine for Connoisseurs*, November 1937.

Burlington Arts Club. *Catalogue of a Collection of Counterfeits*. London, 1924.

Burroughs, Alan. *Art Criticism from a Laboratory*. Boston, 1938.

Le Cahier des Arts. Vermeer de Delft. Brussels, 1938.

Cellini, Pico. *Paragon*. Rome, May 1955.

Chaplin, V. T. J. "La Mésadventure des Cochons." *Le Journal*, February 11, 1935. (Millet–Cazot)

Chapman, Joseph M. "Chapman Reports." *Art in America*, October–November 1965.

Colin, Ralph F. "Fakes and Frauds in the Art World." *Art in America*, April 1963.

———, and Dudley T. Easby, Jr. "The Legal Aspects of Forgery and the Protection of the Expert." Metropolitan Museum of Art *Bulletin*, February 1968.

Coremans, Paul B. "Paintings." *Magazine of Art*, May 1948.

———. *Van Meegeren's Faked Vermeers and de Houghs*. Amsterdam: 1949.

Cürlis, Hans. "Alceo Dossena," film script, "Schaffende Hande." Berlin: Institut fur Kulturforschung, n.d.

Dagbladet (Daily News). "Three False Munchs." Oslo, January 14, 1956.

De Boer, H., and Pieter Koomen. *Han Van Meegeren, Teehemingen I*. The Hague, 1942. (An album of Van Meegeren's drawings, a copy of which was given to Hitler.)

Decker, Karl. "How and Why the Mona Lisa Was Stolen." *Saturday Evening Post*, June 25, 1932.

Decoen, Jean. *Vermeer—Van Meegeren—Retour à la Verité: Deux Authentiques*. Rotterdam: 1951.

———. "Les Faux Vermeer de Van Meegeren Sont-ils Faux Meegeren?" *Beaux Arts*, August 23, 1946.

———. "Encore Van Meegeren." *Beaux Arts*, August 6, 1948.

De la Faille, Bart. *Catalogue Raisonné*. 1927.

———. *Les Faux Van Goghs*. Paris and Brussels: 1930.

———. "Reponse à l'Article de Elie Faure." *l'Art Vivant*, June 15, 1930.

Demeure, Fernand. *Les Impostures de l'Art*. Paris: 1951.

Dreeves, William K. "Frauds and Forgeries." In *Fine Arts Insurance*, New York: 1938.

Duveen, James Henry. "How Pierpont Morgan Bought 'Mistakes.'" In *Secrets of an Art Dealer*, New York: 1938.

Easby, Dudley T., Jr., with Ralph E. Colin. "The Legal Aspects of Forgery and the Protection of the Expert." *Art Forgery*, The Metropolitan Museum of Art *Bulletin*, February 1968.

Edgell, G. H. "Report of the Directors." *Bulletin of the Museum of Fine Arts*, Boston: 1962.

Edgell, G. H., Edwin J. Hipkiss, and W. J. Young. "A Modified Tomb Monument of the Italian Renaissance." Ibid.

Esterow, Milton. *The Art Stealers*. New York: 1966.

———. "Metropolitan Finds Its Greek Horse Fake." *New York Times*, December 7, 1967.

Eudel, Paul. *Le Truquage*, Paris: 1903.

———. *Trucs et Truquers*, Paris: 1907.

Eyre, John R. *The Two Mona Lisas*. London, 1923.

Faure, Elie. "A Propos les Faux Van Goghs." *l'Art Vivant*, April 1, 1930.

Feller, Robert A. *Combining Art and Science*. The National Gallery of Art Research Project in Artists' Materials, Washington: 1965. (Reprinted from *Rutgers Alumni Magazine*, November 1965.)

———, and Sheldon Keck. "Detection of an Epoxy-Resin Coating on a Seventeenth Century Painting." *Studies in Conservation*, February 1964.

Fogg Museum of Art. *Art: Genuine or Counterfeit*. Exhibit catalogue, Cambridge, Mass., 1940.

Forrer, L. *Biographical Dictionary of Medallists*, vol. 5. London, 1912.

Fournier, Marthe. *De la Protection des Parties dans les Ventes d'Antiquités*. Paris, 1936.

France-Soir. November 23, 1967.

Friedlander, Max J. *Genuine and Counterfeit: Experiences of a Connoisseur*. New York, 1930.

———. *Art and Connoisseurship*. London, 1942.

Froentjes, W. *Revue de Criminologie et de Police Technique—l'Affaire van Meegeren*. Geneva, 1949.

Gill, William J. "The Collector's Puzzling Path." *Life*, November 2, 1962.

Grant, J. *A Pillage of Art*. New York, 1966.

Graves, Dorothy M. "Dossena Forgery Analyzed." *Art News*, January 26, 1929.

Hahn, Harry. *The Rape of La Belle*. Kansas City, 1946.

Hannema, Dirk. *Het Museum Boymans*. Rotterdam, 1935.

Herbert, Robert L. *Barbizon Revisited*. Boston, 1962.

Hoeber, Arthur. *The Barbizon Painters*. New York, 1915.

Hodes, Scott. *The Law of Art and Antiques*. Dobbs Ferry, N.Y., 1966.

Hours, Madeleine. "Radiographies de Tableaux de Leonardo da Vinci." *La Revue des Arts*, December 1952.

———. *Secrets of the Great Masters: A Study of Artistic Techniques*. New York, 1968.

Hoving, Thomas P. F. "The Game of Duplicity." *Art Forgery*, The Metropolitan Museum of Art *Bulletin*, February 1968.

Huntford, Roland. "Curator Said to Have Sold Munch's Works." *London Observer*, April 23, 1968.

Huth, Hans. "The Gentle Art of Faking." *Apollo*, April 1936.

Illustrated London News. On Van Meegeren: November 3, November 8, November 24, 1945.

Irving, Clifford. "Fake." *Look*, December 10, 1968: excerpt from *Fake*, New York, 1969.

Isnard, Guy. *Les Pirates de la Peinture*. Paris, 1955.

———. *Faux et Imitations dans l'Art*. 2 vols., Paris, 1959 and 1960.

Joni, J. F. *Affairs of a Painter*. London, 1936.

Jousseaume, F. *Les Vandales du Louvre*. Paris, 1910.

Kaplan, Abraham, Samuel A. Berger, and George I. Gross. *The Rosso Case*. New York, 1934.

Keck, Sheldon. "The Laboratory Detection of Fraud." *Magazine of Art*, May 1948.

———, and Robert L. Feller. "Detection of an Epoxy-Resin Coating on a Seventeenth Century Painting." *Studies in Conservation*, February 1964.

Keisch, Bernard. *Scientific Evidence in Art Authentication: Problems in Interpretation*. Address before International Academy of Law and Science, reprinted from *Lex et Scientia;* Washington, 1968.

———. "Dating Works Through Their Natural Radioactivity: Improvements and Applications." *Science*, April 26, 1968.

———. "Discriminating Radioactivity Measurements of Lead: New Tool for Authentication." *Curator*, no. 1, 1968.

———, R. L. Feller, A. S. Levine, R. R. Edwards. "Dating and Authenticating Works of Art by Measurement of Natural Alpha Emitters." *Science*, March 10, 1967.

Kilbracken, John (pseud.: John Godley). *Master Art Forger*. New York, 1951.

———. *Van Meegeren, Master Forger*. New York, 1968.

Kohler, Ellen A. "Ultimatum to Terra-Cotta Forgers." *Expedition*, Winter, 1967.

Kramer, Hilton. "On Fakes, Frauds, and Forgeries." *New York Times*, January 7, 1968.

Kurz, Otto. *Fakes*, 2nd ed. New York, 1967.

Lagrange, Francis. *Flag on Devil's Island*. Garden City, 1961.

Laurie, A. P. *New Light on Old Masters*. New York, 1935.

———. *The Pigments and Mediums of the Old Masters*. London, 1914.

Lefkowitz, Louis J. (interview). "The Art Frauds Legislation." *Art Forgery*, Metropolitan Museum of Art *Bulletin*, February 1968.

Lukomskii, G. K. *L'Art Etrusque*. Paris, 1930.

Lusetti, Walter. *Alceo Dossena, scultore*. Rome, 1955.

MacDougall, Curtis D. *Hoaxes*. 2nd rev. ed., New York, 1958.

Mailfert, André. *Au Pays des Antiquaires*. Paris, 1935.

———. "Comment On Fabrique les Faux Fragonard ou les Faux Utrillo." *Paris-Midi*, January 31, 1935.

"Make the Punishment Fit the Crime." *Apollo*, December 1947.

Malingue, Maurice. *Les Faux Tableaux*. Paris. (Gauguin)

Margat. *Traité de Jocondologie*.

Mather, Frank Jewett. *Western European Painting of the Renaissance*. New York, 1966.

Mayer, Ralph. *The Artist's Handbook of Materials and Techniques*. New York, rev. ed., 1957.

McWhirter, William A. "How Art Swindlers Duped a Virtuous Millionaire." *Life*, July 7, 1967.

Mendax, Fritz. *Art Fakes and Forgeries*. New York, 1956.

Minns, E. H. *Scythians and Greeks*. Cambridge, 1913.

Nå: Interview with Langaard re Caspersen, January 12, 1959.
National Art Galleries, New York. *Sculpture by Alceo Dossena.* New York, 1933.
The National Gallery of Art. *Scientific Investigation.* From *A Twenty-five Year Report*, Washington, 1966.
Netherlands News. "Unmasking of Clever Dutch Nazi Art Forgery." New York, July 11, 1945.
———. "Mad Genius Creates Another Vermeer." September 10, 1945.
New Statesman. "Chrysler's Controversial Century." December 14, 1962.
Noble, Joseph V. *The Techniques of Painted Attic Pottery.* New York, 1965.
———. "The Forgery of Our Greek Bronze Horse." *Art Forgery*, Metropolitan Museum of Art *Bulletin*, February 1968.
Nobili, R. *The Gentle Art of Faking.* London, 1922.
L'oeuvre. November 20, 1926. (Mona Lisa)
Otis Art Institute. *The Vernon Mona Lisa.* Los Angeles, 1964.
Oudgaarden, L., *Rotterdam.* Rotterdam, 1958.
Pars, H. H. *Pictures in Peril.* New York, 1957.
Parsons, H. W. "Art of Fake Etruscan Art." *Art News*, February 1962.
Pater, W. "The Renaissance." *Fortnightly Review*, London, 1869.
Pease, Murray. "Science Backs the Art Detective." *Art News*, March 1948.
Peterson, Frederick A. "Falsification of Tribal and Pre-Columbian Art." *Encyclopedia of World Art*, New York, 1961.
Prodan, Mario. "Falsification of Oriental Works." *Encyclopedia of World Art.* New York, 1961.
Pulitzer, Henry F. *Where Is the Mona Lisa?* London, 1967.
Reinach, S. *Revue Archaeologique*, p. 105ff., Ser. 4, vol. 2, 1903. (Rouchomovsky)
———. *Les Arts*, p. 19ff., May 1903.
Reinhardt, Hans. *The Story of Rotterdam.* Rotterdam, 1955.
Reisner, George Robert. *Fakes and Forgeries in the Fine Arts.* New York Special Libraries Association, 1950.
Richter, Gisela M. A. *The Etruscan Terra Cotta Warriors.* Metropolitan Museum of Art papers no. 6, New York, 1937.
———. *Handbook of the Classical Collection.* New York, 1917 and 1927.
———. "Dossena, His Works and His Lesson." *Art News*, February 2, 1929.
———. "Forgeries of Greek Sculpture." Metropolitan Museum of Art *Bulletin*, 1929.
Rigby, Douglas and Elizabeth. *Lock, Stock and Barrel.* New York, 1944.
Riis, P. J. *An Introduction to Etruscan Art.* Copenhagen, 1953.
Rorimer, James Joseph. *Ultra-Violet Rays and Their Use in the Examination of Works of Art.* New York, 1931.
Rosenberg, Adolph. *Leonardo da Vinci.* Bielefeld and Leipzig, 1903.
Rouault, Georges. *Le Faux dans l'Art et dans l'Histoire.* Paris, 1955. (Catalogue for an international exposition, Grand Palais.)
Rouchomovsky, Israel. *Mein Leben und Mein Arbeit.* Paris, 1928.
———. *Anthropology*, p. 113, 1807; p. 245, 1903: reply to Von Stern.

Rousseau, Theodore. "The Stylistic Detection of Forgeries." *Art Forgery*. Metropolitan Museum of Art *Bulletin*, February 1968.

Savage, George. *Forgeries, Fakes, and Reproductions: A Handbook for the Art Dealer and Collector*. New York and Washington, 1963.

Schüller, Sepp. *Forgers, Dealers, Experts*. New York, 1960.

Sensier, Alfred. *Jean-François Millet, Peasant and Painter*. Boston, 1881.

Sparkes, Boyden. "What the Tourist Buys." *Saturday Evening Post*, 1926.

Steege, K. R. "Dossena Executes Many Orders." *Art News*, December 14, 1929.

Steegmuller, Francis. *Appolinaire, Poet Among Painters*. New York, 1963.

Teitze, Hans. *Genuine and False: Copies, Imitations, Forgeries*. New York, 1948.

———. *Metropolitan Museum Studies*, vol. 5. New York, 1934–36.

Treue, William. *Art Plunder*. London, 1960.

Urbani, Giovanni. "Falsification of Medieval and Modern Art." *Encyclopedia of World Art*. New York, 1961.

Van de Waal, H. *Aspects of Art Forgery*. The Hague, 1962. (Report of a symposium sponsored by the Institute of Criminology at Leiden.)

Vlad Borrelli, Licia. "History of Falsification." *Encyclopedia of World Art*. New York, 1961.

———. "Procedures for Identification of Forgery." Ibid.

Von Stern. *Anthropology*. p. 732. 1896. (on Rouchomovsky)

Walker, R. A. *How to Detect Beardsley Forgeries*. London, 1950.

Wallace, Irving. "The Man Who Swindled Goering." *Saturday Evening Post*, January 11, 1947.

Wallace, Robert. *The World of Leonardo*. New York, 1966.

"What about My Millet?" *Literary Digest*, June 14, 1930.

"Which Smile Is the Mona Lisa's?" *Life*, September 26, 1955.

Whitney, Frederick Allen. *Bulletin of Cleveland Museum of Art*, April 1929. (on Dossena)

Williamson, George Charles. *Stories of an Expert*. London, 1925.

Wurtenberger, Thomas. "Criminological and Criminal-Law Problems of the Forgery of Paintings." *See* Van de Waal, 1962.

Wraight, Robert. *The Art Game*. New York, 1965.